OBSERVATIONAL CINEMA

T0326725

OBSERVATIONAL CINEMA

Anthropology, Film, and the Exploration of Social Life

ANNA GRIMSHAW
AND AMANDA RAVETZ

Indiana University Press
Bloomington and Indianapolis

This book is a publication of

Indiana University Press
601 North Morton Street
Bloomington, IN 47404-3797 USA

www.iupress.indiana.edu

Telephone orders	800-842-6796
Fax orders	812-855-7931
Orders by e-mail	iuporder@indiana.edu

Library of Congress Cataloging-in-Publication Data

Grimshaw, Anna.
    Observational cinema ; anthropology, film, and the exploration of social life /
Anna Grimshaw and Amanda Ravetz.
        p.   cm.
    Includes bibliographical references and index.
    ISBN 978-0-253-35424-2 (cloth : alk. paper) — ISBN 978-0-253-22158-2 (pbk. :
alk. paper) 1. Motion pictures in ethnology. 2. Visual anthropology. 3. Art and
anthropology. I. Ravetz, Amanda. II. Title.
    GN347.G753   2009
    305.8—dc22

                                        2009020624

1 2 3 4 5 14 13 12 11 10 09

In Memory
of
Jim Bracewell
and
Eric Wade

CONTENTS

PREFACE

Observational cinema is one of the most ubiquitous terms in visual anthropology. More often than not, it seems synonymous with the genre of ethnographic film itself. Once hailed as a radical breakthrough in the established conventions of documentary and ethnographic filmmaking, observational cinema quickly fell out of favor. It was widely criticized as a form of scientism in which a supposedly detached camera served to objectify and dehumanize the human subjects of its gaze. Paradoxically, despite extensive critique, observational cinema has continued to be a crucial point of reference for those concerned with the exploration of social life.

In this book we make a new case for observational cinema. It looks forward rather than backward; it is expansive rather than prescriptive. Crucial to it is a shift of theoretical perspective. Returning observational cinema to its Bazinian roots, we argue that traditional interpretive frameworks drawn from science and semiotics have obscured the genre's identity as a sensuous, interpretive, and phenomenologically inflected mode of inquiry. We explore its distinctiveness as a way of knowing, highlighting the challenge represented by observational cinema to the discursive conventions of a textual anthropology. Far from an illustrative endeavor or anachronistic survival in an age of dialogic and reflexive scholarship, we underline the intellectual seriousness of observational work and argue for its significance as an example of experimental practice.

The term "observational cinema" appeared during the 1970s. It started circulating as a description of developments that emerged from a dialogue between anthropologists and documentary filmmakers. "Observational" was used to refer to an approach that differed in important ways from how the camera had hitherto been used in the documentation of social and cultural mores. On the one hand, it indicated a departure from the kind of anthropological filmmaking that was pursued in accordance with a certain scientific paradigm, where the camera was used as a recording instrument to generate data for study and analysis. On the other hand, it served to differentiate the new approach from film essays and other didactic forms organized around overarching themes, in which cultural particularities served to illustrate a series of general propositions about humanity. The observational filmmakers broke with both of these models. They pioneered a new kind of practice that challenged existing conceptions of documentary cinema and anthropology.[1]

Observational Cinema locates changes in ethnographic filmmaking within a broader historical landscape. The observational turn was part of a more general shift in postwar cinema. Beginning with Italian neorealism and continuing in subsequent decades as a central tenet of documentary practice, the commitment to observation was counter-posed to what had gone before. It became the watchword of a cinematic movement that repudiated rhetoric, grandiosity, editorializing, expert summary, and the use of pictures to illustrate ideas. Filmmakers now claimed to take up a different position with respect to the world. They sought to insert themselves into it, relinquishing their privileged perspective in favor of an openness to being shaped by particular situations and relationships they encountered. Observation was first and foremost understood to be an ethical stance. From this followed innovations in filmmaking techniques and representational forms.

One of our objectives in this book is to examine the origins of observational cinema and to trace the process by which the genre took shape. We will chart differing understandings of the observational impulse as it came to be expressed through selected bodies of work. How did the commitment to engaging with the world differently find expression through specific innovations in filmmaking techniques? What does observation involve as an ethnographic practice? If it is about directing attention in particular ways, how do observations constitute anthropological knowledge? In addressing these questions, we have in mind, of course, the broader project of anthropology itself. Although observation has long been central to the rhetoric of the modern fieldwork project, its significance as an epistemology and methodology merits further scrutiny.

The book comes out of our extended engagement with questions of observational cinema in a number of contexts. We had long been struck by the depth and richness of the genre but we were perplexed by the fact that our experience of working with its techniques was often at odds with much of what we read in the critical literature. But just as we became increasingly impatient with the established discourse, so too we were frustrated by our own confusion as to what was properly constitutive of the form. We wanted to transcend our intuitive sense of observational cinema's significance and articulate a more coherent argument for its value as a means for engaging with social and cultural realities. *Observational Cinema* is our attempt to achieve this task.

Unfolding over a period of almost ten years, this project has moved through different phases as our interests have evolved and changed. At times our work has converged, at other times it has diverged, taking us along quite separate paths of inquiry. What has been interesting—and surprising—to us has been the continuing importance of observational cinema to our endeavors. It has endured as a conceptual and methodological point of reference, enabling us to reflexively evaluate the scope and direction of our ongoing work. We have been intrigued by the fact that we have returned again and again to it from different places in our research.

The initial focus for our engagement was ethnographic filmmaking. Each of us sought to use observational techniques within specific fieldwork projects, but our orientation toward this work was shaped by our diverse backgrounds and training. During the late 1970s, Amanda Ravetz trained as a painter at London's Central School of Art and Design. It was a time when the ideal of art as an expression of universal truth had crumbled under social and political pressure. The following decade, she began to work directly in and onto the landscape, making earth drawings and using her body to perform carefully choreographed ritualized actions in an attempt to bring a more situated and sensory perspective into her work. This shift in her artistic practice opened up broader questions about social and relational ways of seeing and experiencing the environment. Having worked with the medium of paint, and then with the materiality of her body, Ravetz found herself gravitating toward certain areas of anthropology and visual anthropology (in particular, observational cinema), since they offered her a way of combining, and extending, her interests in embodied knowledge, painterly observation, and social inquiry.

Anna Grimshaw's involvement with ethnographic filmmaking grew out of a long-standing engagement with the possibilities of an experimental anthropology. The crisis in representation symbolized by the publication of *Writing Culture* (Clifford and Marcus 1986) had underlined the acknowledged, if little discussed, discrepancy between the experiences and encounters of ethnographic fieldwork and the established modes of anthropological textuality. Grimshaw's imaginative memoir *Servants of the Buddha* (1992) was written in response to this problem. Later, in moving into the field of visual anthropology, she discovered that it offered a new context for the exploration of the sensory, material, and subjective dimensions of fieldwork. Following a period of training at Britain's National Film and Television School, Grimshaw began to develop her own observational filmmaking practice. It became an integral part of her investigation of technique and forms of knowledge in anthropological research.[2]

The Granada Centre for Visual Anthropology at the University of Manchester was an early site for our exchanges. Ironically, as Ravetz was moving away from art practice and into anthropology, Grimshaw was beginning to develop a series of collaborations with artists. Not surprisingly, the developing conversation between us has involved a constant tracking back and forth across the art and anthropology divide. Observational cinema was the focus of our initial exchanges, but we quickly found that it did not confine us to the narrow field of ethnographic film. Instead, understood more broadly as a certain kind of epistemological inquiry, we found that it could serve as the interpretive ground for considering a range of visual practices that cut across conventional areas of specialization.[3]

At first sight *Observational Cinema* might appear to be addressed to a limited audience of anthropologists and filmmakers. However, from the outset, we have conceived of our project as an open and expansive one. We are especially mindful that the development of our work has taken place in the context of changing academic interests and the realignment of existing areas of disciplinary specialization. There have been a number of significant changes. First of all, there has been a renaissance in the largely moribund anthropology of art. Secondly, a new dialogue has begun to take shape between artists and anthropologists. Finally—and perhaps most importantly—visual anthropology has begun to emerge as the critical site for a convergence of different perspectives around the visual. Until recently, the latter was largely synonymous with ethnographic filmmaking, and, as such, it was all too easy to regard it as about the acquisition of technical skills in the pursuit of a "pictorial" or illustrative anthropology rather than a different kind of anthropological endeavor. The diversification of visual anthropology, coupled with the clarification of its own distinctive intellectual agenda, has transformed what was hitherto viewed as a marginal or separate sub-discipline into an expansive inter-disciplinary site. One of the distinctive features of this development has been the renewed interest in harnessing conceptual exploration to innovations in technique and form.

At the heart of the book lies the question of practice itself. One of our primary purposes is to move away from general statements about observational cinema to consider specific instances of practice. Hence, in the narrative that follows, we focus on the work of a handful of filmmakers. This may seem unduly restrictive, given the potential range of examples. But, by employing a case study method, our intention is to identify some of the key elements that constitute an observational approach while simultaneously highlighting significant variations in interpretations of the observational task. For, contrary to much critical opinion, this genre of filmmaking is authored. But the nature of authorship is fluid—that is, it is conceived as a process, something that emerges from, and is profoundly shaped by, the complex interweaving of subjectivities that come together in the making and viewing of the work.

In writing *Observational Cinema,* we have drawn on three distinctive fields of scholarship—notably, history of science, film studies, and, of course, anthropology. Let us now briefly explain how work pursued within these respective fields has influenced our own project. First of all, we have found that our concern with practice overlaps significantly with perspectives developing in the history of science, where observation has come to be conceptualized in terms of sites, technologies, techniques, skills, and performances.[4] Understood in this way, observation is taken to involve the special training of the senses. It is a training that is both reflexive and rigorous. It requires schooling in the use of technology and instrumentation; it takes place in particular locations of practice (for example, the theater, field, laboratory, or archive); and it hinges on recognizable performances and displays of knowledge (charts, tables, and graphs). Central is the distinction between commonplace or everyday and disciplined observation. Learning to observe scientifically involves learning to see objects in a way that conforms to certain codes and expectations. It also hinges upon discrimination, the selection of particular objects to the exclusion of other potential foci of human concern.

The framework offered by the history of science has been enormously valuable to us. It has opened up new ways of thinking about observational cinema, enabling us to move beyond the familiar critical terrain of visual anthropology and to articulate a rather different set of questions than the ones conventionally associated with the genre. For example, what special skills and training are involved in developing an observational approach as a filmmaker? What, where, and how is observation performed? What technologies are involved? How are observations organized and constituted as different sorts of knowledge? By asking such questions, we attempt to place observational cinema within a broader context of social and scientific inquiry.

Secondly, the field of film studies has been important in shaping our project. We take seriously the aesthetics of ethnographic work. For, like many commentators, we are dissatisfied with technologically dominated discussions of the documentary. Our concern is to examine how observational practice finds expression in the form of the films themselves. Hence our discussion of the genre is anchored in the details of certain examples. It may seem that we often belabor the details but the devil is, precisely, in the details. Certainly commonplace assumptions about observational cinema's "plain style" or naïve realism do not take us very far in understanding questions of aesthetics. But if the relationship between techniques and forms of knowledge is to be taken seriously, we must examine carefully not just *what* filmmakers attend to but, crucially, *how* they attend to social and cultural phenomena. This means acknowledging the forms of authorship in observational cinema. However, in borrowing from cinema studies the notion of ethnographic film-as-text, we are also mindful of the ethnographic film as *not text*. It is this question that lies at the heart of our engagement with the discipline of anthropology.

Finally, our ideas have been profoundly influenced by changing analytical perspectives that have marked anthropology's recent history. By this we refer to work expressive of the discipline's post-semiotic moment; that is, work that might be loosely termed *phenomenological* in its orientation. The renewed interest in material, emotional or affective, bodily, and sensory ways of being in the world has been critical to our rethinking observational cinema. It has enabled a shift in the terms of debate, away from observational filmmaking as a kind of bad science to acknowledge it for what it is—a mode of inquiry that sticks close to lived experience and that seeks to render the finely grained texture of lived experience.

The book is organized into three major parts. We begin by tracing the emergence of observational cinema as a distinctive genre and take as our starting point the key essays of Roger Sandall ("Observation and Identity," 1972) and Colin Young ("Observational Cinema," 1975). Writing in response to the rise of a new kind of ethnographic filmmaking, both authors sought to identify its distinguishing characteristics, and their suggestive accounts establish important ground for a fuller investigation of the genre's antecedents. Not least, the essays of Sandall and Young remind us of the significance of André Bazin to any discussion of observational cinema. Although the debt is left largely implicit, we will argue that Bazin's discussion of the work of Italian directors like Rossellini and De Sica is immensely valuable in gauging the influence of neorealism (and fiction films) on subsequent cinemas of reality. Not least, the French film critic insisted on the ethical basis of the stance adopted by the Italian postwar filmmakers. It had a renewed commitment to observation at its core—one that was subsequently taken up by the American documentary filmmakers of the 1960s. In looking at the work of several prominent figures— most notably that of Robert Drew, the Maysles brothers, and Frederick Wiseman, we seek to highlight how from the beginning the principle of observation was interpreted in very distinctive ways. A discussion of developments in the broader project of postwar documentary cinema provides the context for our examination of the rise of observational filmmaking within ethnographic inquiry.

The middle part of *Observational Cinema* is built around two case studies—the work of Herb Di Gioia and David Hancock, on the one hand, and that of David MacDougall, on the other. Di Gioia, Hancock, and MacDougall were crucial pioneers of the approach that came to be known in anthropological circles as observational cinema.[5] They were associated with the Ethnographic Film Program founded in 1966 by Colin Young and Walter Goldschmidt at the University of California in Los Angeles.[6] For Di Gioia, Hancock, and MacDougall, the term "observation" did not designate an approach that required adherence to fixed principles and prescribed methods. Indeed, the term was not one that they themselves used much at the time. Hence, in charting the development of their observational practice, we draw attention to its essentially ad hoc, improvisatory qualities. Not least, we are concerned to link innovations in their filmmaking technique to the specific relationships and contexts in which their respective projects were developed.

We begin with a discussion of the films that Herb Di Gioia made with his partner David Hancock during the early 1970s. It charts what we call *an observational cinema in the making*. It is one that diverges in interesting ways from the one pursued at around the same time by David MacDougall. Although Di Gioia and Hancock are perhaps less well-known figures than some of their other contemporaries, they produced an early body of work that allows us to track the uneven and rather uncertain process by which an observational approach was forged through practice.

David MacDougall, by contrast, has long been one of the most prominent figures within the observational tradition. Beginning with his classic film *To Live with Herds* (1972), MacDougall's engagement with the tradition as both theorist and practitioner has spanned more than three decades. During this time, the emphasis and direction of his research has shifted as his research has unfolded in diverse cultural sites. However, in describing his project as an *observational cinema on the move,* we highlight the consistent and yet changing nature of the observational sensibility that runs through his work. We take MacDougall's *Doon School* series (2000–2004) as the focus for our discussion, suggesting that it is crucial to understanding the nature and scope of a new non-textual anthropology— and the role of observational cinema within it.

The book's final part explores observational approaches within contemporary ethnographic research. We begin by putting to one side the narrow ocular frameworks by which such work has been judged and we ask instead, how does one learn to observe? The perspective we develop hinges upon an interpretation of observational filmmaking as a form of skilled practice. It is predicated on a retuning of the senses inseparable from a reorientation of the ethnographer's body such that new kinds of knowledge come into view. We suggest that rather than understanding an observational approach as a preliminary to anthropology proper, it constitutes a form of intellectual inquiry in its own right. Although often considered to be descriptive rather than analytical, we argue for its importance as an anthropological way of knowing. Drawing on examples of work produced in selected sites of observational practice, we seek to highlight the elements that comprise this alternative mode of inquiry.

Central to *Observational Cinema* is the notion of an experimental anthropology. We recognize, however, that there is something of a paradox here. For on the one hand, we are making an argument in the book for the distinctiveness of observational work, while, on the other hand, we are concerned to resist its enclosure within a tight, prescriptive framework. If, indeed, there is a good deal of fluidity in the interpretation of the observational task, why do we continue to hold on to the idea that there is something unique about it? This is the challenge of the latter part of the book. Here we chart new directions in the project. Our interest is in highlighting contemporary innovations that remain identifiably "observational" and yet push at the existing limits of practice.

Using selected examples (MacDougall, Castaing-Taylor and Barbash, Stefani), we trace a number of significant changes in observational cinema —most notably, the foregrounding of aesthetic and narrative experimentation and the movement of work from the conventional screening room into the gallery. We are interested in exploring the ways in which these kinds of observational projects converge with certain preoccupations in contemporary art practice. By this we have in mind the possibility of a experimental anthropology that eschews pre-fabricated knowledge in favor of tracking the real, addressing the gap between what can be known and what remains emergent. For true to its Bazinian roots, an observational sensibility is attuned to the alchemy implicit in the experience of worlds at once imagined and yet concrete and sensory. As such, it cannot be conceived as something fixed or immutable—a point of arrival. Instead, it becomes a site for radical departures in anthropological work.

ACKNOWLEDGMENTS

We have incurred many debts in the course of writing this book. Our original decision to embark on a study of observational cinema was made when we taught together at the Granada Centre for Visual Anthropology, University of Manchester. Our early ideas were shaped in important ways by exchanges with Roger Crittenden, Mark Harris, Penny Harvey, Tim Ingold, Erik Knudsen, Peter Wade, Cristina Grasseni, Penny Moore, and Rosie Read.

The main body of the book was drafted after we had taken up new academic positions. In 2003, Anna Grimshaw moved to the Graduate Institute of the Liberal Arts at Emory University. There she benefited greatly from the advice and intellectual support of her colleagues. An invitation in 2006 to participate in the History of Observation Project at the Max Planck Institute for the History of Science, Berlin, provided a stimulating context in which to extend the initial conception of the book. She is especially grateful to Lorraine Daston and Fernando Vidal for making this possible.

From 2004 to 2007, Amanda Ravetz held an Arts and Humanities Research Council Fellowship at Manchester Metropolitan University. She is grateful to the many individuals there who have helped nurture the ideas developed in this book—particularly John van Aitken, Jim Aulich, Jane Brake, Pavel Büchler, Steve Dixon, Simon Faulkner, John Hyatt, Ian Rawlinson, Leon Wainwright, and Jane Webb. Curators Bryony Bond, James Hutchinson, and Lesley Young and the artists and anthropologists who attended the Connecting Art and Anthropology Workshop also made important and lively contributions.

Both of us continue to learn from our students—Donna Mote, James Redfield, Lawrence Cassidy, Heide Imai, Elizabeth Kealy-Morris, and Naomi Kendrick. Filmmakers Ilisa Barbash, Lucien Castaing-Taylor, Herb Di Gioia, and Eva Stefani have been unfailingly helpful, sparing precious time to make their work available and answering our queries. Paul Stoller has been a most generous and insightful reader. We have greatly benefited from David MacDougall's engagement with our project. He combed the manuscript with an attentive eye, and offered encouragement and constructive criticism in equal measure. He pressed us on many points, forcing us to clarify our broader arguments and to attend more carefully to the many smaller details of our thesis. Without his intervention, this book would have been much the poorer. Rebecca Tolen and Laura MacLeod at Indiana University Press have moved this project along with remarkable speed and efficiency. We are very grateful to them for their commitment to the book and their support.

The final stages of the book were undertaken in Manchester and Machiasport, Maine. Writing is never an isolated task. David Freedberg and Joe Ravetz have been much-valued companions on our long journey to completion.

Anna Grimshaw would like to thank Emory University for sabbatical leaves awarded in 2006 and 2008. She is also grateful to the Woodruff Fund and the Fox Center for Humanistic Inquiry for resources that have facilitated research in connection with the project. Funding from the Arts and Humanities Research Council and the Manchester Institute for Research and Innovation in Art and Design (MIRIAD) enabled Amanda Ravetz to undertake the work necessary to complete this book.

Early versions of parts of this manuscript were published in *Visual Anthropology Review* (chapters 3 and 4) and the *Journal of the Royal Anthropological Institute* (chapter 5). We remain grateful to the editors and reviewers of these journals for their many useful comments and suggestions.

Stills and photographs are courtesy of the Bridgewater Film Company, the British Film Institute, Lucien Castaing-Taylor, Drew Associates, Herb Di Gioia, Sally Hancock, David MacDougall, Maysles Films, Norman Miller, and Eva Stefani. The cover photograph is by Sally Hancock. Every effort has been made to contact all copyright holders. The publishers will be pleased to make good in future editions any errors or omissions brought to their attention.

OBSERVATIONAL CINEMA

PART ONE

PART ONE

CHAPTER ONE
What Is Observational Cinema?

This opening chapter takes its title from the collected essays of the French film critic André Bazin. The two volumes of his writing, published posthumously as *What Is Cinema?* establish important foundations for understanding observational cinema. But before turning attention to Bazin's work, we discuss some of the critical writing that accompanied the new mode of ethnographic filmmaking. In particular, we focus on two commentaries that appeared in the early 1970s. The first, written in 1972 by the anthropologist Roger Sandall, introduced the term "observational" as a description of a certain kind of documentary, but it was a second article by Colin Young published some three years later that served to decisively name the genre.[1]

"Observational cinema" was coined to designate films that represented a significant break with earlier anthropological approaches toward the recording of social and cultural practice. Although filmmaking (and photography) became marginalized by a professionalizing discipline following the Malinowskian revolution of the 1920s, the use of a camera in fieldwork situations did not completely disappear. A number of anthropologists continued to pursue the early interest of Haddon, Boas, and others. Most notably, during the 1930s, Margaret Mead in collaboration with Gregory Bateson had developed an ambitious comparative project in Bali and New Guinea (later publishing their photo-essay, *Balinese Character,* and film series, *Character Formation in Different Cultures*). Their work was framed according to a scientific model with a clear distinction drawn between recording (data) and analysis (findings). Running in parallel with this kind of anthropological filmmaking was a very different enterprise, one animated by broad, ambitious questions about the nature of humanity and exemplified by the work of Robert Gardner (*Dead Birds,*

Rivers of Sand). Here cultural details were mobilized in the service of epic themes—the nature of warfare and the struggle between the sexes.

Observational cinema was predicated on a repudiation of methods that fragmented ethnographic realities as a preliminary to reassembling them in accordance with a conceptual framework imposed from elsewhere. It was linked to a different epistemology and aesthetic. It was grounded in the ethnographic encounter itself—and it was fundamentally cinematic, not literary. Specifically, it involved the abandonment of ethnographic interpretation as explanation and argument in favor of a different kind of interpretive logic—one that was filmic rather than derived from written text. Since the observational paradigm is sometimes thought to imply an absence of rigor or abdication of analytical intent, it is important to emphasize that from the very beginning it had its own analytical procedures. Given that these did not conform to existing norms, they often went unrecognized. As many observational filmmakers discovered, one of the challenges they faced was how to persuade audiences otherwise.

If Sandall was the first to offer a label for the new approaches in ethnographic filmmaking, Young's essay was quickly adopted as a sort of manifesto for the genre.[2] Although neither author offered a closely argued case, their essays established *observation* as central to any discussion of the new direction in ethnographic filmmaking. Both were writing in response to developments they perceived to be occurring at the time. Like their distinguished predecessor, Bazin, Young and Sandall were witnesses to changes in filmmaking practice, and their commentaries were contemporaneous with what they described. Hence we can read their essays as reports on work in progress, representing the authors' respective attempts to clarify the nature and scope of the new practice and to evaluate its significance. Of course, Young himself had been instrumental in creating a context in which experimentation could take place. His Ethnographic Film Program at UCLA had attracted an unusual group of anthropologists and filmmakers, eager to share ideas and experiment with practice. It functioned as an important incubator of observational cinema.

Writing in the British journal *Sight and Sound*, Sandall framed his explorations of the observational film with statements by D. H. Lawrence and André Bazin. For Sandall, the significance of these writers lay in their interest in an aesthetic that respected things for what they were, for their irreducibility and singularity. Drawing on Bazin's notion of a cinema of duration, he underlined the centrality of preserving unities of time and space to an observational sensibility. He pointed to the completeness with which John Marshall, David and Judith MacDougall, and Herb Di Gioia and David Hancock recorded moments of cultural life, holding together dense webs of relationships in the face of the impulse to fragment. Their work manifested a resistance to what Sandall termed "interpretation." By this he was referring to a different kind of aesthetic approach in which objects were appropriated by and overwhelmed by the sensibility of the filmmaker. "Direction inhibits: observation frees," he declared, positing seeing over assertion, wholeness over parts, matter over symbolic meaning, specificity over abstraction.[3]

We can leave to one side Sandall's technologically driven argument and his occasional lapses into the discourse of science (evidence, truth, fact, proof) and instead appreciate the importance of his essay in identifying the aesthetic structure that underpinned the observational turn in ethnographic filmmaking. Many of the features that Bazin made central to his conception of a new cinema of reality may be discerned in the observational film as Sandall described it. There was indeed a renewed respect for context, a foregrounding of relationships, connections and continuities rather than an isolation of discrete segments or parts. Moreover, the new work was intended to be suggestive rather than declarative. Above all, Sandall grasped the quality of irreducibility that marked the observational film from the very beginning—that is, the unresolved tension between the subject and the frame of the work. For practitioners of the observational approach this tension has always lain at the heart of the matter, evidence of an engagement with the world predicated on a respect for what Sandall (quoting Bazin) called "the singular individuality of things."[4] To observe, as Sandall made clear, involved attending to the world—actively, passionately, concretely—while, at the same time, relinquishing the desire to control, circumscribe or appropriate it.

Although Sandall made his debt to Bazin explicit in his commentary on observational film, it was left largely implicit in Young's writing. Nevertheless, Bazin's influence may be discerned in the account that Young offered of the new techniques being pioneered by ethnographic filmmakers. Importantly, Young began his discussion by clarifying several frequently misunderstood aspects of the observational approach. First of all, he sought to dispel the common myth that observation was synonymous with objectivity. Next he underlined the intimate, engaged observational camera. Far from being detached or remote, he reminded his readers that the exploration of social life could not be carried out with a camera used as a "surveyor's instrument" but hinged upon the forging of close, personal relationships with subjects. Lastly, Young rejected the notion that observational filmmaking involved an invisible camera, what is often referred to as a "fly on the wall" approach, explaining "the ideal was never to pretend that the camera was not there—the ideal was to try to photograph and record 'normal' behavior. Clearly what finally has to be understood by this idea is that normal behavior being filmed is the behavior that is normal for the subjects under the circumstances, including, but not exclusively, the fact they are being filmed."[5] Given the clarity of Young's statement with respect to these issues, it is surprising to discover that thirty years later such misconceptions still continue to cloud discussions of observational cinema.

In his essay, Young offered a sketchy history of observational cinema, linking its emergence as a genre with earlier innovations in cinematic form, most notably those associated with the *cinéma vérité* movement and Italian neorealism. Taking the 1960s documentary renaissance in France and the United States as his first point of reference, he suggested that the kinds of films made by Rouch, Leacock, Pennebaker, and the Maysles brothers sharply exposed the limitations of conventional cinema. For Young this new body of work challenged what he called "highly manipulative classical melodrama" as well as "didactic educational films."[6] The distinction he was drawing turned upon questions of power and control. He suggested that the significance of the *cinéma vérité* films lay in the new relationship posited between filmmakers and their audiences. They opened up a space for engagement. No longer patronized or manipulated, the viewer was now included as an active participant in the generation of the film's meaning.

Young understood the films of Italian neorealism to be important precursors of *cinéma vérité*. He celebrated in them "the low key of the drama, the attention to lifelike detail, and the willingness to have the dramatic development, in its details, verified by us against our own experience as the film progressed."[7] Such characteristics he took to be expressive of a shift away from the controlling perspective of the film's director toward an embracing of life itself. However, according to Young, the innovative potential of work produced by the Italian directors and later by *cinéma vérité* filmmakers was not fully realized. He followed other commentators in pointing out that many of the 1960s American *cinéma vérité* films remained tied to the classic model of conflict-based drama.[8] Narratives were still structured around a crisis and its resolution: "At that stage what had happened was a change in morality and tactics during shooting, but not yet a change in overall aesthetic. That change had to come when film-makers went after more open-ended subjects."[9] The change happened a decade later and with it observational cinema was born.

We may read Young's interpretation of observational cinema as part of a broader narrative about post–World War II cinema. Central to it was the emergence of a new humanism. It animated the work of many film-makers who, in the aftermath of revolution, war, and enormous social dislocation, sought to make cinema an integral part of the rebuilding of society. Work produced after 1945—in its scale, subject matter, and aes-thetic form—was conceived as an alternative to the rhetoric and bombast that had marked so much of early twentieth-century cinema, whether it be the films coming out of Hollywood, post-revolutionary Russia, or European fascism. Even the interwar documentaries of John Grierson and his group had turned working men into heroes, transforming the degradation of wage labor into a grandiose sacrifice to the spectacular machine of modern industry.

The movement that Young traced in his essay had at its core a break with cinema conceived as spectacle. Beginning with the early work of Méliès and Griffith, cinema's pioneers made ever greater claims for their medium, and their message had become ever more explicit. As Young noted, this kind of cinema left little to the imagination. It also lacked human scale. The films made later, most notably in Italy, were marked by their sobriety and humanity—indeed humility. In place of tales of epic scope and struggle, interest was focused on small-scale dramas dis-tinguished by their human detail. The affective quality of this work, its "truth," stemmed from an appeal to personal experience.

Observational cinema involved a scaling down too. Young described a genre that resisted grand claims, either for science or art. The films con-sidered to be exemplary were unassuming, understated, modest, quiet, painstakingly built from an amassing of detail. They were often decep-tively simple. Instead of talking over subjects or lecturing their audience, the new ethnographic filmmakers carefully attended to the texture of lived experience. Significantly, they appeared to be out of step with the directions in which text-based anthropology was moving at the time. For here concerns with ethnographic particularities were pushed aside in favor of the more muscular or herculean endeavors of theory, Marxism, and interpretation.

Crucial to Young's account was the distinction he drew between films that *show* and those than *tell*. Echoing Sandall's characterization of approaches built around *seeing* as opposed to those built around *assertion*, Young likewise sought to identify work that he believed invited discovery and work that made this difficult. Citing *The Nuer*, a film made by Robert Gardner, Hilary Harris, and George Breidenbach, as an example of the latter, he expressed dissatisfaction at the intrusion of the filmmakers at every point of the film. In particular, he criticized the fragmentation of events according to an analytical structure that precluded alternative explorations and understandings of the material. By contrast, he pointed to John Marshall's *Bitter Melons* and David and Judith MacDougall's *To Live with Herds* as films that presented experiential and interpretive possibilities rather than explanatory and definitive statements.

Young shared Sandall's view of the figures at the heart of the observational movement. Especially prominent were the partnerships of David and Judith MacDougall and Herb Di Gioia and David Hancock. For Young—as for Sandall—it was the work of these filmmakers, in its intense engagement with the details of everyday life, that challenged the limitations of didactic and conflict-driven cinema. In writing about the new approach, Young made it clear that observation did not merely refer to a developed visual attentiveness among the ethnographic filmmakers. He reminded his readers that it encompassed the aural too. For alongside a heightened sensitivity toward the details of gesture, movement, and expression, there was an increased concern with sound that included, of course, language. No longer dominated by the single voice of an anonymous narrator, the observational film brought into focus a range of different voices, ways of speaking, and contexts of speaking.

At the heart of Young's essay lay the question of the relationships that observational filmmakers sought to forge with their subjects and audience. They were expected to be of a fundamentally different kind from the ones characteristic of the fiction film and the classic documentary. Instead of being circumscribed by conventional hierarchies built around an assumption of directorial authority, there was now an attempt to cede control of the film—to render it a fluid process shaped through the intervention of subjects, the interruption of unexpected or spontaneous

Still from *To Live with Herds* (1972). *Courtesy of David MacDougall.*

events, and the empathetic or imaginative participation of the viewer. If the American *cinéma vérité* filmmakers had been pioneers in this regard, the observational filmmakers attempted to take it further. Films were now expected to *follow* from extended, long-term relationships rather than for relationships to function instrumentally as vehicles for "getting" the film. Moreover, the texture and quality of these relationships were considered part of the work itself and were woven into it as an integral part of the process. This did not necessarily mean that they were foregrounded—in fact quite the opposite—but they were understood to be the indispensable epistemological and ethical foundations of observational cinema.

The essays by Sandall and Young were critical in establishing the parameters of the new kind of ethnographic film. Both writers identified its distinctive aesthetic. Central was a commitment to the spatial unity of events and to duration. In particular, they underlined importance of continuity (within the shot, between image and sound, between shooting and editing) and context (emplacement, the holding together of figure and ground) to observational cinema.[10] Interestingly, each writer built his narrative around the notion of *observation*—though neither offered a definition of this key term. As we have seen in the case of Sandall, observation was opposed to what he called "interpretation." It was about the empirical, the specific, the concrete. It involved preserving what he called the "identity" of the subject. In his view, the observational film was to be evaluated according to different criteria than those used in the case of conventional film, that is, on the basis of what he called its "evidence" and not according to the sophistication of its rhetoric or the intricacy of its meaning. Sandall was not making a case here for the objectivity of the new kind of film or for its technological superiority—though his comments might easily be mistaken for such.

If such questions remained unresolved in Sandall's account, Young was more unequivocal. From the outset he made it clear that his notion of observation implied neither the objectivity nor the invisibility of the observer, reminding his readers that the camera was always selective, partial, subjective, and situated. Like Sandall, Young was using the term "observation" in a very particular way. Both writers were describing something other than a purely visual strategy on the part of the filmmaker.[11] They referred to a particular ethical stance—in which "to observe" meant "to respect" or "to comply with." In this sense, the choice of the term "observation" resembles that made by Jonathan Crary in his book *Techniques of the Observer.* Although Crary's interests are different, the distinction he drew here between the spectator and observer is valuable for our purposes: "Most dictionaries," Crary explains, "make little semantic distinction between the words 'observer' and 'spectator,' and common usage renders them effectively synonymous. I have chosen the term *observer* mainly for its etymological resonance. Unlike *spectare,* the Latin root for spectator, the root for 'observe' does not literally mean to 'look at.' Spectator also carries specific connotations, especially in the context of nineteenth century culture, that I prefer to avoid—namely, of one who is a passive onlooker at a spectacle, as at an art gallery or theater. In a sense more pertinent to my study, observare means 'to conform one's action, to comply with,' as in observing rules, codes, regulations and practices."[12]

We will see in later sections of the book that much of the critical discourse surrounding observational cinema has been predicated upon an understanding of observation as about spectatorship. By contrast, we will follow Crary's example, approaching observation as a skilled practice that hinges upon a particular kind of active and disciplined engagement with the world.

At the beginning of this chapter we noted the centrality of Bazin's critical writing to our project. Although he haunts much of the writing on observational cinema, his influence has remained largely implicit (Sandall being a significant exception).[13] The neglect of Bazin by the theorists and practitioners of ethnographic filmmaking may, however, be understood as part of the more general disregard of his work following his death in 1958. For despite his importance in establishing film studies as a respectable and legitimate form of intellectual endeavor, Bazin's style of criticism quickly lost favor. The structuralist revolution that swept through intellectual circles over the course of the next decade largely consigned his work to obscurity. Bazin's humanism, his phenomenological orientation, his commitment to "ontological realism," and his interest in engaging a broad public in questions of cinema were deemed to be relics of an earlier age. Now critics wrote for one another in the dense language of semiotics. The author was dead, long live signifying systems![14]

Bazin, however, is indispensable to our task. Not only is he one of the leading commentators on the moment in cinematic history often cited in discussions of observational filmmaking—Italian neorealism—but the ideas he articulated through his discussion of key figures such as Rossellini and De Sica provide the framework for thinking about the aesthetics and epistemology of observational cinema. As we will discover, the questions at the heart of Bazin's appreciation of postwar Italian cinema—for example, the role of director, the length of the shot, the construction of scenes, the influence of classical dramaturgy—are crucial to understanding the work of Herb Di Gioia and David Hancock and David and Judith MacDougall made some twenty years later.

Bazin's essays began to appear during the 1940s. Through his writing he sought to develop the range of critical tools he believed necessary to any proper engagement with cinema. Such tools were not already in existence. Hitherto many intellectuals had ignored the emergence of cinema, dismissing it as a cheap, popular entertainment or judging it according to frameworks deriving from literature and fine art.[15] Bazin's perspective was different. He was concerned to establish the principles of a criticism founded upon a respect for cinema's distinctive qualities as a new aesthetic form. His writing documented this process. At its core lay his response to individual films. Bazin's method was exemplary and, more than fifty years after its formulation, it remains a model for anyone concerned with the development of critical perspectives toward ethnographic filmmaking. One of his biographers, Dudley Andrew, described it in the following way: "Bazin's usual procedure was to watch a film closely, appreciating its special values and noting its difficulties or contradictions. Then he would imagine the kind of film it was or was trying to be, placing it within a genre or fabricating a genre, constantly reverting to examples taken from this film and others like it. Finally, these 'laws' would be seen within the context of an entire theory of cinema. Thus Bazin begins with the most particular facts available, the film or films before his eyes, and through a process of logical and imaginative reflection, he arrives at a general theory."[16]

We can see here that the foundation of Bazin's method was attention to detail. It involved a close and meticulous observation of the cinematic reality that unfolded before him. From this initial focus Bazin progressively widened his frame to encompass the scope of the filmmaker's project, its location within certain general aesthetic parameters that were themselves located within a particular interpretation of the evolution of the form, until finally, Bazin was able to articulate a more general theory of cinema. Generosity was one of the critic's most noted gifts. This quality manifested itself in Bazin's willingness to yield to the work, to surrender to the spirit of a particular film, while never losing sight of his responsibility to articulate a critical judgment of it. The two poles of his sensibility were always fully engaged.

Bazin's two early essays, "The Ontology of the Photographic Image" (1945) and "The Myth of Total Cinema" (1946), laid the foundations for the particular inquiry that he sought to pursue through the Italian films made in the immediate aftermath of the Second World War.[17] The significance of Italian neorealism lay in its closeness to the theory of cinema that he was beginning to articulate through his writing. For Bazin, films such as Rossellini's *Paisà* (1946) or De Sica's *Bicycle Thief* (1948) were important concrete manifestations of the more philosophical notions that underpinned his approach toward understanding the new aesthetic form. Importantly, his commentary on the work of the Italian neorealist directors was contemporary with the development of the movement itself. There was a tangible sense of anticipation and discovery as both filmmakers and critics explored the creative possibilities for cinema in the postwar world.

André Bazin (n.d.). *The British Film Institute.*

Beginning with his extended essay "An Aesthetic of Reality: Cinematic Realism and the Italian School of Liberation" (1948), Bazin made the question of neorealist cinema a central part of his writing for almost a decade.[18] He wrote about particular films as they were released, noting the new and unusual features that different directors introduced into their work, highlighting contrasts between the sensibilities of key figures—and only belatedly attempting to make any general statement about the form. Bazin's open letter to the critic Guido Aristarco, "In Defence of Rossellini," written in 1955, was perhaps the closest he came toward articulating a broad definition of neorealist cinema.[19] Nevertheless, there is much to be gleaned from Bazin's essays of the period.

Rossellini's film *Rome, Open City* (1945) has long stood as the symbol of a new moment in the history of cinema. It marked the emergence of the birth of Italian neorealism, a movement most identified with figures such as Visconti, De Sica, Zavattini, Fellini, and, of course, Rossellini himself.[20] The films that constituted this movement were made in the immediate aftermath of the war and occupation. One of their primary themes was the reconstruction of society, a process that was explored from the bottom up. The Italian neorealist directors sought to rediscover humanity, locating it among "ordinary" people who were struggling to make new lives for themselves in the midst of the ruins. The bomb-scarred cityscape that became emblematic of their work served not as a backdrop to human relationships but as an integral part of the story itself. Neorealist cinema framed people within the landscape, the landscape understood as expressive not just of geography, history, society—but subjectivity too. If Rossellini's moving portrayal of life under occupation inaugurated the cinema of reconstruction, critics usually cite De Sica's film *Umberto D* (1952) as marking its end. In less than a decade, the human solidarity and social optimism that once so engaged the Italian directors had given way to a different perception of the world. Filmmakers increasingly depicted a world of fragments, isolation, and despair. The cinema of the 1950s turned inward. Rossellini, Fellini, and, above all, Antonioni began to probe a new, interior landscape—what might be called the problem of the soul.

Central to Bazin's understanding of Italian neorealist cinema was his acknowledgement of the unique historical moment in which it emerged. But he was also aware of its important continuities with the past. He readily acknowledged that the work of Rossellini and others was less of a radical break and more a development of certain trends that had been set in motion before the war. Nevertheless, Bazin was interested in the unusual confluence of factors—social, economic, political, aesthetic—that defined what he took to be a distinctive new stage in the evolution of cinema. He recognized the profound involvement of the Italian directors in the historical moment that they set out to document. For Bazin, the primary significance of their work lay in the distinctive perspective, what he called "revolutionary humanism," that was articulated toward contemporary realities. Secondary to it, but nevertheless important, were the specific filmmaking techniques that were hailed as emblematic of the movement (e.g., location shooting and the use of non-professional actors).[21]

Bazin was especially interested in two of the postwar Italian directors. The first was Rossellini. His trilogy of films—*Rome, Open City; Paisà;* and *Germany Year Zero*—was made at the end of the war and represented the early phase of neorealist cinema. The second was De Sica, whose films *Bicycle Thief* and *Umberto D* were made a few years later and reflected the changing social and political conditions in postwar Italy. For Bazin the work of these figures formed the basis for his exploration of cinematic realism—its critical features and its history and development.

Although *Rome, Open City* has long held a special place in discussions of the new Italian cinema, Bazin recognized *Paisà* as the more unusual and interesting film. While critics have never denied the emotional force of Rossellini's tale of the resistance and betrayal in occupied Rome, the extent to which the first part of his war trilogy represented a radical break with existing cinematic forms has always been in doubt. From Bazin onward, *Rome, Open City* has been seen as a synthetic work, one that was as much indebted to existing conventions (like melodrama) as a harbinger of something new. For all of the film's documentary-like texture, the central drama was a familiar story of the struggle of good over evil told in the terms of a classic narrative.[22] According to Bazin, it was *Paisà* that marked what he called the "decisive step forward" in the evolution of realism in cinema.[23]

The second part of Rossellini's war trilogy shared with *Rome, Open City* a concern with events that were happening at the time of the film's making—namely the liberation of Fascist Italy by Allied forces. But the way Rossellini excavated this historical situation was, Bazin suggested, bolder and more radical than in the earlier film. He described *Paisà* as a kind of "reconstituted reportage," the "documentary" quality of the film interpreted as an expression of the unusual closeness between the filmmaker and the events, situations, and human relationships that he was exploring.[24] For Bazin, the importance of *Paisà* lay in Rossellini's innovative approach toward subject matter and toward the aesthetic possibilities of the film medium. He understood the reconstruction of cinema to be an integral part of the social reconstruction that followed the devastation of war. As a consequence, the Italian filmmakers like Rossellini worked at ground level rather than from an elevated or privileged position—and their innovations followed from this fundamental reorganization of perspective. Rossellini's camera was now located differently in the world—what it saw and how it saw were inextricably connected.

Bazin likened the second part of Rossellini's war trilogy to a series of short stories. He noted that by contrast with the first film, *Rome, Open City*, there was no overarching narrative, only episodes that had no connection with one another beyond their shared historical ground. Importantly, there was no "progression" in the movement of Rossellini's film. Each episode had its own tempo. Moreover, *Paisà* was distinguished by its fragmentary, elliptical quality. In particular, Bazin drew attention to the centrality of "image facts" to the construction of the film. He contrasted these cinematic units with individual shots that function as the basic narrative elements of the montage-based film.[25]

Bazin's discussion of *Paisà* also included comments on the quality of its camera work. He had already noted that "[t]he Italian camera retains something of the human quality of the Bell and Howell newsreel camera, a projection of eye and hand, almost a living part of the operator, instantly in tune with his awareness."[26] In the case of *Paisà*, Bazin was interested in the unusual mobility and location of Rossellini's camera. Unlike the conventional Hollywood camera that had a "god-like" quality, an ability to see everything, Rossellini's camera was partial and situated, grounded as it was at the level of human experience. As Bazin pointed out, this was nowhere more strikingly manifest than in the last part of *Paisà*. Located alongside the partisans in the dense reeds of the Po delta, the camera's perspective precisely mirrored that of Rossellini's characters as they moved across a dangerous and mysterious landscape that hovered between sky and water. For Bazin, the unique dramatic texture of *Paisà's* concluding episode owed as much to the placement of Rossellini's camera as to the nature of the events that it depicted.

The features that Bazin identified in *Paisà* he took to be evidence of a new phase in realist cinema. However, he was the first to acknowledge a paradox here—that the realism of Rossellini was an artful construction. It was not simply "found" but rather self-consciously fashioned, declaring "realism in art can be achieved only in one way—through artifice."[27] What Bazin celebrated in *Paisà* was Rossellini's respect for the ambiguous and continuous nature of the real. This was rendered through the use of specific techniques—most notably the image fact, the fluid, informal camera style, and the non-montage-based editing approach. All of these devices served to open up a distinctive cinematic space that invited exploration

Still from *Paisà* (1946). *The British Film Institute.*

and active engagement on the part of the viewer. For Bazin, Rossellini's great achievement—paralleled by Orson Welles's development of deep-focus photography—was to eschew the conventions of both Hollywood and montage-based cinema that circumscribed or foreclosed interpretive possibilities.

Bazin's engagement with the work of Rossellini marked the first stage in his documentation of Italian neorealist cinema.[28] At the time of his writing, the movement itself was still in the process of emerging and he was in an enviable position as a critic. He observed the new cinema in the making. The work that followed *Paisà*—films made by Visconti and Fellini but, most of all, those made by De Sica—allowed Bazin to extend and refine his ideas as he sought to map the changing complexion of neorealism through the late 1940s and early 1950s. Given the commitment of the Italian directors to locating their work in society, it was inevitable that their cinema would change as postwar conditions changed. Bazin was among the first to acknowledge his doubt as to whether there was any future for neorealist cinema once the crisis of the war and occupation had passed.[29] Increasingly, however, he came to recognize the films of De Sica as crucial to understanding the contours of a later neorealist cinema. He celebrated films like *Bicycle Thief* (1948) and *Umberto D* (1952) as important stages in the evolution of neorealist cinema, describing the former as "the ultimate expression of neorealism," only to later revise his opinion in favor of the latter work. If ultimately less "perfect" than *Bicycle Thief*, the cinematic ambition of *Umberto D* was, according to Bazin, far greater.[30]

In his review of *Bicycle Thief*, Bazin considered the extent to which its content and techniques conformed to certain expectations of the neorealist film. He highlighted De Sica's interest in what might be characterized as "ordinary" people and everydayness rather than extraordinary personalities, situations, or events.[31] Additionally, he noted his commitment to filming in the world rather than the studio and his use of non-professional actors or people playing their own lives.[32] But in proclaiming De Sica's work "neorealist," Bazin also suggested that *Bicycle Thief* pointed the way forward. He was especially interested in De Sica's innovative handling of drama and narrative structure, celebrating the filmmaker's skill in articulating a powerful thesis about contemporary society without producing a piece of propaganda or didactic intervention: "Events and people are never introduced in support of a social thesis—but the thesis emerges fully armed and all the more irrefutable because it is presented to us as something thrown into the bargain. It is our intelligence that discerns and shapes it, not the film. De Sica wins every play on the board without ever having made a bet."[33] According to Bazin, De Sica went further than the earlier neorealist filmmakers in abandoning conventions of acting and performance. There was also less of a commitment to a dramatic scenario and story. Instead De Sica's film involved an "unfolding" in which individual moments were not ranked hierarchically but each had its own individual weight and meaning. The film's dramatic intensity emerged not from "tension" but from what Bazin called the "summation" of events.[34]

Bazin considered *Umberto D* to be a less perfectly realized piece of work than De Sica's *Bicycle Thief*, but he declared its break with classical dramaturgy to be much more audacious. For here he believed that De Sica had moved more decisively away from both spectacle and conventional narrative. "The narrative unit is not the episode, the event, the sudden turn of events, or the character of its protagonists," Bazin explained, "it is the succession of concrete instants of life, no one of which can be said to be more important than another, for their ontological equality destroys drama at its very basis."[35] Although other critics were largely indifferent

Still from *Bicycle Thief* (1948). *The British Film Institute.*

to *Umberto D,* Bazin hailed the film as a masterpiece. It allowed him to glimpse the possibility of what he called a "cinema of duration."[36] All of his writing had been directed toward the clarification and articulation of precisely this notion.

For Bazin, a cinema of duration represented the most complete expression of his conception of realist cinema. He identified two scenes in *Umberto D* as important examples of what he had in mind. In the first, Umberto D takes to his bed in the belief he has a fever; in the second, the maid awakens and goes to the kitchen to make coffee.[37] According to conventional expectations, both scenes are unremarkable, commonplace episodes devoid of obvious drama or tension, and yet, as Bazin points out, the way that they are filmed by De Sica—his profound respect for their spatial and temporal continuity—yields sequences of remarkable beauty and insight. These moments of revelation were not so much "created" as "found," plucked from life as it unfolded. Nevertheless, as Bazin

acknowledged in his discussion of *Umberto D*, such revelations were neither accidental nor haphazard but depended crucially upon the use of aesthetic techniques. No one, he reminded his readers, planned his scenarios
with more care and detail than De Sica.

Bazin's essays on Italian neorealist cinema were an integral part of
his attempt to articulate a theory of cinema. In tracing the evolution of
cinematic language, an aesthetic that owed nothing to established forms
of art and literature, he drew a distinction between "those directors who
put their faith in the image and those who put their faith in reality."[38] The
former, exemplified by the Soviet school of montage, broke up the inherent continuity of the real, reorganizing it according to an a priori logic that
was external to the events and situations depicted. The latter, filmmakers such as Flaherty, Renoir, and, above all, the postwar Italian directors,
worked differently. In repudiating the primacy of montage, Bazin argued
that they developed techniques that served to render the fundamental
integrity and ambiguity of the real. These techniques included deep-focus
photography, the use of long, unbroken sequences, and the preservation
of the spatial and temporal unity of events. It meant an emphasis on
shooting rather than editing, scenes rather than shots. Filmmakers framed
interpretive possibilities through relationships of proximity rather than
asserting meaning or association through radical juxtaposition. For Bazin,
montage was about "the creation of a sense or meaning not objectively
contained in the images themselves but derived exclusively from their
juxtaposition."[39] By contrast, in the work of Murnau or Flaherty, he continued, "montage plays no part, unless it be the negative one of inevitable
elimination where reality superabounds. The camera cannot see everything at once but it makes sure not to lose any part of what it chooses to
see. What matters to Flaherty, confronted with Nanook hunting the seal,
is the relation between Nanook and the animal; the actual length of the
waiting period. Montage could suggest the time involved. Flaherty however confines himself to showing the actual waiting period; the length of
the hunt is the very substance of the image, its true object. Thus in the
film this episode requires one set-up. Will anyone deny that it is thereby
much more moving than a montage by attraction?"[40]

The filmmakers who interested Bazin—Murnau, Welles, Renoir,
Flaherty, Rossellini, and De Sica—all shared a particular way of attending
to the world. It involved a refusal to "add" to reality. Instead, reality was subjected to what one commentator called a "long hard gaze."[41] Here we find

the origins of Sandall's distinction between contrasting principles of inter-pretation and observation, since following Bazin he too described a film-making engagement with the world that was premised on the irreducibility of things, their singular individuality.[42] Bazin had been especially keen to point out that there was nothing passive about taking up such a stance, nor was it predicated on any abdication of judgment. It was an interrogation of the world but of a different sort than that of montage-based cinema. Filmmakers were now less directors and more *filters,* drawing their audi-ences into an active exploration of the world created through cinema.[43]

Bazin's approach to cinema was profoundly humanistic, informed by ideas derived from phenomenology and existentialism. At the core of his theory of cinema was a commitment to reality. Fundamental was "Bazin's belief in the ontological priority and primacy of the real, the idea that there is a reality independent of human consciousness which pre-exists and is greater than any representation of it."[44] Cinema, in Bazinian terms, then was about revelations of the real understood to be infinitely myste-rious. Its unique qualities derived from the "redemptive" power of the image. For the image was both *materially connected* to the real—existing as a "trace" or an "imprint" created by light falling on the film's negative and rendered visible by means of mechanical processing; and it was a *representation* of the real—and, as such, it transcended the contingencies of space and time, preserved as a moment that lived in defiance of the inevitable processes of change and decay.

Despite many years of obscurity, there is today evidence of a renewed interest in Bazin's writings. The field of cinema studies, like that of anthropology, has been marked by a change in its theoretical paradigms. The resurgence of phenemenologically oriented work promises to greatly enhance any understanding of the nature and scope of observational cinema. Although "observational" was not a term used by Bazin in his discussion of cinematic language, his influence may be discerned in the way that Sandall and Young characterized the changes they witnessed in anthropological filmmaking practice. They shared with Bazin a profound interest in a particular kind of filmmaking sensibility. It is distinguished by the intensity, steadfastness, and, crucially, *expansiveness* of the filmmak-er's attention. Bazin's biographer characterized it thus: "The neorealist cameraman lifts himself above the everyday perception not by means of technical tricks or manipulation of what is photographed but simply by the intensity of his attention, which makes certain details stand out. He

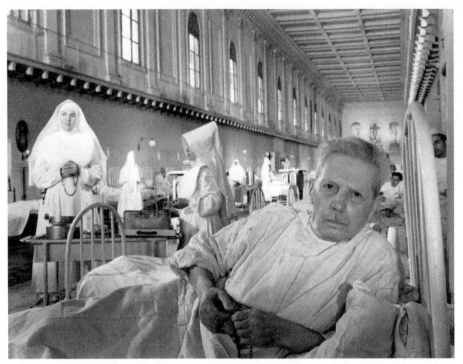

Still from *Umberto D* (1952). *The British Film Institute.*

becomes a filter, Bazin suggests, changing nothing, but letting through a steady stream of facts coming from a particular frequency of light."[45]

Whether explicitly acknowledged or not, Bazin's general orientation toward questions of cinema coupled with his interest in the work of particular directors offered—and continues to offer—both a framework and a set of critical tools for interpreting developments in ethnographic cinema during the late 1960s and early 1970s. His discussion of the evolution of cinematic language provides a context for thinking critically about the connections between observational filmmakers like Herb Di Gioia and David Hancock or David and Judith MacDougall and their precursors such as Flaherty, Rossellini, and De Sica. A fuller engagement with Bazin's work brings up a number of questions. To what extent was the observational movement in ethnographic filmmaking an extension of the kind of cinematic realism that he sought to trace and articulate through his writing? How useful are the concepts he developed with respect to Italian neorealist cinema—that is, how might Bazin's notions of the "image fact," duration, deep-focus photography, the long shot, the scene / *mise-en-scène,* the director as filter help us in understanding the techniques of the new ethnographic filmmakers?

In drawing on Bazin's writing, we also acknowledge the complex relationship between ethics and aesthetics in moments of cinematic innovation. He was the first to acknowledge the ethical basis of innovations in the techniques of cinematic realism and their historical contingency. The realist impulse was always, as he put it, "more a reaction than a truth."[46] It is important to bear this in mind when evaluating observational cinema. For the advocacy by Sandall, Young, and Bazin of a particular filmmaking sensibility (subsequently termed "observational") was partly conceived in response to what they perceived to be the excessive subjectivity and rhetoric of existing forms. Hence the emphasis placed on the cultivation of distinctive features was intended to clearly demarcate this form of filmmaking engagement with the world from others. Observational cinema was self-consciously authored, but it was also conceived as an extension of human consciousness, an almost objective correlative of what the filmmaker sees, hears, and feels. The terms used by Bazin and later commentators—including circumspection, objectivity, detachment—were attempts to characterize these qualities and to distinguish them from existing cinematic forms. Critics, however, have often understood them differently, building them into a discourse about observational cinema that has been remarkably difficult to dislodge.

CHAPTER 2

Social Observers: Robert Drew, Albert and David Maysles, Frederick Wiseman

The notion of observation as a central tenet of documentary cinema appeared in America during the 1960s. It was the touchstone of the movement variously described as *direct cinema* or *cinéma vérité*. In particular, it was used in connection with the work of Robert Drew, Richard Leacock, D. A. Pennebaker, the Maysles brothers, and Frederick Wiseman. Observation became a key concept for practitioners and critics alike, describing a new filmmaking approach that was hailed as a radical break with established forms of documenting social life. Put most simply, it was understood as a commitment to "showing," not telling—that is, in place of narrated films with their summary and expert opinion, audiences were now to be presented with materials generated from recording events, situations, and relationships as they unfolded in specific social and cultural contexts. Moreover, in the absence of the conventional devices that rendered viewers passive, audiences were now expected to engage actively with what was presented, to evaluate the different kinds of evidence and interpret the significance of what they were being shown.

The observational movement in postwar American documentary cinema is commonly linked to changes in filmmaking technology. Developments in recording equipment, most notably the switch from heavy tripod-based cameras to relatively lightweight handheld ones and the ability of filmmakers to record sound synchronous with the image, have long been invoked as the driving force behind changes in the subject matter, techniques, and aesthetics of 1960s documentary cinema. For filmmakers like Drew or Leacock, the technological breakthrough was also an epistemological breakthrough, making possible work that they believed lay closer to reality than the highly mediated films of their

Griersonian predecessors.[1] Not surprisingly, the loud and excited proc-lamations of this revolutionary moment in documentary cinema were swiftly challenged. It took little time for critics to point out, for example, the continuing dependence of Drew or Leacock on conventions of plot and character. But it was the problematic truth claims associated with the new kind of observational filmmaking that were most consistently and ruthlessly undermined.[2]

Although we are mindful of the arguments and extensive commen-tary surrounding *cinéma vérité,* in this chapter we suggest a different way of looking at the work of the 1960s documentary filmmakers.[3] Putting to one side the vexed questions of truth, objectivity, and the "really" real, we will instead examine how observation was interpreted by certain promi-nent figures at the time. As a principle, it was central to the rhetoric of the new documentary movement and it served as the basis for distinguishing the new kind of documentary from the older discursive forms. But what did this mean exactly? How was the commitment to observation trans-lated into actual practice? In proposing to explore work by Robert Drew, Albert and David Maysles, and Frederick Wiseman through the prism of observation, our intention is to pose new questions about a much dis-cussed form and to highlight the variation found in documentary projects pursued at this time. Even a cursory glance at the work of these filmmak-ers reveals strikingly different understandings of the observational task.

Our concern then will not be with exposing discrepancies between the rhetoric of observation and its practice, or evaluating the status of truth claims. Instead we will take selected films as the focus for investigat-ing the nature of filmmakers' practice. In developing this approach, we have taken our cue from the growing dissatisfaction among commenta-tors about the kind of debate that has focused around American *cinéma vérité.* For, over the last four decades, much of the discussion has been conducted discursively, by means of assertions and refutations rather than being engaged with the details of the work itself. The rhetoric surround-ing this mode of documentary filmmaking seems to have developed a life of its own, as Jeanne Hall remarks. The energy expended in argument has often been at the expense of critical attention to those films considered to be representative of the genre.[4]

This chapter is built around an examination of *Primary* (1960), *Salesman* (1968), and *Titicut Follies* (1967). We investigate what observation entails in the documentation of social realities. Most importantly, however, we seek to analyze the films for what they *are* rather for what they *are not*.[5] We draw on the three fields of inquiry that we first outlined in the preface. First of all, our discussion has been importantly shaped by studies in the history of science on observational practices. Hence in this part of the book—and in subsequent ones—we will be attentive to where observational work is carried out (sites), to what is observed (objects), to how observation is effected (techniques and technologies), and to the ways in which observations are organized and presented as knowledge about the world (the representational form / film text).[6] Such a framework has helped us to move beyond the familiar critical terrain that surrounds *cinéma vérité*, enabling us to change the questions asked of documentary materials from the 1960s. For, despite its frequent use as a general description, the meaning of observation within specific contexts of filmmaking practice has yet to be closely scrutinized.

The new possibilities offered by history of science perspectives might appear, at first sight, to sit awkwardly with approaches emerging from film studies, the second field of inquiry to inform our research. Somewhat to our surprise, however, we discovered that they complemented, indeed enhanced, existing work on the documentary. By looking carefully at the detail of certain films, we follow other writers in acknowledging the complexity of the documentary as an aesthetic construction. The danger, as Grant has pointed out, is that "[d]ocumentaries are almost always discussed *as documentaries* rather than closely read as film texts."[7] We take seriously the formal strategies of *Primary, Salesman,* and *Titicut Follies,* asking what camera style, the use of sound, and approaches toward editing can tell us about how individual filmmakers have understood their role as observers. What kind of evidence does a film provide of observation conceptualized as a specialized activity rooted in distinctive sites, skills, technologies, and modes of knowledge? In combining approaches from the history of science and film studies, we hope to more effectively address observation as a complex phenomenon that encompasses the technical and the aesthetic, skill and intuition, discipline and innovation.

Finally, our discussion of *Primary, Salesman,* and *Titicut Follies* is animated by questions that originate in the discipline of anthropology. Given our interest in the observational turn in ethnographic filmmaking, we take up Young's suggestion that the American documentaries of the 1960s might be considered important precursors of later developments in anthropological cinema.[8] Hence we explore the extent to which the approaches of Drew, the Maysles brothers, and Wiseman mirror those that are characteristic of the fieldwork-based discipline. Certainly we recognize that the three films at the heart of this chapter are major contributions to an ethnography of 1960s America. Our intention is not to quibble over whether these films meet some kind of criteria necessary for them to be considered legitimate anthropology or not. Instead, we are interested in identifying the points of convergence—and divergence—between the observational practices of documentary filmmakers who were affected in some way by journalism and those for whom anthropology provided the more obvious reference point.

We begin with *Primary,* the film made in 1960 by Drew Associates about the battle between John F. Kennedy and Hubert Humphrey for the Democratic presidential nomination. This film has long been central to the debates about *cinéma vérité.* At the time of its release, it was hailed by its makers as a breakthrough, a symbol of the revolution—conceptual and technical—in non-fiction filmmaking. According to Robert Drew, *Primary* was "received as a kind of documentary second coming."[9] Other commentators were also swept up in the hyperbole. Subsequently, however, critics treated such claims with considerably more skepticism.[10] Was *Primary* indeed more truthful? Were the filmmakers offering their audiences any less of a manipulated view of reality? Were the film's techniques actually different from those of conventional fiction and documentary films and so on? In the narrative that follows, we make the film itself the focus of critical attention. We explore the distinctive features of *Primary* as evidence of a particular interpretation of what observation might entail in documentary. What did Drew and his collaborators observe and how did they understand their role as observers? What techniques and technologies defined this role and how were observations structured and given meaningful form?

Primary

Primary follows John F. Kennedy and Hubert Humphrey in their attempt to be selected as the Democratic candidate for the White House. It charts their changing fortunes through the Wisconsin primary of 1960. The film was made with a number of crews, each one following a different point of action. *Primary* cuts between the two candidates as they embark on a round of public activities in the hope of winning votes. From spontaneous handshaking on the street, to lively banter with schoolgirls, to radio phone-in shows, speeches to farm workers, and appearances at political rallies, the filmmakers present the unfolding drama that reaches its climax on polling day. Kennedy wins but only by a narrow margin, and the two candidates embark on the next stage of their attempt at securing the White House nomination.

The film was the result of a collective effort. It was shot and edited by several filmmakers associated with the former *Life* magazine journalist-turned-producer Robert Drew. Drew was a pivotal figure in the emergence of *cinéma vérité*. Impatient with older forms of documentary cinema, what he called "lectures with picture illustrations," he was determined to forge a new approach that was based upon different premises: recording live events as they happened, communicating to audiences the experience of "being there"; storytelling in place of argument, expert summary, and information.[11] Drew attracted other young filmmakers who were also seeking to break with the old forms and hierarchies of documentary cinema. Most notable among these were Richard Leacock, D. A. Pennebaker, and David and Albert Maysles.

The concerns of *Primary* were very much a reflection of Drew's own concerns. Given his commitment to a different kind of reporting responsive to the new politics of the times, it was perhaps not surprising that many of the early films made politics itself the object of observation. This meant politics not with a capital P but politics understood as performance, process, ritual rather than as a matter of ideals, substantive issues, articulations of policy, or meetings of world leaders. To conceive of politics in this way necessitated changes in the conventional sites, techniques, and technologies of film observation. Moreover, it is important to acknowledge that *Primary* is as much about journalism and the media as it is about two presidential hopefuls. For running throughout is the implicit contrast between forms of traditional journalism and Drew's approach represented by the film itself.[12]

Primary was largely shot on the run. It involved leaving the controlled conditions of the photo opportunity and formal interview for a politics located on the street, in meeting halls and backrooms, in campaign buses and voting booths—and, of course, in recording studios approached as sites of performance and choreography. According to O'Connell, what Drew and his associates understood was "the attraction, the distinctiveness, of *Primary* was more than the camera simply moving off the tripod and following the character; they sensed that, in *Primary*, in the hands of a skilled observer, the camera was finally free enough of its former inflexibilities to begin, at long last, to 'see.'"[13]

So what did a "skilled observer" mean in this context? For Drew, the role of the observer was about witnessing. It involved being there when things happened. It was about following events, approached not as a series of statements about what was happening or had happened but as a process of unfolding relationships in which small clues like gestures, facial expression, body posture had revelatory potential. Above all, Drew and his filmmakers were looking for what they called "moments"—Humphrey falling asleep in the car, Jackie Kennedy's fidgeting hands, Kennedy's sweeping entrance to the Milwaukee rally. Observation then meant the development of a particular kind of alertness to the unexpected. It meant being open to the spontaneous or to the overlooked as potentially yielding new insight into a situation or personality. These skills hinged greatly on intuition and on the fine-tuning of the senses. Filmmakers had to learn to anticipate. They also had to learn to discriminate between banal, everyday occurrences and moments of revelation, even if the latter were often not known until a much later stage in the project. Despite the considerable shooting to editing ratio that followed from the new documentary approach, the filmmakers working with Drew on *Primary* were highly selective observers. They made countless decisions about where to place themselves, how to film, when to film, when to stop filming—and, crucially, when *not* to stop filming. These decisions could not be made in advance but were forged within the context of recording itself.

By the conventional standards of the day, *Primary* is remarkably informal. Certainly it has none of the stiffness characteristic of an earlier style of political documentary, when public figures were presented in carefully chosen situations with enormous deference and distance. Drew's filmmakers hover at the shoulder of Kennedy; they squeeze into a car with Humphrey as he dozes; they overhear the whispered exchanges and confidences around Jackie Kennedy; they observe the exhausted figure of Kennedy, smoking a cigarette, as he waits nervously for the election results to be announced. Using handheld camera and sound equipment, Leacock, Al Maysles, Pennebaker, and Macartney-Filgate were attempting to be part of what they were filming. At times they moved easily alongside the candidates, at other times they situated themselves amid excited clusters of people waiting to catch a glimpse of Kennedy.

Still from *Primary* (1960). *Courtesy of Robert Drew.*

From the beginning of the film, there is a tangible sense of a living, breathing camera—one that is animated by what is happening around it. Occasionally, there is a bravura display of agility, such as Al Maysles's famous tracking shot of Kennedy arriving at a political rally in Milwaukee. For the most part, however, the filmmakers are *with* people, close enough to be jostled, crowded, and carried along by the momentum of unfolding events. They are part of the ritual process of politics, folded into the performance for the duration of the show. Although *Primary* was shot by a number of different individuals, the camera work is remarkable in conveying a consistent sense of openness toward subjects. It expresses a curiosity about them and an affectionate regard for them. Not least, this is conveyed by the many shots of individual faces in the film. There is something unusual about the way that the camera looks directly at people, attending to them without objectifying its subjects, rendering them at once recognizable and enigmatic.[14]

The audio track of *Primary* is made up of synchronous sound, dubbed sound, sound bites, audio montage, music, and narration. Given Drew's commitment to a reporting style anchored in "picture" rather than "word logic," it is not surprising to find that these different devices are used in support of the film's strong, compelling images. Sound is used to enhance the momentum of the work, to provide context and background information, to bridge different parts of the film and to shore up the feeling of "being there." Undoubtedly, *Primary* has remained memorable over the years because of its many arresting images, but it also serves to indicate the importance of different sorts of sound to the new documentary approach being forged by Drew and his collaborators. Not least, the film demonstrates the creative possibilities opened up by abandoning the single, dominant voice of the narrator. *Primary* allows us to hear *voices*. They are strikingly varied in pitch, tone, and forms of expression, alerting us to the complex role of language as a mode of communication.

Watching *Primary* almost fifty years after its making, one is impressed by the energy and spirited exuberance of the film. It derives partly from the dynamic images, the music, an urgent narration, and from the particular image-sound juxtapositions. But equally the techniques of editing were crucial in establishing the film's distinctive rhythm and tempo. The filmmakers themselves—Leacock, Maysles, and Pennebaker—were involved in cutting the material that they had shot, but it was Robert Drew who oversaw the process and assumed editorial control. He was, after all, the person responsible for trying to sell the project to the different parties, from the candidates to the television executives. Hence it was only to be expected that Drew's specific concerns would be central in the editing and final presentation of the footage.

The framework for the editing of particular scenes in *Primary* is one of drama. Shots rather than extended sequences are the basis of construction and they keep the film moving—so, too, the constant cutting back and forth between the two candidates, Humphrey and Kennedy. Commenting on Drew's work more generally, the film editor Patricia Jaffe pointed out that much of it is, as she puts it, "flawed by pushing the material into a mold where none existed. This tendency to create a story or constant excitement, to keep the film moving from one headline to another, is a result of Drew's inclination and experience. Basically as a journalist, he feels it necessary to keep the audience at a high pitch of interest and excitement."[15] Certainly in *Primary* we can see this at work. Storytelling and human drama are at the heart of the film. Priority is given to images, and the film is organized around a succession of strong pictures. Drew covers all the angles of the story by employing multiple camera crews. The use of handheld equipment is intended to generate rough, informal material that by virtue of its spontaneity and immediacy enables viewers to imagine "being there."

It was clear from the beginning that Drew had a very clear sense of his agenda. *Primary* was both filmed and edited according to it. As a work of journalism, it necessitated the investigation of a particular story. This involved going behind the scenes of a political campaign, seeking out unusual moments and encounters in an attempt to offer his audience a new perspective on the world in which it lived. The prescience of *Primary* derives from the film's acknowledgement of the centrality of images and image making to American postwar politics. The conception of journalism that Drew deemed appropriate to the times, with an emphasis on pictures, not text, on crafted performances rather than occasions of formal rhetoric, was profoundly expressive of the new social contract. It was a vision of American society first brilliantly articulated by Orson Welles in *Citizen Kane.*

Given Drew's interpretation of his task, it was not surprising that he chose to observe certain aspects of American society and to observe them in a very particular way. His films tended to be defined by action, by a tight time frame, and by a limited engagement between filmmakers and subjects. In the case of *Primary,* the film was shot by multiple crews over a short period of time. There was no sustained research beforehand. Drew simply asked his collaborators to go along for the ride, to throw themselves into the filmmaking and to manage the interpersonal relationships as best they could. As *Primary* shows, the relationships between the filmmakers and their subjects were fleeting, made on the move—and, importantly, they did not develop in any significant way over the course of the film.

The filmmakers who worked with Drew in the early 1960s quickly grew impatient with his agenda. Leacock, Pennebaker, and Albert Maysles had never shared his journalistic interpretation of the documentary project, nor had they ever envisaged television as the primary site for the films they made. Moreover, Drew's position within the world of network television led him increasingly to insist on the kinds of devices that his movement claimed to have abandoned—most notably narration. By 1963 the breakup of the group that Drew had assembled for the making of *Primary* was inevitable. Leacock, Pennebaker, and Albert Maysles began to carve out their own individual trajectories as filmmakers. Although they remained committed collectively to the notion of observation (as fundamentally about showing, not telling), each one worked with it in his own way. In the hands of individual practitioners, it came to be interpreted differently, taking on a distinctive shape and form that was expressive of specific filmmaking personalities. Far from being an anonymous approach, it was obvious from the beginning that observational filmmaking was an authored genre. But the nature of authorship was unusual and complex. It was forged in the space between filmmaker, subjects, and audience. The resulting work profoundly reflected the perceptual register of individual filmmakers, but it was a register shaped and realized through the processes of making and viewing themselves. The centrality of this question to observational filmmaking approaches may be seen in the case of *Salesman,* a film made by Albert and David Maysles some six years after *Primary.*

Salesman

Salesman opens with a hand turning the pages of the Bible. The knotted fingers run across the page and we hear the soft voice of a salesman. The shot widens to reveal Paul Brennan (the Badger), a slight man with a neat, dark suit and earnest expression, in the home of a potential customer. The young woman listens politely, the restlessness of her small child serving as a welcome distraction from the awkwardness of the sales encounter. For Brennan does not let up, his patter continuing, intensifying, quietly insistent, even as we sense the moment to clinch the deal has already been lost. Eventually, the child breaks away from his mother and moves over to the piano. Brennan finally accepts defeat. For a moment the camera lingers on his face. The film cuts, moving from this extended first scene to three other salesmen (introduced by their names and nicknames, the Rabbit, the Gipper, the Bull) glimpsed at different moments in their door-to-door transactions. The situation appears to be the same in each case but, as we discover, with each encounter something new is revealed.

The opening scene of *Salesman* establishes the distinctive approach of the filmmakers toward their subject—not just what aspects of American life they had chosen to observe but the particular way that they went about observing them. Most obviously, it announces the centrality of Bible selling to the film. It is repeated countless times over the course of ninety minutes. But, from the outset, the Maysles brothers show selling to be a highly skilled practice involving an intricate choreography between the different parties. It is a performance that demands improvisation, poetry, humor, persistence, and sheer hard work. Moreover, it requires a keen sensitivity to the dynamics and tempo of individual transactions. With each encounter, we are reminded of the fundamental contradiction between faith and money that lies at the heart of the enterprise. But *Salesman* is the story of particular human subjects. It is not an abstract exploration of the paradoxes of capitalism or the hypocrisy at the heart of American society.

The filmmakers' concerns are revealed in the techniques that they use in the first sequence. There are no preliminaries. There is no narration and no introductory text. We are simply placed in the midst of Brennan's sales pitch. The camera hovers close to the subjects, encompassing at once the details and scope of the scene. Patiently it attends to the tangled web of relationships that constitute the interaction—relationships between hand and page, between language and silence, speech and gesture, body posture and movement, people and the material context of the encounter. It is a reflection of the unusual skill and sensitivity of Albert and David Maysles that in less than two minutes we are aware of a drama unfolding around the camera. Referring to this as *drama,* however, is to risk inflating a moment that is so much more delicately felt as unease or discomfort at Brennan's persistence in seeking to close the deal. For to describe it in such conventional terms would be to upset the carefully wrought scale of the scene that is emblematic of the film as a whole. In their opening shots, the Maysles seek to persuade us that there is something important at stake here, even if it does not involve action or crisis. The tension of *Salesman* is the inverse of Drew's action-based dramas, since actions fail to produce results. The poignancy of the film inheres in disappointment, futility, and failure.

Salesman was filmed by Albert Maysles, the cameraman responsible for the famous seventy-four-second tracking shot of Kennedy in *Primary,* now working with his brother, David, as the film's sound recordist. It was partly conceived in response to their own experiences of door-to-door selling as young men but, more importantly, it was a reflection of their personal experiences growing up in an Irish neighborhood in the Boston suburbs. The subjects of the film resembled men they had known. What intrigued the Maysles—and emerged at the heart of their observation—was the profound disjuncture between who people were and the jobs they did. And, as they discovered, both humor and tragedy lay in this slippage.[16]

The Maysles followed the four-man team from the Mid-American Bible Company over the course of a six-week sales tour that began in the outskirts of Boston and eventually took them to Florida. They tracked the salesmen as they doggedly moved across bleak urban landscapes and unpromising suburban streets, searching for addresses, knocking on doors, seeking to secure that elusive sale. The lonely housewife is their prey. The film offers a glimpse of the lives of women who are at home all day and, for the most part, it is a pretty bleak picture—women marooned in domestic isolation, strapped for cash, and reluctant to make financial decisions without their husband's approval. At every turn *Salesman* is a reminder of the rhetoric of American dream and its reality.

The salesmen's failure to sell is a personal failure—as Kenny, the team's "motivator"—repeatedly reminds the Badger, the Rabbit, the Bull, and the Gipper. Urging them on with his aggressive, self-satisfied oratory, he becomes the antithesis of the quiet dignity of his men. Interspersed with door-to-door selling, sales conferences, and Kenny's interventions, the Maysles show us moments from the downtime that the men spend together in anonymous motel rooms. The film reveals the good-natured banter among the men that grows out of affection and familiarity with one another. The camaraderie, however, is always tinged with awkwardness. There is solidarity but there is also personal isolation—and there is, of course, the unspoken rivalry between the men. As the film slowly closes in around Brennan, the poignancy of his plight emerges as much from the scenes with his co-workers as the futile exchanges with potential customers. Failure can be corrosive. And it is the almost imperceptible withdrawal of Brennan's fellow men that makes his desolation ever more haunting.

Salesman represented a notable shift on the part of the filmmakers away from a concern with observing large moments in American life to the scrutiny of small, intense ones. The Maysles were interested in evoking emotional texture rather than documenting action. They worked from the ground upward, intensively exploring the lives of a handful of subjects situated in the world in very particular ways. The remarkable achievement of *Salesman* lies in the fact that its apparent limitation is the basis of its strength. For it is, paradoxically, the narrowness of the film's focus that makes the broader questions about American idealism and individual experience all the more compelling.

Still from *Salesman* (1968). *Courtesy of Albert Maysles.*

The Maysles shared with Robert Drew and the other observational filmmakers of the 1960s a commitment to locating their practice in the world.
Their agenda was, however, distinctive. With *Salesman,* the Maysles began
to pry open the complex, affective landscape of modern America. In taking this as the object of their inquiry, they developed methods of working
that differed in significant ways from those pioneered in the making of
Primary and other early classics. The restless energy and heroic endeavors
of Drew and his *cinéma vérité* filmmakers were not of much use in exploring the more nebulous terrain of aspiration, failure, and disappointment.
The Maysles had to carve out their own approach. Although at first glance
it appeared to be built around the very same techniques and technologies as other kinds of observational documentary (the use of handheld
equipment, synchronous sound, etc.), there were a number of subtle and
important differences that are worthy of closer investigation.

From the outset, the relationship between the filmmakers and their
subjects was a central part of *Salesman.* Unlike the Drew films, the Maysles
did not attempt to cover all the angles, employing multiple camera crews
in order to capture moments of crisis or drama. Despite following four

subjects, David and Al worked in partnership as a single unit. They lived and traveled with the men over an extended period of time such that their presence came to be woven into the fabric of the film itself. The filmmakers sought to find a position *alongside* the Bible sellers. By this we refer to proximity, a filmmaking position that both encompassed closeness and distance. *Salesman* came out of the filmmakers' curiosity about, and empathy for, their subjects—using the camera with love, as Al Maysles has described it.[17] At its core was the forging of trust. It involved neither a blind identification with the men nor an aloof judgment of them. It required something much more difficult and demanding—namely, being able to look subjects in the eye and to have the courage not to turn away in the face of awkward situations or encounters. The Maysles show us unscrupulous selling tactics, including Brennan's deliberate misrepresentation of himself to a young housewife desperately trying to avoid having to make the down payment. Although these scenes are hard to watch, they are filmed with compassion and understanding such that they are intended not to alienate us from Brennan (to expose him in some way) but to deepen our sense of connection with him.[18] The contrast with Frederick Wiseman could not be starker. He is an unflinching filmmaker too. The affective quality of his work, however, is radically different.

In order to make *Salesman,* Al Maysles adapted the existing recording technology so that the camera became a physical extension of his body.[19] This was not a technical exercise. It was about making it possible for him to relate to people in a very specific way. As Maysles recognized, to evoke the emotional texture of people's lives necessitated a human camera. He humanized the camera by making it a part of his body. This did not constitute a disavowal of technological mediation in the documentation of the world. It was about placing the experiencing body at the center of the filmmaking encounter. Hence for Al Maysles to take up a position with his subjects, to locate himself within their existential space, is an attempt to refract something of this through his own body.

We have already seen in the case of *Primary* that observation was directed toward action and the style of the film took on some of the qualities of what was being documented. Like their subjects, Drew's filmmakers were men of action, people doing things in the world, following movement, capturing drama, energetically seeking out strong, dynamic images. Despite the rhetoric, there was an emphasis on striking individual shots rather than extended, continuous takes, and synchronous sound made up only a small part of the film's audio track. The camera and sound techniques of *Salesman* are quite different, reflecting the new documentary agenda that the filmmakers sought to articulate. "I don't think in terms of actions and reactions," Al Maysles once explained. "I don't think in technical terms at all, but rather of what I want to get, and what I really want to get is a front-head-on look at the person who is talking at the time. I'm not thinking of an artistic shot or an artistic composition of shots, though that's important. I suppose that approach makes the editing more difficult, but I feel that it is one of the reasons why the human content of the film is so strong and so totally convincing, because my concentration is on what I feel I have to get of the person, rather than some artistic thing I am trying to prove."[20]

Al Maysles's camera work is notable for its attentiveness to the human scale of things. It conveys a physical closeness to subjects and yet is respectful of human distance (as we will see, this contrasts with Wiseman's extreme close-up style that distorts the human body). In *Salesman,* Maysles's camera is unhurried, patiently taking in the whole scene that unfolds around it. The richness of these extended sequences partly stems from the filmmaker's keen sensitivity to background and his commitment to placing people in the material contexts of their lives. For Al Maysles alerts us to the importance of how people live, to what they have around them (the proud owners of the new stereo, the anonymity of motel rooms), using his camera to gather up a wealth of everyday detail that is central to the filmmakers' interpretation of their subject matter. Bible selling is embedded in a matrix of social and material relationships in which nuances of gesture, posture, facial expression, the style of furniture, the cut of a suit are laden with cultural meaning. Of course, language is crucial to this activity too. And David Maysles's approach as sound recordist, in its rendering of the sheer diversity and complexity of speech (and silence), serves to mirror the meticulousness of the film's camera style. He too worked by humanizing the recording technology, rejecting the use of a boom microphone, for example. For the most part, *Salesman* is built upon the use of synchronous sound. Far from restricting the communicative potential of language, this device opens up a range of new possibilities. The contextualization of speech lays bare the dense context within which language functions—who is speaking, to whom, in what way, and under what circumstances.[21] Not least, the film reveals the clumsiness of language—the missed connections, misunderstandings, the profound gaps between meaningful human communication and the language of selling.

The modesty of *Salesman*'s subjects found its reflection in the modesty of its filmmakers. There is no artificial inflation of events or interactions, no demonstrations of virtuosity (as in *Primary*). Moreover, the Maysles remind us of the enigmatic nature of subjectivity. Although their film allows us to approach the lives of their subjects, it does not assume the knowability of another person's experience. They hint at the interior life of Brennan, for example, and suggest possible feelings and emotions, but they do not seek to explain him.[22] For the Maysles, observing the Bible salesmen did not mean closing in around them, tightly scrutinizing their subjects in a way that gave them no room to breathe. On the contrary, their film opens out. It both allows their subjects to breathe and generates a space for empathetic connection.

The renewed commitment to observation in postwar American documentary had at its core the notion of filmmaker as witness—the filmmaker was present when things happened rather than reconstructing or commenting on them after the event. The resulting film constituted a report on what had been experienced firsthand. It was not an objective record but an eyewitness account with all its limitations and partiality. The persuasiveness of the representation lay not in its completeness but in the opposite. The flaws, the tangible evidence of the human observer on the scene, offered important clues in judging the final representation of witnessed events. Given the centrality of firsthand observation to this kind of documentary, the question of who takes responsibility for the editing of the footage has long been an important one. In many cases, there was a commitment to the notion that editing was to be carried out by the original witness to the events rather than someone outside the relationships and experiences of the filmmaking encounter. This was something Drew recognized, even if he was not entirely successful in making it part of his practice. The Maysles, however, have always proceeded differently. Typically they use an outside editor—indeed Al Maysles does not get involved in editing at all. With *Salesman,* the hundred or so hours of footage generated over the course of six weeks was fashioned into the ninety-minute film by Charlotte Zwerin, an editor whose understanding of Brennan and his team was entirely based upon the celluloid materials with which she worked. Of course, Zwerin's decisions as an editor were to some extent circumscribed by the recording techniques used by the Maysles at the time of filming. Nevertheless, the overall shape and texture of the final piece was created by someone removed from the relationships and contexts of filming. The issues that follow from this kind of arrangement are important to consider in any discussion of observational practice. Our concern here is not to understand them as a betrayal of ideals or as further evidence of the discrepancy between what is claimed for *cinéma vérité* and what is actually practiced. Instead, we explore what is instructive—and revealing—when the editor works in a way that is different from how the material has been shot.

Although as documentary filmmakers the Maysles were committed to exploring the experiential texture of contemporary life, *Salesman* (like *Primary*) was organized according to the norms of dramatic narrative. The film is not action-led, but it charts a familiar emotional journey that begins with hope and ends in despair. This is Brennan's journey and he is quickly identified as the character around whom *Salesman* is built. It is the Chicago sales conference that indicates the centrality of his fate to the film. From the moment we see Brennan framed against a drab city landscape juxtaposed with an audio track taken from the meeting to which he is heading, we know that his trajectory has become the central narrative thread of the film.

Zwerin has often been criticized for this particular segment of *Salesman*. Certainly it signals her continuing attachment to established narrative conventions, despite the more open-ended, exploratory filmmaking approach pursued by the Maysles. More specifically, this section of the film has attracted comment because of Zwerin's use of non-synchronous sound over the images of Brennan, thereby imputing certain thoughts and feelings to him that the visual evidence does not necessarily support. It is not the purported "untruthfulness" of this juxtaposition that is the problem here but rather that it runs counter to the observational style of the filming. The device is unnecessary. Zwerin's intervention was conceived in response to what she saw as a weakness in the film.[23] Paradoxically, however, it serves to expose not the weakness but the strength of the original material. Zwerin makes explicit what the filmmakers left implicit and, in so doing, she circumscribes the potential resonance of the scene. The shot of Brennan's face against a train window, silhouetted against a bleak cityscape, said everything without having to say anything. Without the added audio track, an imaginative space opens up, inviting a response from the viewer that is infinitely more nuanced and subtle than the one offered by the film's editor.

The final scene of *Salesman* is also interesting in this respect. For here, too, we sense a conflict between the way that the material has been shot and how the editor seeks to work with it. We see Brennan with the members of the sales team in yet another impersonal motel room. He prepares to leave, his defeat palpable. In order to conclude the film, Zwerin constructs this scene entirely through editing, bringing together a range of single shots that originated in different locations. The dramatic effect is distinctive, as Bazin famously pointed out in his discussion of the seal hunt in Flaherty's *Nanook of the North*. For the relationships suggested by Zwerin are not integral to the material; instead, montage functions as the basis for the creation of meaning. Meaning does not emerge from the images themselves but from their combination or juxtaposition and, as Bazin was the first to point out, a montage-based sequence engaged the spectator in an entirely different way from a *mise-en-scène* approach.[24] Although Zwerin's constructed scene brings closure to the film, its style sits awkwardly with the broader interest of the filmmakers in preserving the spatial unity of events and the inherently ambiguous nature of the real.

The flaws in *Salesman* are not a reflection of some kind of cheating. Their significance follows from what they make manifest in observational filmmaking as a practice. It is the Maysles's commitment to forging new techniques as an integral part of observing the world differently (that is, attending to the emotional texture of "ordinary" people's lives) that renders conventional editorial interventions problematic. The problem with Zwerin's use of devices taken from the conventional narrative film is that at best they are redundant, at worst they cut across the film's carefully judged sensibility. What *Salesman* lays bare is the centrality of human relationships and human perspectives to observational work. The unfolding encounter between subjects and filmmakers is woven into every scene of the film, even if it remains implicit rather than explicitly acknowledged. The problem with Zwerin's approach is that it is "privileged." It denies the human basis of what it is we are seeing and hearing, disrupting the ongoing negotiation between the subjects, filmmakers, and viewers.[25]

Titicut Follies

When the observational technique works, it puts you in the middle of the events and asks you to think through your own relationship to what you're seeing and hearing, which I think is more interesting for the viewer. The real film takes place where the mind or the eye of the viewer meets the screen and interprets, in a sense participates in, what they're seeing and hearing.

—*FREDERICK WISEMAN*, Cineaste *interview with Cynthia Lucia (1994)*

The work of Frederick Wiseman is critical to our discussion of the rise of observation as a postwar filmmaking practice. His films have often been characterized as "observational."[26] Moreover, it is a term that he uses himself to describe the style that has come to be the hallmark of his work. Despite modifications here and there, Wiseman's approach has not fundamentally changed over the course of forty years. His films have remained remarkably consistent in their focus and their aesthetic design. In the final part of this chapter we examine what observation means in the context of Wiseman's project. What is the nature of his commitment to observation as a principle of investigation and how is this expressed as a filmmaking practice? Our exploration of this central axis in Wiseman's work is driven by his importance as one of the leading figures in the American postwar documentary cinema. But also we are interested in indicating some of the continuities and contrasts between his work and that of his contemporaries, most notably Drew and the Maysles brothers. As in the preceding parts of this chapter, our interest in Wiseman's observational practices is partly filtered through an anthropological framework. Like the films of Drew and the Maysles, Wiseman's work is ethnographic too. One of our concerns is to establish a basis for comparing his techniques of social inquiry with those later developed in the context of an explicitly ethnographic cinema.

Wiseman's early film *Titicut Follies* (1967) appeared at the end of the decade that began with *Primary*.[27] Wiseman had never been part of Drew's circle, coming to filmmaking from a background in law. Although he worked with many of the same techniques and technologies that characterized the early *cinéma vérité* films, it was clear from the outset that Wiseman's project diverged from that of his contemporaries. Not least, his vision of American society was much bleaker than that offered by Drew, Leacock, Pennebaker, and even the Maysles. In place of celebrity, drama, heroic endeavors, and personal crises, Wiseman focused his attention on institutions and the workings of power. America as a buoyant society in movement, made and remade through individual agency, became something quite different—a world at once enclosed, oppressive, and profoundly dehumanizing.

Titicut Follies opens with a musical revue. Wiseman presents us with a group of performers running through a song and dance routine. There is nothing to suggest that this group is made up of staff and patients of Bridgewater, a secure hospital located on the outskirts of Boston. The film abruptly shifts from this opening sequence to a scene of men getting undressed and being forced to stand naked as guards sort through their discarded clothes. It then moves to an extended interaction between a psychiatrist and patient about his sexual life and offenses against young girls. From here the film unfolds as a series of episodes from the life of an institution. We watch patients being washed and shaved, forcibly fed, taunted by guards about the state of their cell; groups of confused, shuffling men; nakedness, a birthday celebration with party games, "consultations" between doctors and patients, verbal outbursts and spontaneous speechmaking by inmates; and the preparation of a corpse for burial. Wiseman's documentation of institutional life constitutes a devastating critique of Bridgewater—its cruelty and callousness conveyed as much in innumerable small gestures and everyday humiliations as in the more explicit and horrifying moments of violence.

The film came out of Wiseman's moral indignation in the face of conditions he had encountered at Bridgewater while teaching as a young lawyer in Boston. He wanted to make the public aware of where they were sending people and of the muddle in the judicial system that consigned both the sick and the criminal to the same inadequate facility.[28] His film was conceived as a contribution to public awareness and social reform. Although its focus is a single institution, *Titicut Follies* is an investigation of how America deals with the mentally ill. It raises questions about the nature of madness (echoes of Jean Rouch's film *Les Maîtres Fous* here), about how illness is constructed, managed, and contained by the work of an institution. But to explain it in such terms is to deny the work's extraordinary visceral power. For, above all, Wiseman makes his viewers confront a part of American society that had remained largely hidden from view, forcing it upon them in an unusually raw and unsparing way.

To describe *Titicut Follies* as an observational film is to refer to observation as both a principle and practice in Wiseman's project. From the outset, Wiseman was dedicated to working with film in the service of social observation, an inquiry understood to involve looking closely,

Still from *Titicut Follies* (1967). © *1967 Bridgewater Film Company, Inc.*

attentively, and critically at the world in which we live. This serves as the ethical basis for the techniques Wiseman used as a filmmaker. Like many other prominent figures in the 1960s documentary movement, he was committed to recording things as they happened rather than as recollected or explained after the fact, and he expected his audience to play an active role in interpreting and evaluating the material he presented to it. Wiseman also dispensed with narration, music, interviews, and expert summary characteristic of the conventional documentary. Eschewing the tripod and working with a minimal crew (consisting of himself as sound recordist and cameraman John Marshall),[29] he sought to insert himself unobtrusively into the institutional context, taking up a position of witness, and he took sole responsibility for the editing of the material into the final film. Although, in important ways, the techniques and technologies of Wiseman's filmmaking overlap with those of people like Leacock or the Maysles, *Titicut Follies* reveals the distinctive character of his observational practice. The film establishes the unique filmmaking personality of Wiseman and the particular conditions that have shaped it.

Let us now examine more closely what observation as a practice involves in the case of *Titicut Follies*. Aside from the broad contours of the filmmaking approach indicated above, Wiseman uses very carefully selected techniques. His interpretation of observation is complicated by the fact that he does not shoot the film himself but instead always works with a cameraman—in this case, John Marshall. Hence we must reconcile how the film is shot, where the camera is placed, how it frames what it sees, with the manner in which sound is recorded and used with images, and how, as director, Wiseman constructs this through combinations of shots and juxtapositions of scenes.

In the opening sequence of *Titicut Follies,* Marshall's camera is situated in the audience of Bridgewater's theater. It looks out across a dark auditorium toward the harshly lit performers on stage. An abrupt change of location follows, as Wiseman cuts from the performance to a guard ordering an inmate to remove his clothes. This takes us by surprise, immediately alerting us to the uncertain and uneasy world of Wiseman's film. It is a moment of disorientation that resonates throughout the film, since we are never once able to situate ourselves in Bridgewater. Wiseman's extensive use of close-up shots renders an institutional space that is unrelenting in its dreary architecture, its enclosure and anonymity, but also one that is deeply confusing. It is a kaleidoscope of hard surfaces and angular spaces—walls, bars, cells, narrow corridors, tight spaces—that we traverse without ever getting our bearings. Over the course of almost ninety minutes, Wiseman never allows us to know where we are, how we have gotten from one place to another, or where anything is in relation to anything else. This sense of disorientation and claustrophobia is generated by the tight frame of the camera that precludes our developing a perspective on things and by an editing style built around discontinuity and unusual juxtapositions. But it is also exacerbated by the role that sound plays in the film. It is remorseless, an unending stream of harsh noise—barked orders, shouting, taunting, arguments, confrontations, squeaking doors, footsteps on hard floors, keys jangling, a siren, singing, television sound, a ringing telephone, and so on.

Titicut Follies is made up of a series of scenes that begin and end abruptly. Wiseman cuts into events or encounters that are already unfolding and he leaves them before closure. Often he inter-cuts different scenes. For example, in one of the most discussed parts of the film, he juxtaposes the force-feeding of one patient with footage of the preparation of his body for burial (this is also the only moment of silence). Wiseman has often been criticized for heavy-handedness in this sequence, but it is a strategy that he signals early in the work and one that he uses in different ways throughout it. Shortly after the opening revue, Wiseman inserts us into a conversation between one of Bridgewater's psychiatrists and a sex offender, cutting away from it to the earlier scene of men being stripped of their clothing, before returning us to the interview once more. Aside from the disruption of spatial and temporal integrity created by this editing strategy, the interaction between doctor and patient is also shot in a manner that underlines the subversion of context. It is a scene largely constructed around close-up shots of the two participants seen separately rather than held together as participants in conversation. Moreover, they are suspended in a kind of limbo, the camera pressing up against their faces and obliterating any kind of background. The doctor and his patient are neither situated in time nor space, nor in relation to each other. This is repeated elsewhere in the film. The camera systematically isolates individuals from one another, removing context or reducing it to a blank wall against which reverberate the harsh sounds of institutional life.

Of all the observational filmmakers of the 1960s, Wiseman has perhaps been the most consistent in retaining the central link between the shooting and editing phases of his project. But, as we have already noted, there are unusual complications in his case. Although his own firsthand observations at the time of recording are the material with which he works as the film's sole editor, the footage itself is not generated by him but by his cameraman. Wiseman has described editing as a sort of "thinking through," an analytical process that gives meaning to what has been recorded. Despite the intense observation undertaken during the filming stage, Wiseman privileges editing as the crucial stage when the intellectual work of filmmaking occurs: "It's a matter of the final film being both a report of what you find and a reflection of your experiences and feelings about what you find. So it's really a matter of trying to think your way through the material."[30] The way he carries out this task and articulates what he calls a "theory" of the witnessed events is distinctive. In an extended account of Wiseman's editing techniques, Nichols points to the "mosaic" structure of his films.[31] By this he refers to the overall organization of the work according not to the usual conventions of argument, narrative, or chronology but by means of metaphor or patterns of poetic association. However, the individual parts of the film, what he calls *tes-*

serae, are "narrative-like," edited according to conventions of continuity. It is the juxtaposition of these segments that make up the mosaic, requiring the viewer to actively explore connections and resonances that emerge within and between the different parts of the film.

Titicut Follies was an early attempt by Wiseman to develop an editing form consistent with his understanding of observation as a filmmaking practice. It is one that may be characterized as "theme and variations"—a central, underlying principle serves to anchor a series of self-contained and yet interlinked episodes or encounters. It involves drawing on film-making approaches that are organized around opposing cinematic principles. On the one hand, we may recognize elements of a Bazinian aesthetic in the assembly of scenes according to principles of spatial and temporary continuity, while on the other hand Wiseman works with a montage approach built upon radical juxtaposition. As Nichols points out, it is through this representational form that Wiseman articulates his theory of what has been observed. It is an expression of the filmmaker's assumption "that social events are multiply-caused, and must be analyzed as a web of interconnecting influences and patterns. It is dialectical rather than mechanical."[32] Although critics have pointed to the continuing attachment to narrative in *Titicut Follies,* its "day in the life" structure, and the broader metaphorical movement from life to death (symbolized by Malinowski's fate), the film demands a particular kind of engagement by the viewer. Wiseman asks his audience to work critically with the materials he presents. One of the consequences of this method is that Wiseman's films are, paradoxically, both open and closed. Undoubtedly, such ambiguity greatly contributes to the uneasiness of the viewing experience. For there is, at one and the same time, the sense that the filmmaker is withholding judgment *and* conveying to us the strength of feeling about what has been observed.

Titicut Follies has often been discussed in terms of its voyeurism, the way that a detached camera takes up a position of unwavering scrutiny, subjecting its helpless victims to the power and cruelty of an inhuman gaze. Indeed, it consistently refuses to avert its gaze—forcing us to watch beyond any point of decency and respect. But the film could also be described in opposite terms. For the impact of *Titicut Follies* also stems from the problem of proximity, the violent assault that the film inflicts on the viewer's senses. It is as though Wiseman is saying to us: see this, hear this, smell this, touch this, taste this. To say that our noses have been rubbed in it seems an apt phrase to the physical sensation of having been sullied by the film. The conflict between distance and proximity that makes viewing so uncomfortable emerges, of course, from the dissonance between Wiseman's detachment as the film's director and the visceral quality of Marshall's embodied camerawork. This tension runs through every scene of *Titicut Follies* and is inherent to the film's power.

If *Titicut Follies* establishes the objects and methods that have come to characterize Wiseman's project, it also offers important clues as to how he understands his role as an observer. In this film we see how the institution as a social microcosm serves as the focus for documentary inquiry and that its observation depends upon certain techniques—taking up a position inside, seeking out particular encounters and moments of confrontation, attending carefully to visual and aural details such as hands, eyes, mouths, and so on. But *Titicut Follies* raises a crucial question about the observer himself. It is one that reverberates throughout Wiseman's work as it has unfolded in different settings. Where exactly is the filmmaker positioned in the world that he documents and what are the implications of this position? For it seems that one of the vexing aspects of Wiseman's observational practice is that it is predicated on not being *with* any of the subjects of his film.[33] And it is this withholding that has sometimes provoked a crisis in the aftermath of filming—nowhere more acutely than in the case of *Titicut Follies*.

Wiseman follows a particular procedure in the development of his film projects. It raises interesting questions about the nature of his observational practice, shedding some light on the ethical issues posed by his approach and alerting us to how Wiseman's conception of his task might differ from that of an anthropological filmmaker. Although Wiseman was familiar with Bridgewater, he did not carry out background research nor did he spend any extended period in the hospital before he started filming. With *Titicut Follies* (and his other work), Wiseman received permission by means of consent rather than release forms: "The ground rules which I always operate under are that I don't get written releases, but I get consents."[34] His negotiation of access is predicated on his autonomy as a filmmaker and, once granted permission, he moves freely through spaces and among its subjects.

Wiseman's working method hinges upon gaining access rather than developing trust—and significantly, it does not involve the development of close or extended relationships with his subjects. However, in allowing

Wiseman access to their institutional world, it is not hard to see how subjects come to assume there is a relationship of trust, that the filmmaker is with them or alongside them, and that there will be some overlap between how he sees their world and how they see it. This never happens—and, as a consequence, subjects often feel betrayed.

From the opening shot of *Titicut Follies,* Wiseman suggests a refusal to take up a position with his subjects. Marshall's camera hovers above and behind the audience that is watching the show but is not situated in the audience, just as it is neither with the guards nor with the patients in the following scene. To use MacDougall's notion again, we might call Wiseman's observational style "privileged" since it does not manifest the characteristics of human observation.[35] This is revealed in different ways. His perspective as a filmmaker is not a situated or partial one. The picture of Bridgewater that Wiseman presents in *Titicut Follies* is not one that his subjects could articulate. His refusal to align himself with patients, doctors, guards, visitors finds expression in the constant breach of norms concerning social distance, the dissection of the body into parts (eyes, mouths, heads), and the inter-cutting of scenes that serves to subvert any human point of view.

In taking a number of key films from the 1960s, our objective has been to use the notion of observation as a way of articulating a fresh perspective on one of the most discussed moments in the history of documentary cinema. We have sought to shift attention away from the rhetorical claims and counter-claims that have surrounded *cinéma vérité* from the very beginning in favor of a focus on the work itself. Although the term "observation" has often been used in connection with the films of Drew, Leacock, Maysles, and Wiseman, it has remained at the level of general description. Moreover, observation has become a loaded term, filled with negative connotations—detachment, passivity, objectivity, objectification, the "uninvolved bystander" as Barnouw once put it.[36] Putting to one side the emotive associations of the term, we have sought then to explore how different filmmakers have interpreted it as a practice. What, where, how have they observed? Employed as a critical tool in this way, it quickly becomes clear that the notion of observation is more complex and diverse than perhaps commentators have been willing to acknowledge. It involves distinctive objects, sites, techniques, technologies, and forms of knowledge.

Our second concern in this chapter has been to establish the grounds for thinking about the American documentaries of the 1960s as important precursors of the observational turn in ethnographic filmmaking. As Young and others have suggested, the work of people like Leacock, Pennebaker, the Maysles, and others stands between Italian neorealism and the kind of anthropological cinema that began to emerge in the late 1960s and early 1970s. To what extent might *Primary, Salesman,* and *Titicut Follies* be understood as part of a Bazinian project? Did this work represent an extension of the new cinema of reality that Bazin sought to articulate in his writings, or was this challenge taken up only later by the ethnographic filmmakers? In the next chapters we will look more closely at these questions.

PART TWO

CHAPTER 3

Observational Cinema in the Making:
The Work of Herb Di Gioia and David Hancock

The observational turn in ethnographic filmmaking began as a series of ad hoc innovations by filmmakers working in a range of different social and cultural settings. Although these developments are often discussed as if they constituted a coherent movement, it is important to acknowledge that from the outset there was considerable variation in the interpretation of observation as a filmmaking practice. Moreover, the term "observational" was not used by the filmmakers themselves at the time of their experimentation with new techniques. It was the writing of Sandall and, above all, Young that served to give a name and identity to what were essentially independent initiatives. Once described in this way, however, commentators and practitioners were quick to use the term, passing it into common currency as a description of a distinctive approach within ethnographic cinema.

Observational cinema was always something of a quiet revolution. Unlike Robert Drew, Richard Leacock, and the other leading proponents of *cinéma vérité* who loudly proclaimed a radical break with established cinematic principles and practices, the observational filmmakers were much more modest in their claims. Their reluctance to "talk up" their films has often been misunderstood as naïveté or a refusal to acknowledge the complexity of issues raised by the presence of the camera in fieldwork situations. But looked at another way, it is in the apparent simplicity of observational cinema that its real challenge lies. For while the genre is profoundly subversive of conventional expectations of drama, explanation, action, character development, and so on, the nature of this subversion is at once elusive and interesting.

From the beginning, observational work has baffled anthropological viewers, opening up a sharp division between those who are indifferent, impatient, and sometimes intensely irritated by it and others who are plainly entranced. The diversity of response partly stems from the fact that perhaps more than any other filmmaking approach, the observational one represents a significant departure from textual models of engagement. To "read" an observational film is always to risk screening out what is distinctive to it as a form of expression. The observational film confounds certain assumptions—not by means of a direct challenge but through a kind of withholding. It is in the absence of something expected (e.g., an explanation) that a sense of uncertainty begins to develop in the viewer, precipitating disengagement and a dismissal of the film. It is as though this uncertainty opens up a gap that somehow must be filled. Certainly ambiguity does not sit well with a social science discipline, and anthropologists in general are rather uneasy with open interpretative spaces. A closer examination of instances of observational practice will allow for a fuller appreciation of how this kind of filmmaking is constituted as a mode of analysis and interpretation, even if it is one that differs significantly from that familiar to textual anthropologists.

Among the early pioneers of observational cinema were Herb Di Gioia and David Hancock. Although not formally trained as anthropologists, their work has long been influential in ethnographic filmmaking circles, and it stands as a valuable model of what might be called "an observational cinema in the making." The films Di Gioia and Hancock produced during the early 1970s, while not as well known as those of David and Judith MacDougall, allow us to chart innovations in practice that followed from their attempt to take up a new position as filmmakers with respect to their subjects and audiences. An examination of their four-part Vermont People series (*Duwayne Masure* [1971], *Chester Grimes* [1972], *Peter Murray* [1975], *Peter and Jane Flint* [1975]) along with *Naim and Jabar* (part of Norman Miller's *Faces of Change* series, 1974) will serve to focus questions raised by the attempt to move beyond the conventions associated with both documentary and anthropological filmmaking. For, as Di Gioia and Hancock discovered, their commitment to developing different kinds of relationships created unanticipated difficulties at the level of technique. These could not be envisaged in advance but emerged through practice itself. Understood in these terms, the observational turn in ethnographic filmmaking appears less a manifesto-driven movement (like *Dogme,* for example) or merely an outcome of technological changes and more a process, a series of improvisations devised by individual film-makers feeling their way toward something new.[1]

Herb Di Gioia and David Hancock met at UCLA in the 1960s. It was a vibrant place, politically and intellectually. New ideas swirled around the campus and students flourished amid a heady atmosphere of change and experimentation. Filmmaking was no exception. Situated on the doorstep of Hollywood, UCLA had always drawn on the expertise of distinguished directors, but it was also a magnet for a range of work being produced on both sides of the Atlantic and that included fiction and documentary as well as avant-garde and art films. In his brief memoir of the period, David MacDougall conveys something of the excitement and creative energy experienced by students at the time. "It was," he explains, "a period of innovation and ferment both in politics and in documentary and fiction filmmaking. To be a film student then was to be caught up in the belief that cinema was being reinvented, and that anything could come of it. UCLA was a particularly exciting place to be, for there we felt many cross-currents—'underground' films from San Francisco and New York; the new independent Hollywood cinema; the 'direct cinema' of Richard Leacock, the Maysles brothers (Albert and David), Frederick Wiseman; *cinéma vérité* from Montreal and Paris; the films of late Italian neorealism; and the revolutionary experiments of the *Nouvelle Vague*."[2]

As film students, Di Gioia and Hancock (along with David and Judith MacDougall) found themselves drawn to the new initiative launched in 1966 by Colin Young, UCLA's director of Theater Arts. Young, in part-nership with his colleague in the Anthropology Department, Walter Goldschmidt, had set up an Ethnographic Film Program that was intended to facilitate a new creative dialogue between anthropologists and film-makers.[3] Young's background had been in philosophy and filmmaking, but a fortuitous encounter with the anthropologist Edmund Carpenter led to his interest in exploring potential collaborative ground between different fields of endeavor. When Di Gioia joined the program, he had already decided to make films about aspects of life that he knew and about the people he lived alongside in Vermont, where he had settled with his family. He was open-minded, however, about whether to pursue such work as fiction or documentary. Like others in the circle around Young, Di Gioia's own cinematic interests were varied. Not surprisingly, given his own background, the classic films of Italian neorealism were important influences—but so, too, was the work of Renoir, Antonioni, Truffaut, and Godard, and, of course, Flaherty.[4] Di Gioia quickly formed a close partnership with David Hancock, another member of Young's program, and together they began to explore the possibilities of developing a film project in Vermont.[5] With Di Gioia mainly in the role of sound recordist and Hancock as camera operator, they set out to both discover a new subject matter for documentary and a new way of working. These two parts of their enterprise were integrally connected, forged as part of a single process.

There were a number of aspects of the collaboration between Di Gioia and Hancock that marked it out as unusual in terms of the UCLA Ethnographic Film Program. For example, their fieldsite was located within the United States rather than in a place of significant cultural and linguistic unfamiliarity. Hence, unlike many of the other projects associated with Young and Goldschmidt, theirs required neither the assistance of a formally trained anthropologist nor a translator. Although Young had long envisaged the anthropologist-filmmaker as a single person, there was still often a separation between areas of expertise. The anthropologist was expected to bring linguistic and cultural fluency to a project, while the filmmaker contributed skills in recording and editing.[6]

The creative partnership between Di Gioia and Hancock, however, was cut short by the tragically premature death of Hancock in 1976 at the age of thirty. At the time they had completed four films in their Vermont series and *Naim and Jabar*.[7] After Hancock's death, Di Gioia remained an active member of filmmaking circles but increasingly channeled his energies into teaching. The work of his students has been critical in continuing and extending the observational approach that he had first explored with Hancock.

The films produced by Di Gioia and Hancock have been often overlooked in accounts of observational cinema. Partly this has been due to the fact that the work has not been easily available. Despite many screenings during the 1970s, the films gradually disappeared from circulation, becoming ever more difficult to see since they were never transferred to video. Moreover, commentators have also been slow to recognize Di Gioia's significance as a teacher. For his contribution to the observational tradition has lain as much in the output of his students as in his own original film work. As we will see later, he had a very keen sense of the importance of pedagogy. His approach was distinctive, carefully honed over many years, but it has remained largely implicit, emerging from what was presented to him by his students rather than a formal articulation of theory or principles of practice.[8]

The Films

The first film in Di Gioia's and Hancock's Vermont People series was *Duwayne Masure*. Made in Sutton during the winter of 1970, its focus was a rough and ready character who had captured Di Gioia's imagination some years earlier. A man who "lived by his wits," Duwayne Masure, his wife, children, grandmother, and cousins made their living by means of farming, logging, and trapping—an eclectic range of activities that frequently blurred the boundary between legality and illegality.

The film, shot in black and white, opens with Duwayne and his brother stuffing an injured, freezing pony into the back of an old Chevrolet. Crunching the deep, packed snow underfoot, their breath rising like spirals of smoke in the frozen air, the filmmakers situate the two men in the midst of a harsh winter landscape. The camera frames the whole scene in depth. It follows the action in the form of a long, unbroken shot that concludes with the film's subjects acknowledging the presence of Di Gioia and Hancock as they drive off toward the farmhouse with their wounded passenger.

A low voice-over describes how terrible the winter is, how boring it is to be imprisoned by the snow week after week. The film cuts to Duwayne Masure, sitting at a kitchen table with a cup of coffee as he reflects on his life. It is a monologue, with its own spontaneous poetry. We begin to understand the precarious nature of Masure's enterprise—and to appreciate the tenacity and ingenuity that such a life demands. It is Masure's enigmatic presence that haunts the film. He is indeed a romantic figure—even though, as we discover, there is little that is romantic in how he makes his livelihood.

Di Gioia and Hancock show us some remarkable scenes. We watch as dead pigs are hauled by a system of ropes and pulleys into a bath to have their skins scraped and cleaned; we listen to the desperate squeal of a pig being led to slaughter, followed by the sounds of its slow death; we witness a deer being skinned and are not spared the horrible noise of its head being removed. But these scenes are counter-posed with others that convey the warmth and intimacy of Masure's family confined together

Duwayne Masure (circa 1970). *Photograph by David Hancock. Courtesy of Sally Hancock.*

through the long, dark winter months. Vermont, as evoked here, is far from the kind of rural idyll that outsiders often imagine. The Vietnam War is part of contemporary experience. And the arrival of "flatlanders" with their summer houses and cars is beginning to impinge on Duwayne's way of life, threatening to disrupt his activities as a poacher of deer.

It is in the film's opening scene that Di Gioia and Hancock establish their approach as filmmakers. Throughout the piece, Hancock's camera frames action as a whole, the zoom being used to explore different parts of the scene and to effect transitions between them. Moreover, the zoom always reveals the exact location of the filmmakers themselves within the situation that is unfolding around the camera. Instead of scenes constituted primarily by means of editing, an assembly of shots brought together after the moment of filming, it is clear that Hancock was working within the classic Bazinian aesthetic that presumed the fundamental continuity of reality.

The particular use of sound, the aural intensity of everyday activities, rendered through the proximity and skill of Di Gioia as sound recordist, coupled with Hancock's close attention to material process, gives the film an unusual texture. From the first scene we are struck by the ease of the relationships and interactions that unfold between Masure and his family and associates, an unfolding that encompasses the filmmakers, too. Nevertheless, rural life is rendered in its full physicality. Work is hard and demanding. It is often dirty, bloody, gruesome, and sometimes cruel. But it demands invention too. Duwayne Masure's survival hinges upon a mixture of charm, stubbornness, cunning, and skill.

Di Gioia and Hancock employ a voice-over by Masure, adapting his spontaneous monologue to provide the film with a narration. It neither explains what we see nor functions as any straightforward explanation of the film's central subject. It represents an attempt by the filmmakers to offer some kind of reflection on the film from within its own logic, rather than imposing this from outside.[9] This device was conceived as a solution to the central problem Di Gioia and Hancock encountered once they decided to let go of the conventions of interview and commentary. But it was not entirely satisfactory, since it seemed to draw attention to the limitations of an observational approach in revealing not much beyond what lay at the surface of things. Moreover, by using Masure's monologue over other scenes in the film, the point of reflection seemed unanchored, originating nowhere in particular, rather than being generated within a specific moment of encounter.

Di Gioia and Hancock were essentially developing their filmmaking approach as they proceeded. It was shaped through a process of trial and error. Abandoning established techniques—such as the gathering of single shots for subsequent editing into scenes and treating formal interviews as unnecessary—was only the first stage. The challenge was then to find new ways of revealing character, situation, action, process, and relationships. These were problems that could not be solved abstractly but they had to be addressed through *practicing* filmmaking in specific contexts.

The questions Di Gioia and Hancock confronted in their first film focused around the complex and enigmatic character of their central subject—how could they suggest something of Masure's agency and consciousness in the world that did not at the same time render him exotic or disreputable?[10] They had sought to achieve this through a close attention to the material process of his life, but they felt that until they added the voice-over a certain kind of reflectiveness continued to elude the film.[11] Their disquiet about how best to provide a point of reflection was a measure of how much further they wanted to take the cinema they had begun to develop. As inexperienced filmmakers they were unsure of what to look for—yet this was not the central problem. Rather, they were still discovering the implications of focusing not so much on questions of what and why (why Masure lived on the margins of legality, what impact Vietnam had on him and others), but on questions of who and how. Masure's life process involved a kind of crafting, shaping and being shaped by his relationships to place—with all the wider political and economic forces that implied. Asking the question "how?" meant focusing on the actuality of these processes. Through making their next film Di Gioia and Hancock began to see more clearly what the possibilities of this way of working were.

Chester Grimes, the second film in the Vermont People series, is also a portrait of a notable local character. It, too, has a memorable opening scene. Chester Grimes drives his great Belgian horses, Tom and Chubb, through the mist toward us. From tiny specks on the horizon, they gradually emerge as a powerful presence in the wooded landscape. Grimes, a stubborn, cantankerous Vermonter, is impatient with the encroachment of a mechanized economy that increasingly threatens his distinctive way of life. He still works with horses, felling trees and cutting logs; his honed skills, like those of the blacksmith, stand in sharp contrast to the indiscriminate motions of machines operated by younger men upon whom Grimes now depends.

Di Gioia and Hancock revealed Grimes to be fiercely independent, tenaciously hanging on to his way of doing things. But there were also intimations of his vulnerability. Picking his way over abandoned farms, he raged against the emergence of land as real estate. No longer productive, it had become private property owned by outsiders who do not work it. The once cultivated fields and orchards have become rough, overgrown places whose value increases precisely by means of a logic that runs counter to the spirit of Grimes's life.

Chester Grimes shares many stylistic features with *Duwayne Masure.* This is not surprising, given that they were made at roughly the same time. The filmmakers, having shot much of *Masure,* had run out of money. To finance their first film they had started working in the woods with Chester Grimes, and they quickly realized that he, too, was potentially a film subject. Chester Grimes was very different when he was in the woods than with outsiders to whom he often liked to play the larger-than-life, colorful old Vermonter. The filmmakers again saw the danger of turning him into a "character." They also knew that he was a strong personality who would assert his agency in the filmmaking process.

This second film underlined the approach that Di Gioia and Hancock were beginning to carve out as filmmakers. *Chester Grimes* is distinctive for its long, unbroken sequences. Again Hancock employs the zoom to explore relationships, using the camera frame to preserve the integrity of particular scenes rather than to create scenes from individual shots by means of editing. Although they primarily filmed in this way, generating a body of footage with its own "organic" unities, they also assembled other kinds of material (voice-over, archive photographs, music) that they intended to use as a way of fleshing out their subject. However, as they edited *Chester Grimes,* Di Gioia became more and more uneasy about how they were working with their materials. He felt that they were "forcing" the film, losing contact with the original spirit of the rushes that more subtly suggested the contours of their subject's experiential world. Di Gioia believed that the portrait they were assembling was not true to what they had come to understand about Grimes from working and filming him in the process of his life.[12]

Di Gioia and Hancock discovered that once they had embarked on a particular path as filmmakers, they had to continue along it. There was no halfway house. The problems posed by their early Vermont work forced them to acknowledge that the kind of film they were committed to making hinged crucially upon its shooting—and that their editing must flow from this. In this regard, *Chester Grimes* was an important breakthrough. The filmmakers discarded all the additional material they had accumulated, including most of the voice-over. They edited what remained into a film that came together into a distinctively loose, delicate form. They recognized that to force the materials to express their ideas rather than their subject's life would have been fundamentally at odds with the footage they had generated working alongside Grimes in the Vermont woods.[13]

Following the completion of their first two Vermont films, Di Gioia and Hancock were hired by the producer Norman Miller to work on a National Science Foundation–funded film series that he was developing across different ecological zones. Their assignment was to shoot a film (with the anthropologist Louis Dupree) in Afghanistan. It was a difficult project. Di Gioia and Hancock were now operating in conditions

Chester Grimes (circa 1971). *Courtesy of Herbert Di Gioia.*

of considerable cultural and linguistic difference, and they were being asked to produce film materials that would fulfill a social science brief.[14] Nevertheless, they made a striking film. It bears many of the hallmarks of their earlier work developed in a radically different setting. *Naim and Jabar* is a moving portrait of fourteen- and fifteen-year-old boys, close friends, whose lives are at a critical juncture. Jabar has completed a year of secondary school in Mazar-i-Sharif and Naim is seeking admission to the same school. For both boys, schooling represents an opportunity for advancement, opening up perspectives beyond the confines of rural life that has condemned their fathers because they have no land.

In the overall scheme of things, getting a place at a secondary school in an Afghan town seems a minor matter, but it is testament to the skill of Di Gioia and Hancock that one feels the full weight of its significance in the lives of the film's subjects. Like the great postwar Italian films, most notably De Sica's *Bicycle Thief, Naim and Jabar* reminds the viewer of the knife-edge upon which poor people live. One stroke of luck—good or bad—changes everything. At the end of the film we know that Naim's failure to be admitted to the school is the moment of separation between the friends, each now embarked on a very different trajectory. The poignancy of this moment is acutely rendered, not only by Jabar's tears and Naim's innocent optimism but by the sheer indifference of the bureaucrats in whose hands the boys' fates has lain. Watching the film today, of course, one cannot but reflect on that fate.

Naim and Jabar begins high in the mountains of northern Afghanistan. A long shot slowly tracks Naim, as he walks through cultivated fields to join other men scything and bundling sheaves of wheat. Through a series of close-ups, we watch the expert way he works. Through this opening passage the filmmakers characteristically locate Naim in the landscape socially and geographically. Likewise, Hancock's camera frames Jabar and his father in the context of their work, making mud bricks and laying them out to dry in the sun. The film is notable for the extremely sparing use of titles and subtitles. The effect is not an exoticization of subjects, as often happens in the absence of translated speech. Instead, we are made aware that subjectivity is constituted in complex ways through sounds, gestures, movement, rhythm. The limitation of the filmmakers' linguistic understanding, paradoxically, allows their subjects to breathe.

For Di Gioia, the experience of making *Naim and Jabar* served to strengthen his initial impulse to pursue work in contexts of greater cultural familiarity. Aside from the frustrations of collaborating with an anthropologist and the difficulties of communication with his Afghan subjects, he was very uneasy filming people with whom he had no long-term relationship. Although Di Gioia was himself a "flatlander," he was concerned to integrate his filmmaking activities with the other parts of his life in Vermont. He wanted to find ways of making his practice an integral part of his continuing relationship with people and place. This ethical commitment was an important factor in shaping the films themselves, affecting the scope and possibilities of formal innovation. Hancock's insight is significant here. In notes cited by Young, he observes: "*Naim and Jabar* is more conventional in its narrative structure than some of our earlier material in Vermont, whose openendedness perhaps represents a greater movement away from traditional dramatic structure."[15]

Naim and Jabar focused a central issue for Di Gioia and Hancock, who were trying to work differently with people's realities. How could they avoid falling back on narrative conventions (e.g., dramatic tension, melodrama, crisis structure) in organizing footage generated through

Herb Di Gioia and Jabar (circa 1972). *Courtesy of Norman Miller.*

the development of new techniques? It was a problem encountered by Flaherty but also critically by Rossellini, De Sica, Zavattini, and by the American *cinéma vérité* filmmakers. According to Young, the breakthrough represented by observational cinema involved precisely this question: "[t]he details of our films must be a substitute for dramatic tension, and the film's authenticity must be a substitute for artificial excitement. This does not rule out the possibility that a film's events will have the weight of general metaphor, but first and foremost they will have meaning within their own context."[16] However, the problem of narrative continued to be a pressing one. It was a problem that the MacDougalls also found themselves facing as they returned from Uganda around the time Di Gioia and Hancock left for Vermont. Hancock's comment on *Naim and Jabar* remains important. He raises the significance of context in the development of the new approach. To what extent were the radical possibilities of observational cinema linked to conditions of cultural sameness? Were their filmmaking techniques inadequate in conditions of difference? Could observational work reveal the strangeness of the familiar itself?

After making *Naim and Jabar*, Di Gioia and Hancock resumed their documentary work in Vermont. They embarked on three new films, two of which were finished before Hancock's untimely death. The completed works, *Peter Murray* and *Peter and Jane Flint,* were portraits of people whose aspirations were not unlike those of Di Gioia's and Hancock's earlier subjects, Duwayne Masure and Chester Grimes. They were committed to small, locally grounded initiatives. Moreover, as Di Gioia has acknowledged, their ideals and motivations overlapped significantly with his own.[17] Just as he was seeking to make his way as a filmmaker in a location that had not traditionally sustained such practice, so too the subjects of the later films (especially the Flints) were struggling to establish themselves in a setting that was not entirely supportive of their enterprise. Exploring the material process by which these incomers sought to build a life for themselves in Vermont became the foundation for Di Gioia's and Hancock's understanding of their own cinematic engagement with the world.

Peter Murray is perhaps the most unusual film Di Gioia and Hancock made in the course of their partnership. It is deceptively simple. *Peter Murray* is about a man making a chair. The entire film unfolds within the confines of his workshop. It begins with the finishing of one chair and follows the process by which he begins a second. The filmmakers attend closely to the different sounds and rhythms of work. Employing his characteristic method of the zoom to move seamlessly between wide shot and close-up, Hancock's camera explores the habitus of its subject, Peter Murray.

Peter Murray begins with a short text that establishes the exact time and place of its making—September 1975 in a workshop at Mad Brook Farm, East Charleston, Vermont. The film opens with a close-up shot of a pair of hands twisting a length of cattail leaves into taut twine. The camera pulls back. We watch Peter Murray as he works to complete the back of a chair, his dexterous hands tightening, winding and threading the twine through its wooden frame. The distinctive sound of the materials is interspersed with Murray's own informal reflections on his practice and its place in his life. The filmmakers' close attention to the details of the task render palpable Murray's sureness of touch. In particular, we note the skillful handling of materials, the sensing of quality and texture, the continual pushing and pulling of matter that constitutes the process by which Murray discovers or uncovers the shape of the chair. As he works, Murray comments on his approach—one that rejects elaborate technology in favor of a simple tool, the knife. In contrast to the cold, hard edges of mechanized production, Murray seeks a more organically grounded relationship with his materials that will yield what he calls the *light* of a piece.

Murray struggles to push the final piece of rush thread through the chair's woven back. With a brief expression of delight, he stands back to contemplate his work. But this involves not so much an external appraisal of the finished form than its habitation. We watch as Murray sits in his completed chair, shifting his body slightly as he adjusts to its shape and contours. Slowly he loosens his fingers and, beginning to rock gently back and forth, he settles into the particular space and movement of the chair. Murray is on his feet again. Now he starts to examine different parts of the seat, the back, turning the frame over, running his hands along the wood, explaining all the while the continuing evolution of the form.

The second part of the film documents the making of another chair. A wide shot opens up the space of Murray's workshop and he begins to cut wood for a new frame. Absorbed in his task, we observe the experienced process of calibration through eye and hand as Murray shapes and aligns the different pieces that comprise the frame without recourse to devices of formal measurement or calculation. There is no spoken commentary, just the alternate sounds of cutting, banging, sawing, trimming, planing, paring of wood. Eventually Murray pauses to reflect on his relationship with the knife. His practice is founded in a direct connection between tool and material, the action of the knife on the wood serving as the basis for exploration and discovery. By working in this manner, Murray says, the form is not fixed or known in advance, determined through the imposition of lines, angles, or edges, but rather emerges in the practice of making itself.

Murray assembles the frame of the second chair and attaches it to the rockers. He prepares to stain the wood. His own immersion in the creative process enables him to "see" the chair, but for those outside it must be rendered visible. Murray's use of wood stain is intended, as he puts it, to bring the chair *out* while inviting the viewer *in*. But we do not see this technique. Instead the film ends as Murray pauses to assess his work. The camera focuses on his face. His eyes, sharp and alert, move back and forth, assessing the emergent form before him. Slowly the camera moves back to leave Murray framed within the contours of his chair.

In the very first shots of *Peter Murray*, Di Gioia and Hancock reveal the nature of the engagement between themselves and their subject and his world. Di Gioia and Hancock situate themselves in close, physical proximity to Murray. Without preliminaries—a conventional establishing shot, for example—the filmmakers insert the viewer directly into the flow of Murray's actions, processes that are already unfolding and will extend beyond the life of the film. Moreover, there is no break as Hancock uses the zoom lens to effect a transition from his initial interest in the detail of Murray's hands to a wider shot that brings together the object, subject, and context. Although the artificial optical effect of the zoom does not correspond to how human beings see, it is used by Hancock to convey something important about human perception, foregrounding relationships rather than abstracting separate visual elements. This concern for how things hold together is signaled from the very beginning—and is critical to the film's aesthetic.

Over the course of fifty minutes, Hancock's camera actively explores what is happening around it. Unconstrained by a tripod, the shots are fluid and expansive, expressive of an embodied technology that captures not just what Murray does but how he does it. Using long takes, Hancock traces the distinctive way that the chair maker handles his materials and the rhythm of his practice. These extended, unbroken shots are not, however, fixed or static. They are dynamic—the energy being generated from within the shot itself by the camera's movement between different points of focus as it probes the relationship between part and whole, action and contemplation, figure and ground. Hancock's camera is perhaps best described as animated. It is alert and engaged, even when completely stationary. There are occasional flaws in the camera work, serving to remind the viewer that the technology is being used as part of a process at human scale. For Hancock uses the camera not to transcend the limitations of the human eye but to create equivalents for its operations. From time to time, Hancock loses focus as he zooms in toward his subject, framing

Peter Murray (circa 1975). *Courtesy of Sally Hancock.*

Murray's face in a tight close-up shot. Getting too close, however, results in distortion and the camera is forced to move back, to find a position that more closely resembles an optimal *human* distance between filmmaker and subject.

The audio track of *Peter Murray* is an integral part of the film's fabric. Throughout the sound is held in synchrony with the image. Hence Murray's informal narration is not separated from his material practice and elevated into a conventional voice-over that "explains" the images. Instead it remains embedded in the process of making, an integral part of a richer soundscape that Di Gioia renders through specific recording techniques. Like his filmmaking partner Hancock, Di Gioia situates himself in close physical proximity to his subject. He, too, inserts himself within Murray's space rather than remaining outside listening in.

Speaking to camera (now a mainstay of documentary) raises questions about whether the camera obliges—or simply stimulates—people to speak. In *Peter Murray* there is no hint of obligation. Murray's talk seems to arise from the grain of his life, a life that now includes the filmmakers.

It has a sensory, poetic quality that Di Gioia carefully renders. As sound recordist, he holds together both speech and context, at the same time as he draws attention to the communicative quality of a range of non-verbal sounds—and, crucially, to the communicative nature of silence itself. Our ears have to be retuned and we must learn to listen in a different way.

The editing style of *Peter Murray* follows directly from Di Gioia's and Hancock's sound recording and camera techniques. Hence the filmmakers seek to respect the organic unity of scenes. Notes made by Hancock on his developing practice with Di Gioia offer further insight into their approach toward editing: "If you have shot in the observational style and wish to edit in a way that respects the integrity of the shooting, all you are doing is providing fewer events and less information than the rushes give. This is why we end up by dropping whole scenes or sequences rather than trying to keep them all, but at shorter length." He continues: "Each scene is made up of discrete pieces of information and behavior and shortening it for dramatic effect would lose the resonances (to use [James] Blue's phrase) and misrepresent the material. More and more we seem to be finding scenes that have no crisis, no main structure or dramatic point, but are composed of the bits of behavior which are the ingredients of our daily lives. Scenes in which nothing appears to be happening dramatically can gradually be revealing. Thus a decision to drop an entire scene does not misrepresent the material to the same extent—we have simply provided less information."[18]

Although Hancock does not specifically refer to *Peter Murray*, his comments help us appreciate the distinctive qualities of this film. He makes us aware of how the film is constituted through a coalescing of sequences, clusters of extended shots, that are intended to frame a range of interpretive possibilities and to engage the viewer in the construction of its meaning. Meaning inheres in constellations of detail as much as in the succession of individual shots. The axiom "less is more" functions in a very particular way here. By including fewer but more extended scenes, the filmmakers seek to generate visual and aural resonances rather than to eliminate them. Paradoxically, the editing of *Peter Murray*, like its shooting, is dependent on knowing when *not* to cut. It depends on holding things together. The filmmakers seek to foreground relationships and continuities and to generate a space for exploration. The film unfolds. Its movement is not straightforwardly linear. *Peter Murray* is a piece that rises and falls, something that breathes.

For Di Gioia and Hancock, *Peter Murray* represented the culmination of their filmmaking approach. It enabled them to grasp what they were trying to achieve as filmmakers.[19] The way Murray worked with his materials served as a kind of mirror to their own practice. It, too, involved a process of discovery that turned on the relinquishing of control in favor of a more open-ended excavation of the materials. Discovering the chair maker's techniques, how he generated form, enabled them to grasp that they too sought to *uncover* inherent shapes and textures, rather than to create form through the imposition of a structure from the outside.[20] Their task, like Murray's, was to uncover the *light* of the piece. This was dependent on an active engagement—a kind of taking in and letting go—by which process the film eventually emerged. Conceiving of their own work in this way allowed Di Gioia and Hancock to glimpse the revelatory—indeed redemptive— possibilities of observational cinema.[21]

The final film in the Vermont People series had an energetic young couple, Peter and Jane Flint, at its center. During the summer of 1974, Di Gioia and Hancock followed Peter and Jane as they sought to establish themselves on the land and develop a small dairy farm. The filmmakers document the hard work, and the unrelenting physical effort, that underpins such an enterprise. There are the day-to-day tasks of bringing in the cattle, feeding, milking, and cleaning out the cowsheds; there are setbacks (the sickness of animals) and small advances (the birth of a calf); there is uncertainty, inexperience, tedium, exhaustion, and moments of joy.

Peter and Jane Flint is built from long, unbroken sequences in which the filmmakers closely follow events that have their own coherence and integrity. These are interspersed with informal conversations in which Peter and Jane, sometimes together, sometimes separately, offer their own commentary on how they have come to choose this kind of life and where they believe it is taking them. Once more this material functions as an important reflexive thread, but it is now woven into the fabric of the film in a way that eluded Di Gioia and Hancock when they were making *Duwayne Masure.* Slowly, *Peter and Jane Flint* evolves into a film with its own distinctive emotional shape. This affective landscape coalesces by means of hints and suggestions, rather than being openly declared or confronted. It is a reflection of the filmmakers' skill that everything remains on a human, everyday scale. At the same time we are offered glimpses of what lies beyond—demands on the body and spirit that the Flints must accept as the price for carving out a life together that is in accordance with their ideals.

Jane Flint, Peter Flint, Herb Di Gioia, and David Hancock (circa 1975). *Courtesy of Sally Hancock.*

Like Di Gioia and Hancock's other films, *Peter and Jane Flint* is constructed from a careful attention to the concrete details and processes of material life. This is the context through which their characters express their subjectivity in the world. *Peter and Jane Flint* has neither obvious drama nor larger-than-life characters. Despite this—in fact, because of it—the film is a poignant piece. More than twenty-five years later, one still wants to know—as with all the subjects of Di Gioia and Hancock's work—what happened to Peter and Jane Flint. Did they manage to build a viable dairy farm? Did they stay together?

An Observational Cinema in the Making

The five films made by Di Gioia and Hancock during the first half of the 1970s represents an *observational cinema in the making*. By casting this body of work in such terms, our intention is to draw attention both to its ethical inflection and to the process by which it took shape. As a series comprising different parts that were made in close succession, it offers an unusual opportunity to examine how the filmmakers' approach was formed through practice. The films stand as a valuable counterpoint to the writing of Sandall and Young, serving to focus discussions about what observation actually involved as a filmmaking practice at the same time as raising questions about its cinematic antecedents—most notably, the classic tradition of Bazinian cinema (especially Italian neorealism) and the American *vérité* documentaries of the 1960s.

The work of Di Gioia and Hancock had at its core a particular ethical commitment—and it is with reference to this that "observational" properly applies. Although barely in circulation at the time (and only later taken up Di Gioia), the term refers to the filmmakers' practice that grew out of, and was shaped by, their long-term commitment to a site, Vermont, and to the people who made their lives there. In developing an approach that refracted their exploration of shared subjectivity, Di Gioia and Hancock sought to be open to the challenges—interpersonal, technical, and aesthetic—that were thrown up by specific relationships and situations. Hence their techniques were both guided by a chosen ethos, yet not specified in advance—rather they devised techniques as they went along. At the same time there was a deliberate attempt *not* to do certain things—for example, interviewing, breaking up scenes into shots, asking people to do things for the camera, looking for "characters" or drama, and so on. One of the challenges of observational work, as we noted earlier, lies here. For it is subversive of expectations by means of a withholding or absence—and, as such, it makes unusual demands not just on audiences but on filmmakers and their subjects too. As Di Gioia and Hancock were also quick to find out, there was nothing passive about this kind of filmmaking. On the contrary, it required of both its subjects and audiences patience, intelligence, concentration, intuition, and empathy.

David Hancock's brief notes about filmmaking offer a tantalizing glimpse into the project that he was pursuing with Di Gioia.[22] His observations, carefully anchored in the details of their own unfolding practice, reveal some of the key ideas that lay behind innovations in their techniques. Significantly, Hancock made it clear from the outset that an open, acknowledged relationship between the filmmakers *as people* and the subjects of the film lay at the heart of their work. Moreover, the agency of the film subjects was recognized to be critical in the fashioning of the work. What he meant by this was not how such a precept now tends to be understood—film subjects themselves using recording technology or participating in the editing room. Instead, Hancock was referring to something different—a crucial but implicit element of their approach—namely, their attempt to make filmmaking an integral part of the daily life they shared with their Vermont subjects such that it was intertwined with the hauling of wood, the making of a chair, the skinning of a pig. It was conceived not as an elevated form of expertise but instead was understood to be a material practice that was shaped in and through these ongoing activities and relationships.

To work in this way necessitated the kind of open, exploratory style that Hancock described in his writing and expressed through his camera work. There was an emphasis on the spatial and temporal integrity of events; a sensitivity to context—that is, what might be considered "background" was essential to any interpretation of foreground; there was a keen sensitivity to the scale and proportion of things; human subjects were approached in the fullness of their bodies—not dissected into a series of parts—eyes, hands, mouth, and so on. To accomplish this, Hancock's shots were long and fluid, sequences were extended and filmed in depth, the zoom was employed: "not merely as a labour-saving elastic telescope but as a device which can show the relationship between two people or two pieces of action in unbroken continuity and duration."[23]

The commitment was to preserving the organic unity and flow of life as it unfolded around the camera and, as Hancock reminds us, shooting and editing were inseparable parts of the same process. Despite the clarity with which Hancock articulated his reflections on their practice, there was still considerable uncertainty surrounding their approach. As Di Gioia and Hancock learned, it was easy to throw off conventions of drama and argument, but the process of then "finding" the film was often difficult and protracted—and there was always the risk that it might end in failure. For, if the film was not already there in the shooting, it could not be "made" in the editing. Editing was not about assembling fragments into a pre-existing framework, but it was—like Murray's chair—more of a process of elimination, the shedding of extraneous elements in order to reveal the essential shape of the piece.

In the case of Di Gioia and Hancock there were additional risks involved in their endeavor. Their work was neither located in a site of significant difference nor was it pursued in accordance with contemporary anthropological frameworks (initiation, ritual, development, gender, and so on). Each of their films was built around a particular individual or individuals understood in the context of their daily lives. This raised significant challenges—why might what seemed to be nothing more than "ordinary" deserve attention?

Observational Cinema and Its Antecedents

The distinctive contours of Di Gioia's and Hancock's project are thrown into sharper relief once they are juxtaposed with similar filmmaking initiatives and contextualized within a broader cinematic landscape. Although changes in ethnographic cinema during the late 1960s and early 1970s are often seen as a development of observational practices first pioneered within American documentary (by, e.g., Leacock, Maysles, and Wiseman), the work of Di Gioia and Hancock suggests that Italian neorealist cinema be understood as their proper precursor. For the cinema of reality articulated by Bazin in his writing seems to find fuller expression here than in the films of the American *vérité* movement. There are overlaps with the latter—not least a shared interest in exploring contemporary American society—but there are also significant differences in terms of subject matter, techniques, and audience engagement. The preoccupation of the 1960s documentary filmmakers with the mediated nature of contemporary experience and the interpenetration of interior and public worlds suggests a closer link with the concerns of American cinema established by Orson Welles's masterpiece *Citizen Kane* than with the kind of European sensibility that was expressed in the late neorealism of De Sica (*Bicycle Thief* or *Umberto D*). Of course, there are important exceptions. Glimpses of a Bazinian cinema can be discerned in Albert and David Maysles's *Salesman* (and especially in their later *Grey Gardens*). On the whole, however, a different aesthetic appears to be at work in the cinema of Di Gioia and Hancock, one that is tied to a different kind of ethical agenda. Certainly the elision of differences between the *vérité* films of the 1960s and the observational work of the 1970s has always been to the latter's cost. It has occluded its fundamentally Bazinian nature, entangling it in the discourses of science, objectivity, and truth through which American filmmakers and their critics have often conducted their debate.

The significance of Bazinian ideas to the understanding of Di Gioia's and Hancock's work is perhaps not surprising, given Di Gioia's upbringing in one of Boston's Italian-American neighborhoods and his love of neorealist cinema. As we have already seen in chapter 1, the work of the postwar Italian directors was crucial to the development of cinematic language that Bazin was seeking to articulate in his essays of the 1940s and 1950s. Watching the Vermont films one senses a deep affinity with their neorealist predecessors. For running through the work there is a respect for the fundamental connections between human beings and the sensible world, a connection characterized by both continuity and ambiguity. Following Bazin, we might say that Di Gioia and Hancock shared with their Italian counterparts the ability "to create a special density within the framework of which they know how to portray an action without separating it from its material context and without loss of that uniquely human quality of which it is an integral part."[24]

Central to Bazin's interpretation of cinematic realism was his appreciation of its ongoing evolution as a form. It was not something static but an approach that was continually in motion, shaped by the ever-shifting conditions of the historical moment in which it was located and the sensibilities of particular filmmakers. He was especially interested in the directions opened up by the cinema of De Sica, since it suggested a significant extension, aesthetically and conceptually, of the work of earlier filmmakers in this tradition. De Sica's long-term collaborator Cesare Zavattini outlined some of the key principles behind this new phase of neorealism in a manifesto of 1953.[25] It offers an important framework for evaluating the project that Di Gioia and Hancock embarked on some twenty years later.

Perhaps the most quoted part of Zavattini's manifesto is his famous declaration that a woman buying a pair of shoes could form the basis of a film lasting two hours. How could an everyday, banal occurrence of this kind have any consequence or worth? But, for Zavattini, to undertake an analysis of such a moment promises, as he puts it, "to open to us a vast and complex world, rich in importance and values, in its practical, social, economic, psychological motives. Banality disappears because each moment is really charged with responsibility. Every moment is infinitely rich. Banality never really existed."[26] He exhorts the filmmaker to again "observe" the world—by this he means to fully confront its detail and material fullness, to embrace what might be overlooked as "ordinary," "banal," without meaning. It necessitates a resistance to the temptation to "extract" from the world, to simplify it and render it as a fiction or story.

The new cinema imagined by Zavattini dispenses with causal narrative in favor of a sort of accretion or dynamic that expands laterally as much as lineally and in which people are not exemplifications of something, metaphors, or representative of larger structures that deny them their unique individuality, their presence (concretely manifest, as Zavattini reminds us, in their "name and surname"). Crucially, it is a cinema dedicated not to emotions such as excitement, anger, disgust, suspense but one intended to stimulate a process of reflection.[27]

Although De Sica's classic films, made in conjunction with Zavattini, failed to fully realize the kind of cinema outlined in the manifesto, they nevertheless afforded a glimpse of its possibilities. Both *Bicycle Thief* and *Umberto D* depended on the use of melodrama and other familiar narrative devices, and the kind of intense analysis of the everyday that was envisaged by Zavattini can be found in only a handful of moments, but where found, it yielded moments of startling clarity, insight—and beauty.[28]

In his 1975 essay, Colin Young suggested that the observational turn in ethnographic filmmaking represented an important stage in the development of cinema. Without making explicit the lineage that Bazin traced through Flaherty, Renoir, Rossellini, and De Sica, he pointed to many of the features discussed above as emblematic of the new work being produced by David and Judith MacDougall and Herb Di Gioia and David Hancock. In the case of the latter, it is possible to trace the reverberations of Zavattini's principle of observation in their films. Their project is anchored in the everyday, in the non-dramatic event, in a conception of human subjectivity that is neither narrowly psychological nor the basis of a social abstraction but instead is approached as a specific human consciousness that arises with and is permeated by the physicality of the world. It was from this principle that their observational practice followed.

To interpret Di Gioia's and Hancock's work through a Bazinian lens is, as we have suggested, to recognize its difference from the kind of project pursued by the American filmmakers of the 1960s. But it also serves to clarify differences with the observational path charted during the same period by David and Judith MacDougall. It could not be otherwise. For, from the beginning, the observational impulse in ethnographic filmmaking was refracted through the different personalities and contexts in which practice was developed. It was never about the acquisition of a "tool kit." It took shape through the ongoing engagement between filmmakers, their subjects, their sites of inquiry—and their audiences.

According to Di Gioia, audiences were initially puzzled and perplexed by the work he made with Hancock.[29] On the one hand, it did not resemble the kind of documentary that had been produced by the *vérité* filmmakers with their tense situations, colorful personalities, high energy, and dramatic momentum. On the other hand, it was not easily identifiable as "anthropological," since (apart from *Naim and Jabar*) it was not obviously located in a place of linguistic and cultural difference. Moreover, viewers were asked to engage intelligently with the films without the assistance of narration, interviews, or a dramatic story. In withholding these devices, Di Gioia and Hancock invited their audiences to embark on the kind of critical engagement of the everyday that Zavattini had proposed in his manifesto. The analytical work necessitated by such a cinema was at first difficult to grasp or even recognize, since it did not proceed according to a familiar logic and it drew upon a different epistemology. Through their techniques, however, Di Gioia and Hancock were attempting to position viewers differently (ethically, intellectually, imaginatively, and sensually) in relationship to their subjects such that new understandings of lived experience, what Zavattini called *dailiness,* might emerge.[30]

Observational cinema is often interpreted as *the* quintessentially anthropological cinema. There is a certain irony in this perception, since many of its leading practitioners (at the time of its inception and today) have had no professional anthropological training, occupying a marginal position—if any at all—with respect to the academic discipline. Neither Herb Di Gioia and David Hancock nor David and Judith MacDougall had backgrounds in anthropology. Colin Young and Walter Goldschmidt intended their UCLA Ethnographic Film Program to be a place in which anthropologists and filmmakers might share ideas and develop innovative forms of collaborative practice. This was remarkably difficult to achieve— as Young and others have subsequently acknowledged.[31] Anthropologists at the time tended to be guarded in their reception of filmmaking. They often found it difficult to regard the medium as anything more than simplifying or popularizing. At best, it was considered useful as an illustrative mechanism for the explanatory categories through which knowledge was legitimately constituted within the discipline. In addition, there was a great deal of confusion about the camera's scientific credentials. These were complicated by an anxiety about cinema's perceived artistic tendencies. Not surprisingly, the kinds of partnerships between anthropologists and filmmakers that Young envisaged were usually marked by tension and did not, on the whole, yield especially innovative work. The partnerships that did flourish, however, were those in which the roles of anthropologist and filmmaker were fused (not always in a single person) and in which the connection to anthropology was less constrained by disciplinary expectations.

The project pursued in Vermont by Di Gioia and Hancock was a profoundly anthropological one, if not formally designated as such. Certainly the filmmakers themselves were not interested in making their anthropology explicit. Rather, they sought to fold it into the film itself. Indeed their experience of working with Louis Dupree in the context of the *Faces of Change* series had left them feeling that their understanding of the anthropological endeavor was at odds with that held by many in the profession.[32] The making of *Naim and Jabar* led Di Gioia and Hancock to confront as problems many of the expectations associated with the discipline as a social science. The emphasis on abstraction and generalization, the broad comparative perspectives and explanatory categories of culture, patterns, and social systems characteristic of 1970s anthropology was inhibiting to the expansive humanist endeavor that they sought to pursue through the medium of cinema.

The position that Di Gioia and Hancock occupied with respect to anthropology (one they shared with their contemporaries the MacDougalls) offered them an unusual space in which to experiment. The cost, of course, was that it was easy for their work to be overlooked or deemed irrelevant as not "proper" anthropology. Moreover, unlike the project developed by David MacDougall that was, from the outset, more engaged—albeit critically—with anthropological frameworks and ideas (development, nationhood, socialization), the observational cinema of Di Gioia and Hancock posed a different and more oblique challenge. It grew out of a commitment to the irreducibility of individual lives in which daily acts of making were understood to open up not only a material but also an existential space. Di Gioia and Hancock conceived of their own work as an *analogous* act of making and being.

CHAPTER 4

Observational Cinema on the Move:
The Work of David MacDougall

For three or so decades, David MacDougall has been a central figure in debates about observational cinema. His position, though, is somewhat paradoxical.[1] He has been one of the leading proponents and one of the leading skeptics. MacDougall's early film *To Live with Herds* (1972) quickly established itself as an important example of observational cinema, while much of his subsequent work (the Turkana trilogy and the collaborations with Australian Aboriginal communities) might be considered a critique of the genre. But if during the 1980s MacDougall moved away from observational cinema toward more explicitly collaborative forms, the pendulum has now begun to swing the other way. Declaring his dissatisfaction with experiments in collaborative authorship that confused rather than clarified the issues of power and representation, MacDougall has returned to making films that are at once more explicitly *observational* and more self-consciously authored. His Sardinian film *Tempus de Baristas* (1993) marked the beginning of this new phase in his anthropological cinema. But it is his more recent work that reveals most tangibly a renewed engagement with the scope and possibilities of an observational cinema.[2]

Our evaluation of MacDougall's work has two parts. In the first, we review his early contributions to debates about the new kind of ethnographic cinema, taking *To Live with Herds* (1972) and his influential essay, "Beyond Observational Cinema" (1998; originally written in 1975), as our initial focus.[3] Both were crucial in establishing a certain discourse and set of expectations about what the observational approach entailed—even if they departed significantly from MacDougall's own understanding of the project. The second and longer part of the chapter is built around a discussion of MacDougall's Doon School series. Between 1997 and 1998,

MacDougall embarked on an extended period of fieldwork at one of India's most famous schools and, from more than eighty hours of footage, he edited five films—*Doon School Chronicles* (2000), *With Morning Hearts* (2001), *Karam in Jaipur* (2001), *The New Boys* (2003), and *The Age of Reason* (2004). The series is distinctive for number of reasons. It was shot on digital video (not film). MacDougall worked alone as camera operator, sound recordist, and editor rather than in conjunction with his long-term filming partner Judith MacDougall or with the assistance of interpreters or translators. The separate parts of the series were not planned in advance or made sequentially. Individual films emerged in the course of the project, prompted by particular subjects or situations—and, crucially, in response to the other films that were taking shape such that films overlapped or developed simultaneously.[4]

By characterizing MacDougall's project as an *observational cinema on the move,* we seek to highlight the extended and changing nature of his engagement with this kind of anthropological filmmaking. It has been clear from the outset that what it means to work in this way has been interpreted differently by individual filmmakers and that, contrary to the popular view, particular sensibilities have been rendered with an unusual clarity through an observational frame.[5] Moreover, as we have noted earlier, the approach itself has never been fixed or static but continues to evolve and be modified as a consequence of specific instances of practice. Drawing on different phases in MacDougall's trajectory, it is possible to indicate something of this openness and fluidity. How might we evaluate such a project and what might be its role in the development of a theoretically and methodologically ambitious visual anthropology?

David MacDougall's approach as a filmmaker, like that of Di Gioia and Hancock, was shaped by the unusual conditions of the late 1960s. Describing the "sea of influences" in which he swam as a student, MacDougall's account of the period offers valuable insight into the lively intellectual context that surrounded the UCLA Ethnographic Film Program.[6] He was challenged and stimulated by a range of political, social, and artistic influences. He read widely (exploring the work of Hegel, Eisenstein, and Merleau-Ponty—even if, by his own admission, he did not fully understand it) and he immersed himself in a rich film culture, one that was greatly enhanced by Young's talent in attracting an eclectic group of filmmakers, anthropologists, and others as contributors to, and participants in, the new initiative that he had launched with Walter Goldschmidt.

In his memoir, MacDougall identified a number of questions about knowledge that concerned those involved in the documentary endeavor at this time. Partly prompted by the cinematic innovations of directors like Godard and his contemporaries in both fiction and documentary, Young expected MacDougall and his cohort, as aspiring filmmakers, to develop a flexible and sophisticated approach toward the evidential capacity of the camera. MacDougall suggested Young's background in philosophy predisposed him to carefully examine matters relating to the nature and status of evidence yielded by the camera.[7] These were not the usual ones about objectivity or "truth." Indeed it was *subjectivity* of the camera that served as a starting point in any discussion about how knowledge was constituted through film itself. Young and his students in the Ethnographic Film Program were committed to what MacDougall calls a "repositioning" of filmmaker, subjects, and audience. It was, he explains, "a way of creating cross-checks on knowledge, a way of creating a triangulation that was for the first time more equitable. The audience and the film subjects had to be drawn more fully into the filming process as confidants and participants. We should be more involved in a common quest for knowledge and the filmmaker less of a magician pulling rabbits out of hats."[8]

The problem of knowledge has remained at the center of MacDougall's own work for almost forty years. What is intriguing is the manner in which he has explored it, subtly interweaving his substantive and reflexive concerns. Despite the changing location and shifting focus of his research, the theme of education or schooling has remained a consistent thread that links *To Live with Herds* and *Kenya Boran* with his later films *Familiar Places, Tempus de Baristas,* and, of course, with the *Doon School* series. From the beginning, MacDougall's probing of his subjects' ways of being in the world has also functioned to illuminate ways of knowing yielded by the camera. Observational cinema has lain at the heart of this endeavor, facilitating a creative synthesis of substance and technique as inseparable elements of his anthropological inquiry. Although not formally designated as such when he began filming with Jie pastoralists in East Africa, the observational approach quickly became the epistemological ground of his work. Initially, it enabled MacDougall to position his developing practice within a broader context of anthropology and cinema, at the same time as it allowed him to identify potential problems or limitations posed by the new approach. More recently, the question of observation itself has become self-consciously articulated as a crucial element in MacDougall's broader project concerned with anthropology, ways of knowing, and the senses.

To Live with Herds

David MacDougall's first film, *To Live with Herds,* is widely acknowledged as one of the classic works of observational cinema.[9] The structural elegance, the distinctive visual and aural texture, the aesthetic completeness or unity of the film, however, belie the uneven process by which it was made. When MacDougall embarked with Judith MacDougall on their particular path as filmmakers, they sought (like Di Gioia and Hancock) to relinquish many of the familiar conventions of documentary cinema (such as commentary, interviews, and so on) without knowing exactly what might follow. In breaking with the norms of the expository film that reported on or reconstructed experience, they too were attempting to render peoples' lives more fully—not in the sense of more accurately or completely but *existentially.* There was an acknowledgment that the fiction film had often been more successful in conveying the emotional texture of peoples' lives and in persuading audiences to engage more actively and imaginatively in the search for meaning. Increasingly, the people around Young were interested in exploring how such a cinema could be generated from documentary principles—that is, how might it emerge not from the studio or the script but from a direct encounter with the world? Moreover, how might its fundamentally humanist impulse be realized in practice—that is, how might its techniques reflect filmmaking not as an industrialized or anonymous system of production but instead as a specific human encounter? By locating this kind of project in East Africa, the MacDougalls confronted additional questions raised by conditions of cultural and linguistic dislocation. These, too, could not be fully articulated in advance and became an integral part of their filmmaking inquiry itself.

"Pastoralism and Prejudice," an essay by the anthropologist Peter Rigby, provided the theoretical framework for MacDougall's work with the Jie herders of Uganda. *To Live with Herds* documents the conflicting perspectives that followed the end of British rule and the foundation of the new nation-state. The film stands as a powerful and moving portrayal of the precarious existence of cattle herders, paying homage to the dignity and resilience of the Jie in the face of change and impoverishment. MacDougall builds a compelling case for the organic integrity of pastoralist life but he does so not by means of conventional argument or drama.[10] For, while the film is both rigorous and passionate, it is never didactic. Instead MacDougall works *cinematically* to persuade, developing camera and sound techniques that are intended to position audiences differently with respect to Jie experience. Hence, in place of summary, viewers are presented with an intimate portrait of particular individual subjects going about their daily lives. Through careful, patient camera work mirrored by the fine-grained detail of the sound track, the filmmaker assembles a case based upon the meticulous amassing of small observations that comprised a series of propositions about the nature of the reality perceived. In using long, unbroken takes with synchronous sound and extended sequences, MacDougall sought to preserve the integrity of events and encounters witnessed, while simultaneously inviting viewers to engage with the materials on their own terms.[11] Crucial to this method, as we have already seen, was the forging of a close relationship between filming and editing such that the latter was not about transforming raw footage into a "final" film but, understood as about the framing of certain interpretive possibilities, editing became a way of both extending and underlining the analytical work inherent in the moment of filming itself.

During the making of *To Live with Herds,* MacDougall discovered that to chart a different filmmaking course was to confront a number of concrete problems. Again, as with Di Gioia and Hancock, these were impossible to anticipate, since the observational approach was essentially formed in and through practice itself. For example, while editing, he struggled to resolve what he subsequently termed "privileged" and "unprivileged" camera styles.[12] He discovered that the techniques he and Judith MacDougall had used while filming the Jie were often at odds with the new position they were seeking to develop in relation to their subjects and audience. At the time of recording they were not aware of the fact that their attempts to find an optimal position as filmmakers undercut the sense of "being there" they were trying to evoke through a humanized, situated camera with its flawed, partial view. A second issue concerned the problem of narrative. For, in abandoning the structuring devices of didactic documentary and the linear causality of dramatic narrative, MacDougall nevertheless had to find ways of ordering and presenting his anthropological understanding. He experimented with a cinematic form derived from Basil Wright's 1934 film, *Song of Ceylon*. In *To Live with Herds*, MacDougall explored questions about modernization, nationhood, and pastoralism through a series of scenes grouped into distinctive parts or chapters and organized according to a symphonic framework. The relationship between the different parts was not then straightforwardly linear but emerged as a series of variations in theme and tempo. Although MacDougall did not couch his argument in the terms typical of expository documentary or textual anthropology, *To Live with Herds* is nevertheless a profoundly analytical piece. In asking his viewers to engage with an argument made through the medium of film, MacDougall raised the possibility that observational techniques might serve as a basis for intellectual inquiry pursued by means of non-textual forms.

Writing some four years after the completion of *To Live with Herds*, MacDougall identified several potential problems in what at the time he designated the "observational" approach. In his essay "Beyond Observational Cinema," he pointed out that despite learning to see again, there was a danger that the observational camera could become closed, distant, and aloof from the human subjects whose lives it sought to render. If the observational filmmaker now followed rather than directed the action, this could easily be misconstrued as a conceit of filming as though the camera was not there. Additionally, MacDougall warned that there was a latent passivity in the approach, since there was not an active searching for information (through, e.g., the asking of questions) but only a recording of the unprovoked—what happened. Working in this way prevented access to underlying or taken-for-granted understandings. As the title of his essay suggested, MacDougall was proposing a further step—one toward what he termed "a participatory cinema."[13]

The essay, written in 1975, was intended as a polemic. It was aimed at those who were arguing for the ideal of a disengaged cinema—or "objective" camera. MacDougall had encountered proponents of this view among some of the anthropologists associated with the UCLA Ethnographic Film Program. Of course, it was also a view expressed by others—most prominently Margaret Mead.[14] Given the eclectic constituency and interdisciplinary brief of the Ethnographic Film Program, it is perhaps no surprise to discover that there was not a shared view as to the direction in which anthropological filmmaking should go.[15] A number of people advocated the absorption of observational approaches into existing

Still from *To Live with Herds* (1972). *Courtesy of David MacDougall.*

industrial models of documentary filmmaking, while others were keen to interpret observation through a scientific paradigm. For filmmakers such as the MacDougalls, and Di Gioia and Hancock, observation meant something quite different—the development of an intimate and authored practice.

It was in this context of debate and dissension that MacDougall attempted to assert one *interpretation* of observational cinema over another. But, despite drawing attention to the participatory qualities of observational filmmaking techniques, his essay became a catalyst for a much cruder polarization that has served to define and confine a good deal of subsequent discussion. Ironically, although the example of MacDougall's own practice demonstrated the participatory potential of an observational sensibility, his discussion was swiftly adopted as a wide-ranging critique of the form. Later, MacDougall acknowledged that his commentary had perhaps implied that observation and participation were opposite sides of the filmmaking coin rather than inseparable elements of a single approach.[16] Certainly at the time of its original publication in 1975, neither film studies nor anthropology had much use for the phenomenological inflections of observational work. The writings of Bazin and Merleau-Ponty had fallen out of favor, with structuralism and semiotics ruling the day. MacDougall himself moved on to explore what he called "participatory" filmmaking and the possibilities of collaborative authorship. During the early 1990s, however, his work took a different turn, throwing again into sharp relief questions about the nature and scope of observational cinema.

The Doon School Project

DOON SCHOOL CHRONICLES

The first film in MacDougall's Doon School series presents an interesting challenge for the reviewer. *Doon School Chronicles* is a dense, complex work. Running at more than two hours in length, it offers both an unusually rich ethnography of one of India's premier educational institutions and a model for a new kind of anthropological inquiry. *Doon School Chronicles* is as much an investigation into the possibility of what MacDougall calls a *visual anthropology* as it is an exploration of school life. For, in understanding this project as an alternative (and a challenge) to established discursive modes of anthropological work, the writer faces a particular problem. How can one effectively communicate the distinctive features of MacDougall's approach by means of a textual form? What, we might ask, is lost in translation?

Doon School Chronicles (2000) inaugurates the cycle of films that MacDougall crafted from over eighty hours of video footage generated during his two years at the school. Located just below the foothills of the Himalayas, in Dehra Dun, northern India, the filmmaker had first come across the school while making *Photo Wallahs* with Judith MacDougall in the nearby hill station of Mussoorie. Later, exchanges with an Indian anthropologist, Sanjay Srivastava, led MacDougall to think seriously about pursuing a project at the Doon School and in 1997 he began filming there.[17]

Although the Doon School has long held a special place in Indian society, it seems important to begin by focusing on MacDougall's project itself. This may seem an obvious point to make, but it is one worth making, since it would be easy enough to preface any consideration of the work with a contextualization of MacDougall's fieldsite that draws on abundant textual sources. To proceed in this way, however, would be to risk interpreting the films in the light of such frameworks rather than considering them as a mode of intellectual investigation in their own right. Hence we will take the work itself as the point of departure. What is the substantive focus of each film? What techniques does MacDougall use as a filmmaker and how are these related to the object of inquiry itself? What anthropological issues are raised by the work? And, finally, how is the Doon School series related to broader questions about observational cinema and non-discursive modes of ethnographic research?

Doon School Chronicles opens with an array of white shirts laid out on the grass to dry. Two women are shaking out other garments, adding them to the configuration of clothes that covers the ground. We see an emerging pattern of blue, gray, and white—even in such a routine task, we begin to appreciate the orderliness of things expressed as a particular aesthetic. Juxtaposed with these opening shots are still images of blue shorts hanging on a clothesline to dry. The film shifts indoors, to a dormitory linen room where shelves are filled with neat piles of folded clothes sorted by type and students' numbers. Each garment is in its place and each garment is accounted for. A worker shows the filmmaker items— socks, pants, shirts, pajamas—that represent the different categories of the pupils' clothing. All, of course, are identical. Reading from his record book, he moves between the numbers on one side of the ledger and the names of the boys that correspond on the other side. Who are these boys, these numbers, we wonder? MacDougall cuts to a series of still images of individual boys photographed from the back. Each one is wearing the Doon School's distinctive gray and blue checked sports shirt. We hear the sound of boys' voices but they are undifferentiated and indistinct. A short text follows: "*A year ago the present members of the Doon School were an assortment of two hundred boys from all over India. Now you can think of yourselves as a pack of cards all with the same pattern of blue and grey on your backs; on the other side is each boy's special character.*" A. E. Foot, Headmaster, 1936. Finally, we see the boys. A line of pupils faces the camera, eager and attentive, waiting for their names to be called. Immediately—and forcibly—we are struck by their diversity. All are wearing identical blue and gray sports shirts, but each boy, for the brief moment we glimpse him, impresses us with his individuality. It is expressed simply and starkly through variation in height, body shape, facial expression, and hair style.

With this, MacDougall announces the film—*Doon School Chronicles: a study in ten parts.*

A closer look at this opening sequence of *Doon School Chronicles* will serve as an important foundation for understanding the piece as a whole. For here MacDougall declares his intentions as anthropologist and filmmaker. Without any preliminaries, MacDougall begins *Doon School Chronicles* by situating the viewer inside a particular place. We are not given any opportunity to contextualize our location, to establish its historical, social, or geographical parameters, since the filmmaker chooses not to approach his subject from a position outside but rather to open his film in the midst of the school landscape. Moreover, our first view of the Doon School is not its classrooms, its historic buildings, its teachers, or, indeed, its pupils. Instead we see a distinctive arrangement of clothing and glimpse a complex army of people whose work ensures the continual reproduction of order. From the outset, MacDougall alerts us to a developed aesthetic at work at the Doon School. It is material and concrete, impinging directly on the bodies that move through its institutional spaces. But it also transcends specific individuals. The images of shirts and shorts evoke absence, hollow receptacles waiting to be animated by the bodies and personalities of particular boys.

The tension between individual and community, uniqueness and anonymity, part and whole emerges as a central question, coalescing from the visual, aural, and textual details that MacDougall gathers in the first three minutes of his film. At the same time, he shows us how he intends to explore these questions as a filmmaker. For example, with his first shot, MacDougall reveals his interest in the material and sensory landscape of the school—how it looks and sounds. This interest represents a reversal of the conventional hierarchy of background and foreground. In *Doon School Chronicles*, MacDougall brings what is often overlooked as merely the setting for cultural practice to the forefront of attention. Thus the landscape—understood as terrain, architecture, objects, shapes, textures, colors, movement, choreography, and so on—comes to be reconfigured as an active agent in, rather than a passive backdrop to, the forging of subjectivity. We first see clothes without bodies, bodies without subjectivity, subordinate staff not pupils, abstract designs not individual personalities.

The opening of *Doon School Chronicles* provides important clues—camera style, use of sound and text, editing approach—as to the kind of analysis that is developed by MacDougall in the ten parts of the film.

Within the pre-title sequence, for instance, we are made aware of the camera's interest in visual patterning as much as in human subjects. Aural communication is not just talk but involves a diffuse texture of sound that expands to include bells, birdsong, footfalls, the hum of human voices, and the echoes of institutional corridors. The filmmaker uses both still and moving images. There is text but no subtitling. Editing is organized around the juxtaposition of different kinds of material such that meanings are suggested rather than demonstrated.

MacDougall's techniques serve then to locate the viewer in the work in very particular ways. From the beginning, we are aware that the *Doon School Chronicles* is being presented as an investigation, an exploratory endeavor in which the filmmaker asks his audience to critically explore the range of materials presented and to participate actively in the making of meaning. The visual and aural texture of the individual shots invites a range of interpretive possibilities that are further extended through an editing approach constructed around the linking of threads and associations through the work as a whole. The use of text is central to the film's construction. Drawing on a range of Doon School sources (its distinguished former pupils, its student newspaper, its first headmaster, A. E. Foot), MacDougall frames each of the different parts or chapters with a quotation. The opening segment of *Doon School Chronicles* reveals how this device functions in the piece as a whole. The quotations, like the other materials of the film, are offered as a series of propositions, rather than explanations. They do not constitute the "analysis" around which "data" is organized. The pieces of text have already been subject to careful scrutiny like the other observations offered by the filmmaker. The analytical structure of MacDougall's inquiry is embedded within the work, disclosing itself cumulatively through the skillful manipulation of textual, visual, aural, experiential, and discursive evidence.

Over the course of ten parts, MacDougall maps different facets of the post-colonial subject as forged within the distinctive landscape and ethos of the Doon School. He reveals the school to be a rich and expansive context for the staging of this subjectivity. In tracing its formation, MacDougall traverses different spaces—dormitories, the theater, dining hall, sports field, laundry room, school grounds, assembly hall, classrooms, corridors, a science laboratory, and school kitchen. He considers its diverse personnel—including teachers, ground staff, laundry and kitchen workers, sign writers, bell ringers, the headmaster, distinguished visitors—and, of course, the pupils themselves. He maps its extraordinary range of activities—from cricket, boxing, and athletics to poetry, science, theater, music making (violin, piano, drumming), filmmaking, and chess playing, to marching and drilling, weighing and measuring, the washing, drying, and stacking of plates. The richness of school life is indeed impressive, but so, too, is its order and rhythm. The Doon School appears as a complex, well-oiled machine in which all the disparate parts appear to mesh and to be self-sustaining. The scenes from the dining hall convey this sense tangibly. It is a dense, crowded, noisy space but when we look more closely we see it is not chaotic—the boys move efficiently through it. MacDougall's subtle juxtaposition of dining hall and kitchen, boys and subordinate staff holds together the different material and symbolic elements in a structure that mirrors the overall structure of the film.

If the opening sequence of *Doon School Chronicles* establishes the contours of MacDougall's inquiry, the subsequent parts represent an extension and development of it. They are not individual pieces that build toward a linear argument but instead they are more akin to a series of digressions that set up alternative perspectives and resonances across the film. The different parts vary in length and focus. Some last for five minutes, others twenty minutes; a number are focused around a person or event (e.g., parts 4 and 6), others comprise more complex and extended explorations of a particular idea or theme (e.g., parts 7 and 8). Although it is our intention to focus on parts 4 and 7 of *Doon School Chronicles* in order to highlight aspects of MacDougall's approach, it is important not to reify the parts as self-contained pieces. For the film comprises a dense network of relationships clustered within parts and cutting across parts. For example, certain motifs—shirts, shorts, shoes, hands—recur at different places in the film, their significance changing and developing through a steady process of accretion.

"*The aim of this school might well be to give you the physique of the savage and the cultivated brain of the civilized man,*" Sir Jagdish Prasad (1937). This text prefaces a tight, choreographed montage of shots. Part 4 of *Doon School Chronicles* is constructed around a series of formal drills that pupils perform on the sports field for the headmaster and a guest seated alongside him in full military uniform. MacDougall's camera is held by the rhythm, synchrony, and configuration of the boys' bodies. His framing foregrounds the abstract qualities of this display—the contrasts of color, the patterning of arms or legs, the order and shape of shared movement.

His ear is alert to the bark of the drill master and to the dull thud of feet on the hard ground. He presents a highly ritualized exhibition of collective identity that melds distinctive subjectivities into a single disciplined body. It is interesting is to see how MacDougall's techniques as a filmmaker mirror the formality and stylization of the cultural performance itself. Part 4 is the most self-consciously abstract of all the parts that make up *Doon School Chronicles*. Lasting barely five minutes, it is put together according to formal aesthetic principles in which line, shape, and tempo replace the imprint of individual human presence. MacDougall uses both still and moving images in his montage assembly, drawing attention to the artifice of his response to the opening text. For the text poses questions that stretch forward and backward across the film—specifically, what is the relationship between a certain discourse of the school and its actual practices?

Part 7 of *Doon School Chronicles* is a different kind of chapter. It is another example of how the filmmaker understands the anthropological potential of his particular medium. For here, too, MacDougall's concern is in pursuing an analysis, but it is one that is radically different from that characteristic of a textual approach. Part 7 is an exploration of ideas that follow from a statement made in 1941 by A. E. Foot, the Doon School's first headmaster: *"At 14 a boy should have acquired habits of competence in various departments of his life . . . at 16 he should be developing his taste . . . At 17 he must acquire a capacity of judgment."* In this complex, extended segment of the film, MacDougall layers different kinds of material and observations in order to address questions of personal motivation, opinion, social responsibility, morality.

Let us briefly consider the forms of evidence presented and manner of their presentation. There are significant shifts of location in part 7 and many unusual juxtapositions of material. It begins in a classroom with a teacher asking pupils to think about learning and social responsibility. From this scene MacDougall cuts to an informal conversation between a handful of boys. They consider the motivations and interests of their fellow pupils, suggesting there is a lack of collective responsibility in the school and that self-interest and materialism are significant features of its moral landscape. Are Doon School boys, they ask themselves, independent agents or do they simply go with the crowd? Prominent in this discussion is a boy (Rohan) with a thoughtful, intelligent face framed by large glasses. We have already encountered him in other parts of the film, talking to MacDougall and offering insights into school life. Here he readily admits that he, too, is not exempt from the criticisms leveled at other boys. The film moves to the dining hall. Although he appears to have left behind particular subjects, MacDougall refers obliquely to the previous discussion of individuality by following another of the film's protagonists (Rishabh) as he negotiates his way through the commotion of the refectory. Amid the crowded space, he appears slightly fragile and uncertain. The scene then shifts toward the materiality of plates, cups, spoons—to the hard, unyielding surfaces that seem to hold everything in place. MacDougall shows us a short sequence of an older pupil being coached for a debate on morality. Next comes a single shot of pupils setting off to race across the sports field. These segments are followed by a discussion between MacDougall and Rohan about what constitutes intelligence. Rohan reflects on this, concluding with the statement that intelligence is perhaps best revealed in how a person reacts to situations. The final sequences of part 7 revolve around a cricket match. Rohan is bowling. MacDougall shows him engaged in an animated discussion with his teammates about the tactics they need to use in order to win. The exchanges become an argument as Rohan tries to stand his ground against the older pupils. Finally, we are returned to the conversation between the filmmaker and Rohan about when to hold on to individual opinion and when to accede to the majority view.

So what is MacDougall doing in this part of the film? Certainly it offers more of a challenge to the viewer than part 4. The latter, while unusually abstract for a piece of anthropology, is nevertheless organized around a single event. However, part 7 of *Doon School Chronicles* might appear at first viewing to be a rambling collection of disparate scraps, a presentation of raw materials and random observations that await organization by means of a theoretical framework. But this would be to assume a lack of intention on the filmmaker's part. Yet if there is one feature that characterizes MacDougall's approach, it is meticulousness. Nothing that he does is left to chance—which is not to say there is no room for the unexpected or spontaneous in his work. Indeed, as MacDougall himself has acknowledged, visual modes are inherently dense and ambiguous.[18] What is often considered problematic, namely the "co-presentation of centered and peripheral details in the same frame" that follows from the analog and uncoded properties of film, serves as the critical foundation for MacDougall's Doon School investigation.[19] Not only is the material

Still from *Doon School Chronicles* (2000). *Courtesy of David MacDougall.*

presented in part 7 already carefully framed and interpreted in ways that acknowledge a surplus of meaning (rather than an attempt to circumscribe it), but the order and tempo of the different sequences have also been finely judged. The filmmaker's intention is to establish a web of associations in which meaning emerges from the complex interplay between individual subjectivities and the material, social, aesthetic, philosophical, and symbolic registers that constitute the Doon School.

Our selection of parts 4 and 7 stems from the fact that they represent the two contrasting perspectives that define the film. In *Doon School Chronicles,* MacDougall is committed to examining the aesthetic texture that characterizes a particular institution but, equally, he is interested in conveying the experience of individual boys who live within it. MacDougall himself has remarked on the tension between these two perspectives, each one marked by a different filmmaking style.[20] The former, as exemplified in part 4, is distinguished by its structural rigor and formality; the latter is characterized by a more open-ended, exploratory style. Although there is a shift from the former to the latter during *Doon School Chronicles,* signaling a broader movement within the film series as a whole, the two perspectives remain distinct. MacDougall resists collapsing one into the other. For the complex interplay between them is, precisely, the focus of anthropological attention.

WITH MORNING HEARTS, KARAM IN JAIPUR, AND THE NEW BOYS

Doon School Chronicles is critical in establishing the distinctive contours of MacDougall's project. MacDougall himself has described this film as the "web" in which the other pieces are suspended.[21] In its expansiveness—geographical, social, educational, and intellectual—it constitutes a charting of the terrain. Acknowledging the unusual anthropological form of this work, one commentator remarked: "No one succeeds in holding a viewer's attention for nearly two-and-a-half hours without recourse to substantial structural artifice, whether intellectually or intuitively deployed . . . the difficulty of approaching these films would reside not in the absence of significant detail but in its proliferation and its density."[22]

If the subsequent films in the Doon series are less ambitious in scope, they are richer and more nuanced in their emotional texture than *Doon School Chronicles.* For MacDougall's attention moves from abstract questions of social aesthetics to a concern with experiential perspectives. In the second and third films, *With Morning Hearts* and *Karam in Jaipur,* he begins to open up the emotional landscape of the school. This shift of focus is indicated in *With Morning Hearts* by the filmmaker's choice of opening text. Taking an extract from a Doon School song, MacDougall raises the question of emotional fortitude that the institution demands of its pupils: *"Call us up with morning faces / And with morning hearts / Eager to labour, eager to be happy / If happiness be our portion / And if the day be marked for sorrow / Strong to endure it."* What does this mean in the lives of individual boys and how does MacDougall set out to explore it?

With Morning Hearts follows a group of boys newly arrived at Foot House, one of the school's "holding houses." Here they learn to adapt themselves to life away from their families. The film chronicles the processes of change and adjustment as the boys prepare themselves for their move into the school proper. At the end of their first year, they will be dispersed into different "main houses," an upheaval that is anticipated with both fear and excitement.

MacDougall begins his film quietly, a moon in the dark sky. The insistent ringing of the school bell breaks through the sound of birds at day-break, and we move indoors to find the boys of Foot House gradually emerging from beneath the bedclothes, drowsy and slow. One by one they begin their tasks—dressing, making their beds, cleaning their teeth, walking together across the school grounds for breakfast at long wooden tables. At each stage, MacDougall's camera is *with* the boys. Never hurried or distracted, it quietly observes the details of the scene that is unfolding around it. Early on, we glimpse one of the new pupils, a small, slight boy dwarfed by his desk who is eagerly seeking to catch the teacher's atten-tion. His arm is up straight, his face is animated, his entire body strain-ing to be noticed. Shortly afterward, Karam talks directly to the camera about arriving at Foot House. He recalls his experiences of the first day and describes his attempts to come to terms with being away from family and home. It is hard not to respond to his appealing vulnerability and his anxiety to please. Karam is a point of reference in *With Morning Hearts* but, unusually, MacDougall does not build the film around him. Certainly it would have been easy enough to follow the process of adaptation to school life through the contrasting experiences of two or three pupils. But MacDougall does not do this. He offers a more diffuse picture of Foot House in which Karam is neither its single focal point nor is he presented in any straightforward way. Indeed we frequently lose sight of him for significant parts of the film. It is only in the next film, *Karam in Jaipur,* that Karam emerges as a subject in his own right.

Over the course of a year, MacDougall documents the process by which the Foot House boys begin to learn the ways of the Doon School. Not least, he reveals that coming to terms with the separation from family involves their coming to terms with each other. Adaptation is both indi-vidual and collective. Through a number of loosely connected scenes—sharing "tuck," eating together, exercise, prayer, play—MacDougall suggests different facets of the socialization process. There are scenes of focused activity interspersed with more extended interactions and encounters. The film reveals how much of the relationships focus on the body. Not only are the boys wedged together by their beds, desks, at the dining table, in their everyday tasks of washing or getting dressed, but they are continually in physical contact with one another—fighting, play-ing, teasing, dancing, throwing their bodies together, tangling and disen-tangling from one another. There is a chaotic exuberance to the informal relationships that the boys pursue within Foot House. It runs counter to the school's ritualized procedures for the disciplining and channeling of their bodily energy.

With Morning Hearts is situated firmly in Foot House. The film confines itself to what happens in a space that serves both as a sanctuary and as a laboratory. For, on the one hand, the holding house shelters the newly arrived boys and prepares them for immersion into school life, while on the other hand, it is a kind of experimental site in which the boys are tested, and test each other, as they seek to fashion community in a new place. Apart from the occasional intervention of the house master or tutor, the boys are largely left to their own devices in working things out. This they do physically and through sustained verbal exchange. Their level of engagement with one another is remarkable. Although homesickness is a shadow that hovers over the film, MacDougall draws attention to the manifold, inventive ways that the boys adapt to their situation and to their fellow Footies. The filmmaker's observational approach renders tangible this process. Locating himself alongside the boys in Foot House, MacDougall shows how social learning is grounded in responses to specific situations, conflicts, and encounters. He documents the creative energy and commitment of Karam and his cohort in fashioning a life for themselves in Foot House without the help of adults. It becomes the basis for their integration into the larger school. For what they build together sustains them in the face of the school's impersonal structures—its architecture, its material culture, its drills, tests, and examinations. Slowly these structures begin to encroach on the world of Foot House, signaling the moment when the boys will exchange the open egalitarianism they have forged together for the formality and hierarchy of the main houses.

The film, loosely organized into parts that mark different stages in the boys' first year at the school, moves inexorably toward this moment. Progressively, too, we feel the pressure of the impending transition. MacDougall solicits comments from a handful of Foot House boys (but not Karam). Each one admits to anxiety and nervousness as they contemplate leaving Foot House and each other for the unknown world of the seniors. What they do know, however, is that the process of learning in the main houses proceeds less by means of trial and error but more through punishment and the threat of punishment. It is a world where boys cannot afford to make mistakes and expect to be excused.

Amid the tangle of boys and bodies in Foot House, MacDougall has made us aware of Karam as he negotiates his way, carefully, hesitantly—

Still from *With Morning Hearts* (2001). *Courtesy of David MacDougall.*

painfully—through his first weeks and months at the school. We observe his actions, for example—there is a long take of him making his bed, attending to every last detail of the action, which lasts for almost a minute. We watch him repeatedly pulling his oversized school clothing over his child's body. We note his different interactions with other boys. From these clues, we begin to develop a sense of him as a person in the world through the web of relationships that connects him with people and things. Much of it is non-verbal and implicit. Nevertheless, Karam remains at a distance. He is a tangible presence within the film and yet he continues to be elusive. For, apart from a brief opening exchange, MacDougall does not ask Karam to explain himself, nor does the filmmaker attempt to do this.

MacDougall continues to trace Karam's trajectory in the sequel to *With Morning Hearts. Karam in Jaipur,* the shortest film in the Doon School series, follows his move into one of the main houses. Dai Vaughan has noted that the slow-motion opening sequence of Karam running is strongly suggestive of escape.[23] But what the film shows, in fact, is the opposite—Karam hunkering down, starting over, establishing his place in the larger school without the help and support of his Foot House friends.

There is a different emotional texture to this film. *With Morning Hearts* was marked by the boundless energy and unlimited curiosity of twelve-year-old boys. In the fluid, affective quality of the second Doon School film, MacDougall rendered something of the openness and generosity of the boys toward one another and toward the world in which they found themselves. The pupils of Foot House always seemed to be in movement, physically and emotionally, sustaining to a remarkable degree a series of ongoing relationships forged through their bodies and verbal exchange. By contrast, the third film, *Karam in Jaipur,* is a quieter, more introspective piece. For, once in the main house, the Doon School boys become more guarded. They are expected to embark on a process of self-discovery that involves coming to terms with who they are and setting their own standards of achievement. Through Karam, MacDougall charts this difficult and seemingly lonely path. It demands reserves of self-confidence, determination, and self-discipline.

MacDougall returns to Foot House in *The New Boys,* the fourth part of his Doon School series. This time he does not document an attenuated process that unfolds over the course of a year as in *With Morning Hearts,* but instead he charts the acute, ragged early weeks that stretch from the day of the boys' arrival in Foot House until their departure at the end of the first term. The dynamic of the new group differs sharply from the one that marked Karam's cohort. It is more divided, fractious, and emotionally raw. This change of mood is subtly suggested in the film's opening shots. MacDougall begins at the school gates, amid the noise and bustle of traffic and people. The world encroaches in the form of parents and their offspring passing through the school gates, and the discordant sounds of the street presage the unfolding of the film's uneven affective landscape. This time MacDougall charts a process of adjustment that is marked by expressions of anger, homesickness, conflict, and unhappiness as much as by empathy and understanding. It is a much more unsettling picture of Foot House than the one represented in *With Morning Hearts.* The boys' encounter with each other and with the culture of the school is fraught with tension. From the very first day, they anxiously struggle with the complex system of rules and established ways of doing things at the school. MacDougall documents these early weeks. The first hopeless attempts to perform drills on the sports field—what one pupil describes as "physical torture," not "physical training"—reveals adaptation to be a physical or bodily process as much as an emotional and intellectual one.

Still from *Karam in Jaipur* (2001). *Courtesy of David MacDougall.*

But above all, *The New Boys* is about Foot House and what happens in this space. Again, the boys are expected to work things out for themselves. However, this time the dynamic of the group is different, and the house master is repeatedly called upon to intervene. MacDougall proposes Foot House as a kind of incubator of social life. What happens here resonates beyond, not just through the school but in the wider world, as the boys themselves recognize at one moment in the film. How can a collective be created from disparate individuals? What role do the emotions play in social life? How do we develop qualities of compassion and understanding?

With Morning Hearts, Karam in Jaipur, and *The New Boys* are distinguished by the modest, unobtrusive camera work that carefully frames subjects in the context of their day-to-day lives. Although here and there MacDougall includes direct, informal exchanges between himself and his subjects, the films are overwhelmingly *observational.* By this we refer to MacDougall's commitment to sharing the experiential space of his subjects, inserting himself in the visual, aural, and temporal landscape through which they move. It is an embodied, sensory participation that constitutes a particular understanding of the world. The understated style that marks these three films follows from MacDougall's commitment to the notion that his subjects are inherently more interesting than himself in this specific filmmaking context. His approach is built upon the recognition that being filmed is neither the only thing happening in subjects' lives, nor the most important one. It would be a mistake, however, to confuse this unobtrusiveness as a filmmaker with his absence from the work. For *With Morning Hearts, Karam in Jaipur,* and *The New Boys* are deeply imprinted with MacDougall's presence in, and his response to, the lives of his subjects. This is conveyed in different aesthetic terms than the first and last parts of the Doon School series. Nevertheless, it must be accounted for in any discussion of the films.

The approach MacDougall pursues in the middle parts of his Doon School project reflects his substantive concerns. His techniques are intended to explore the domain of lived experience, what he calls "social aesthetics"—the way that landscape (understood as sensory, emotional, and material) shapes and is shaped by human subjectivity. Unlike *Doon School Chronicles,* in which the aesthetic and experiential strands were identified but held separate, in the subsequent films MacDougall seeks to find a way of interweaving them. The classic techniques of observational cinema are especially suited to this task.

The three films are built around long, fluid, unbroken camera takes and extended scenes, the use of synchronous sound, a respect for the spatial and temporal integrity of events, and a keen sensitivity to the interplay between foreground and background. By choosing to use these techniques, MacDougall proposes to *show* us rather than tell us about this process. It means filming events, actions, encounters as they happen, attending to their particular rhythm and dynamic as an integral part of what is being communicated. This approach, one that Nichols has called "present-tense representation," constitutes a reversal of the hierarchy characteristic of word-led (through commentary, interview, voice-over, testimony) documentary and ethnographic films.[24] The word-led film is located in a different time and space from the events and relationships represented. It is essentially a recounting that hinges upon abbreviation and synopsis.

Working observationally has always been predicated on different foundations. It hinges upon the dislodging of language as *the* central

structuring device; and, as we have already seen, there are always significant consequences at both the filming and editing stages of the project
of such a move. In *With Morning Hearts, Karam in Jaipur,* and *The New
Boys,* MacDougall neither banishes nor prioritizes language. Instead,
he recontextualizes it, embedding it within a broader and more diverse
range of communicative forms. This includes expression, gesture, bodily
posture, movement, clothing, color, spatial organization. It also encompasses sound. Furthermore, communication occurs not just through the
amassing of details, the accumulation of individual observations, but also
through MacDougall's keen sensitivity to relationships between things,
to the distinctive arrangements, patterns, and textures characteristic of
Doon School life. He makes us aware of the shape of a cup, the particular
way that tea is poured, the place of an egg on a plate, the layout of beds in
the dormitory, the pools of light in the school corridor, the interweaving
of birds, boy's voices, ringing bells, footsteps, the alternating rhythms of
movement and stillness, exertion and repose, and the unfolding choreography of individual and collective, solitariness and communality.

It is within this dense fabric that the filmmaker situates language,
embraced in all its complexity—as expression, performance, information,
conversation, instruction. Indeed, the films reveal that an observational
approach, far from reducing the role of language, serves in fact to expand
it. For MacDougall remains attentive to not just *what* is being said but *how*
things are being said. Moreover, his use of synchronous sound, contrary to
many assumptions, is critical to the opening up, not the closing down, of
language's interpretive possibilities. Framing language within the context
of its use, holding it together with co-existent sounds, silence, and a clus-
ter of visual cues releases the full range of its nuances and ambiguities.[25]

The approach that MacDougall pursues while filming at the Doon
School finds its counterpart in his editing style. We have already seen in
the case of Di Gioia and Hancock the interconnection of shooting and
editing in observational work. Specific choices about what and how to film
have been made at the time of recording such that the footage with which
the filmmaker works in the editing suite cannot then be organized according to different principles—for example, according to those of a word-led
documentary. MacDougall's techniques serve to frame and interpret the
culture of the Doon School in very particular ways. This does not mean
that new discoveries cannot be found in the material (as indeed they are),
but editing becomes a process of choosing less while suggesting more. As

Hancock explained, it involves building the film around fewer observations but denser and more extended ones.

Extended scenes are the basis of MacDougall's construction of *With Morning Hearts, Karam in Jaipur,* and *The New Boys.*[26] But, in contrast with *Doon School Chronicles,* MacDougall uses chronology as the organizing principle of the films' narrative. Unlike the first film, which was not situated temporally (or spatially), the middle body of work is tied to developments that unfold in real time. In the second, third, and fourth parts of the Doon School series, MacDougall presents moments from an ongoing process, positioning the audience alongside himself as witnesses to events and interactions as they happen. Each film is framed by certain questions, and MacDougall uses different devices (text, personal testimony, informal conversation) to suggest the parameters of the inquiry. Although committed to respecting chronology, MacDougall's editing style is nevertheless open; that is, it is not directed toward a single, known outcome. Even at the end of *With Morning Hearts, Karam in Jaipur,* and *The New Boys,* there is a lingering uncertainty, a sense that questions posed have not been definitively resolved. For MacDougall's assiduous documentation of the boys' lives over a specified period of time reminds us of the unevenness of the developmental process. There are small, incremental changes, imperceptible shifts, moments of conflict and ones of harmony, instances of boldness and those of retreat, of collective affirmation and individual isolation. The emphasis of these films is on rendering experience in its fullest sense, not as recounted solely through language. Moreover, MacDougall's refusal to use language as the framework for editing underscores the films' dense interpretive texture. As films, *With Morning Hearts, Karam in Jaipur,* and *The New Boys* expand laterally as much as they develop longitudinally.

THE AGE OF REASON

> *Children have as much a Mind to show that they are free, that their own good Actions come from themselves, that they are absolute and independent as any of the proudest of you grown Men.*
>
> —*JOHN LOCKE (1693)*

The Age of Reason is the last film to be edited from David MacDougall's Doon School material. He has described it as unexpected, something that seemed to emerge spontaneously, at once linked to the other films but also,

Still from *The New Boys* (2003). *Courtesy of David MacDougall.*

in significant ways, set apart from them.[27] It focuses on a young Nepalese boy, Abhishek Shukla. We caught sight of him in MacDougall's previous film, *The New Boys*. Now MacDougall presents a portrait of Abhishek assembled from the materials he shot while filming the spring term in Foot House. However, unlike the earlier film (and the others of the series), the filmmaker explores his own role in the process he is documenting. For his camera and presence function as a kind of umbrella, offering refuge to Abhishek in the course of an unknown and uncertain journey. *The Age of Reason* is built upon a delicate relationship of trust and mutual respect—in which each party is drawn to the other and yet retains a sense of autonomy, scrupulousness, and wary watchfulness. It is both intimate and yet distant, an encounter that involves the careful negotiation of differences of status, generation, and background.

The Age of Reason opens with new boys arriving at Foot House. It is April 1998, MacDougall explains, and he has been filming over an extended period in India's prestigious boarding school, the Doon School. In the midst of the bustle and confusion, MacDougall draws our attention to a slight, intelligent-looking boy. He is alert, wide-eyed, silently but actively taking everything in, both excited and perhaps a little daunted. He is Abhishek Shukla. He seems always to be hovering around the filmmaker, becoming, as MacDougall puts it, "a little like my shadow."

The film has a tripartite structure. Although not identified as such, it resembles the different phases of Van Gennep's ritual passage—separation, liminality, and incorporation. The first part of the film is a kind of diary of the early weeks of Abhishek and his cohort in Foot House. We follow them as they try to adjust to the rules of the classroom, the dormitory, to each other. But as MacDougall points out in his commentary, Abhishek seems much less interested than the other boys in the new ways of the school—since, he suggests, they might be all too familiar to someone who has attended boarding school from the age of six. Certainly we are aware of the animated sounds of Abhishek's cohort playing outside Foot House without him, while he chooses to stay indoors to talk "for hours" to the filmmaker. MacDougall offers glimpses of these extended conversations. Always thoughtful and engaging, Abhishek moves seamlessly between mature reflections on questions of development, history, and Westernization, to the kind of jokes and teasing that children often use in their interactions with adults.

The second part of the film is built around Abhishek's illness. It results in his withdrawal from the life of Foot House and his admittance to the school hospital. It is the filmmaker, however, who acknowledges his intervention in Abhishek's situation, taking him to the doctor and ensuring he has what he needs as he beds down in his hospital ward. The sickness runs its course. For two days, Abhishek seems inaccessible, buried beneath his blankets as he first succumbs to and then emerges from his fever; but, as MacDougall notes, he also seems to have been changed by the experience. He begins to form relationships with older boys in the hospital and when he returns to Foot House he appears to be more at ease and closer in his relationship with others in his cohort. At this juncture in the film, MacDougall admits to being worried about whether his presence is contributing to, or alleviating, Abhishek's attenuated process of adaptation to life at the school. Although, of course, it is *the* question that hovers over the whole piece, the filmmaker refrains from posing it directly to Abhishek himself.

In the final part of *The Age of Reason*, we follow the almost impercept-ible but nevertheless tangible withdrawal of Abhishek from the filmmaker as he increasingly establishes his own trajectory at the school. It starts with an intriguing moment that perhaps marks the turning point in the rela-tionship between subject and filmmaker. Abhishek takes MacDougall on a tour of the school museum, a place of glass cases, stuffed animals, and bottles of curious specimens. At the end Abhishek stands alone framed against an anonymous staircase. "Shall we go back now?" MacDougall suddenly interjects. The filmmaker's suggestion comes as a relief. For, as Vaughan explains, "we sense that he [the filmmaker] may have been led farther into someone else's psyche than he might have wished. It is a haunted moment, and lasts longer in retrospect than in actuality."[28]

The remaining scenes of the film reveal the growing confidence and independence of Abhishek. The camera, however, continues to be an important point of reference as he launches himself into school life. It is as if, in taking these steps, Abhishek still needs to feel the reassuring pres-ence of MacDougall and the camera's acknowledgement of his growing accomplishments. When, after an absence of five months, MacDougall next encounters Abhishek, he is already unreachable. Now, like the filmmaker, we can only watch from a distance as the school closes in around him and he embarks on his journey through adolescence and into adult life.

The Age of Reason is marked by the intimacy and sensitivity of the camera work—characteristics that have distinguished David MacDougall's filmmaking approach from the beginning of his career and are abundantly evident in the Doon School series as a whole. As with much of his work, there is a deceptive simplicity to this last film in the Doon School series. There is nothing apparently self-conscious or mannered about it at all. It never calls attention to itself and yet it is unwavering in its commit-ment to "the singular individuality of things."[29] For, despite its modest, patient style, there is a rigor and meticulousness to the filmmaker's obser-vations that makes specific demands on the viewer. For each scene that MacDougall has selected to chart Abhishek's first weeks in Foot House are dense and complex—in terms of the structure of the image and the rela-tionship between image and sound. For example, we are asked to attend closely to the interplay between foreground and background, we must evaluate what is being said and what is being done, we need to listen carefully not just to what but how things are said, and we have to explore the complex web of associations and resonances between scenes that cuts across the overall movement of the narrative.

In his account of his work at the Doon School, MacDougall describes the essentially open-ended nature of the project. Put in its simplest terms, he explains that "I wanted to find out what it was possible to learn about the school by filming it."[30] Although the recording technology remained the same over the course of his eighteen months of filming, there are important shifts in his approach as he responds to different subjects and situations. Certainly *The Age of Reason* is the most interactive—and personal—film of the series. It is narrated by MacDougall and focuses squarely on his own encounter and changing relationship with one particular pupil. There is an interesting dynamic here not manifest in the other Doon School work, that is, the initiative for the film appears to originate as much with Abhishek as with MacDougall. Not only does Abhishek continually hover around the filmmaker and engage in extended conversations with him (what MacDougall terms "outpourings of talk") but, at various points, he literally leans into the camera to direct its attention in a certain way. His ingenuity in using the camera and the filmmaker's presence to figure out how to negotiate the transition into school life is striking. It seems to be partly about the need to establish his own timing in this process and partly a way of using the camera to make tangible who he is and who he might become.

But if Abhishek asserts his own agency over the filmmaking process, MacDougall has his own reasons for initiating the film too. At the beginning of *The Age of Reason*, in describing Abhishek as rather like his shadow, he raises the possibility that his subject is a kind of double, perhaps another or earlier version of himself. It is surely this sense of overlapping or merging identities that gives the work its unusual tension. There is something risky about the relationship that is being developed through the film. Certainly there are objective inequalities between MacDougall and his subject, ones of age, social standing, education, and experience. The question is not just about how or whether Abhishek will integrate successfully, but it is also—critically—about how the filmmaker will negotiate his responsibility for this crucial phase of his subject's life. In significant ways, MacDougall becomes caught up in this relationship through the actions of his subject, but MacDougall bears the burden of its outcome. With *The Age of Reason*, MacDougall walks a kind of tightrope. On the one side lies sentimentality, on the other, indifference. Maybe it is only through a relationship with a child not one's own that this can be explored. The resolution might be "what we always wanted" as MacDougall puts it at the end of the film. We feel relieved at this outcome but we share, too, the filmmaker's tangible sense of regret and loss.

The film is a testament to the skill of MacDougall—his ability to be a participant in the process and its complex choreography, while at the same time resisting the impetus toward closure or summary. He leaves it open as to where the relationship might lead—until he recognizes the point at which it must be relinquished. It is a balancing act that creates discomfort in the viewer as we wonder how it will be resolved. But *The Age of Reason* also lays bare the problem of responsibility to and for subjects—where the filmmaker ought to intervene, why he or she might be sought out and used by subjects, and so on. Of all the films in the Doon School series, *The Age of Reason* is perhaps the most challenging. It is not the most extended or the most formally inventive work but it poses more acutely than any of the other films the question of the human subject—and the elusive and enigmatic nature of filmmaking itself.[31]

With the Doon School series, MacDougall returned to questions, substantive and methodological, that were first posed in the context of his early East African research. On the one hand, his work at the Doon School can be considered an extension of the filmmaker's long-standing interest in processes of socialization and cultural transmission. On the other hand, it stands as a concrete example of what might comprise a non-textual anthropology and the role of observational filmmaking within it. The two dimensions of the project are intertwined throughout the Doon School films such that it is impossible to disengage one from the other.

For MacDougall, schooling has always been something of a mixed blessing. First addressed as a critical part of his understanding of the situation faced by the Jie herders in post-independence Uganda, he brings it into poignant focus through the example of Moding—the son of one of his Jie subjects whose "cleverness" ensures his social mobility but probably, MacDougall hints, at the cost of his humanity. In *To Live with Herds,* it is precisely through the use of observational techniques that the filmmaker attempts to draw his viewers' attention to what might be lost or displaced by formal education. And what is lost through formal education are other ways of knowing and being in the world, ones occluded or excised by notions of expertise. If the conflict between tradition and modernity,

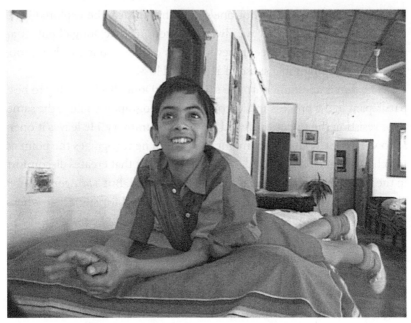

Still from *The Age of Reason* (2004). *Courtesy of David MacDougall.*

people and the state, embodied practice and bureaucratic knowledge subsequently becomes a recurrent theme in MacDougall's work, it also becomes transposed, in the course of his career, into a question about anthropology itself. What are anthropology's ways of knowing? How might they encompass overlooked or intangible areas of experience? How might knowledge (its production, communication, and transmission) be reconceptualized such that it becomes a shared undertaking rather than a matter of specialized and discrete expertise?

The Doon School Project represents a continuation of these preoccupations. Here MacDougall takes the primary site—education itself—as the focus of his investigation. Again, in working observationally, aligning his own practice as a filmmaker with the everyday processes of children's learning (rather than commenting from a place outside of them), MacDougall attempts to generate the conditions in which his own understanding might be transformed by the agency of his subjects.[32] Through filming he found himself documenting the innovative qualities of children—their capacity to think laterally about their and others' lives. His camera revealed them to be adept at working things out in practice and engaging energetically with the material conditions of their existence, both shaping and being shaped by the social and affective landscapes they encountered. His films celebrate the adventurousness of children, their willingness to experiment, and their unusual capacity for generating new social knowledge.

MacDougall's work can be interpreted in a similar light. For, in making the agency of his subjects the foundation of his approach, he allows for a web of resonances to unfold between the boys' active exploration of the world and his own as an anthropological filmmaker. It would be a mistake, however, to regard the observational quality of the Doon School films as evidence of a retreat or as involving the simple replication of techniques used by MacDougall in *To Live with Herds*. For observation functions here as "an expanding point of reference," orienting the filmmaker to the world in a way that makes different kinds of engagement possible.[33] In the Doon School Project, it becomes the basis of an approach that encompasses discrete filmmaking modes—ones that MacDougall has referred to as responsive, interactive, and constructive.[34] Although all three are rooted in observation, their ways of positioning the filmmaker allow him or her to attend to the modulations in perceptual activity and the different sorts of knowledge (experiential, dialogic, abstract) that arise. These are not so much represented by the different films as rendered through the texture of the Doon School series as a whole.

The shift in medium, from film to digital video, further enhanced the scope of MacDougall's observational inquiry, allowing him to embark on an open-ended project that might—or *might not*—have specific films as its outcome. In the case of the Doon School, this led to the creation of a new kind of anthropological form, one akin to a prism in which different but overlapping perspectives are developed around a single site. As we have seen, the films offer a series of crisscrossing pathways and lack a comprehensive framework or clear narrative line. The interpretative possibilities suggested by this unusual structure have a profound effect on what it means to be a viewer of the work. For, in negotiating the connections generated by the different facets of a prism, alternative ways of posing and answering questions emerge. Each viewing results in a further accretion, subverting the notion that intellectual inquiry has either a definitive beginning or end.

One of the challenges of MacDougall's Doon School series is precisely its status as anthropology. How do we go about evaluating it, given that it does not correspond to established disciplinary forms typically expressed through writing? Equally, it confounds many of the common expectations associated with the genre of ethnographic film. It is neither event-driven nor built around characters—and it does not offer an argument articulated through the discursive strategies of narration and interview. As MacDougall himself, quoting Robbe-Grillet, notes—perhaps wryly: "A new form always seems to be more or less an absence of any form at all, since it is unconsciously judged by reference to consecrated forms."[35]

In charting an observational cinema on the move, it becomes clear that for MacDougall (unlike his contemporaries Di Gioia and Hancock), the discipline of anthropology has from the very beginning provided a rich framework for his developing practice. The previous chapter revealed the centrality of making (understood as craft or labor) to the project pursued by Di Gioia and Hancock. Here observation is understood as a yielding, or lending of, the human being to the materiality of life such that the world is disclosed existentially. MacDougall's work, however, is animated differently. Central is the act of questioning itself. Through the medium of film, he asks, "What is knowledge?" Yet despite the different inflections, each of the approaches contains aspects of the other. The Doon School series reveals a filmmaker tirelessly curious, probing knowledge and its formation at every turn. But what also permeates this intellectual landscape is a consciousness that, in filming, MacDougall becomes open to the being of his subjects.

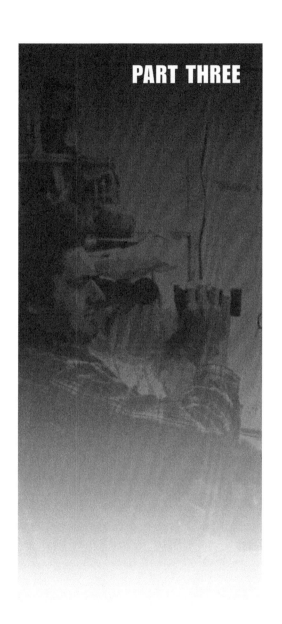

PART THREE

CHAPTER 5

Rethinking Observational Cinema

What is the role of observational filmmaking in contemporary anthropological research? In this chapter, we examine its significance as a particular kind of intellectual inquiry, establishing new ground for its evaluation that depends upon renewed attention to practice. Hence our concern is less with discourses about observational cinema and more with what it means to work with certain techniques in the context of research. For despite the ubiquity of the terms "observational" and "observational film," there is a surprising lack of discussion focused around examples of the work itself. At the beginning of the book we noted the dissatisfaction among film scholars with the dearth of commentary addressing the formal dimensions of the documentary.[1] As Grant pointed out, discussion of documentary film has traditionally focused around issues relating to technology or truth claims at the expense of questions about aesthetics. This is true, too, of much of the writing about ethnographic film. But, with observational cinema, there is an additional problem. The discourse attached to it has come to define the genre so comprehensively that to suggest alternative interpretations can at best appear misguided, at worst outlandish.

Although initially hailed as a breakthrough in ethnographic filmmaking, the early enthusiasm for observational cinema was quickly replaced by more guarded responses—and, eventually, skepticism. Commentators began to identify problems that were believed to be inherent to the genre.[2] From the beginning, the debate was confused by the different understandings and designations assigned to the term "observational" itself. We have already seen that David MacDougall's 1975 essay represented an early intervention.[3] It was quickly followed by others reflecting critical positions articulated from within the fields of anthropology and film studies.

In the case of film studies, one of its leading commentators, Bill

Nichols, identified features such as detachment, passivity, and what he called "'present tense' representation" as important drawbacks of the observational mode.[4] For him, the unacknowledged, non-responsive, and unsituated presence of the filmmaker created conditions for voyeurism, for "ideal" viewing in which viewers were encouraged to empathize with subjects and situations without real consequence. Additionally, he found the problem of meaning—its openness in observational work—troubling. According to Nichols, the absent filmmaker and the lack of commentary and exhaustive description gave the audience both the illusion of an unmediated reality and the space within which it could impose its own meaning according to pre-existing prejudices and assumptions.[5] Hence despite Nichols's appreciation of the qualities of observational cinema—for example, its three-dimensional fullness of scenes; its respect for duration or lived time; and its non-judgmental, affective texture that elicited empathy in the viewer—he advocated the development of a more self-conscious ethnographic cinema that acknowledged the conditions of its own making. Nichols's depiction of observational filmmaking was to represent it as a stage on the way to a more advanced participatory or reflexive mode of documentary.[6]

A second body of critical discourse associated with observational cinema had its origins in anthropology. It was linked to the problem of "visualism." Introduced by Johannes Fabian, this notion swiftly passed into circulation as a critique of the discipline that had, he claimed, "a bias toward vision."[7] Scientific ethnography was represented as a set of techniques and a theory of knowledge with observation at its core. Observation was understood to be synonymous with "visualism," signifying a distanced, disembodied, controlling gaze that objectified human subjects and denied them agency and history. During the 1980s and 1990s this critique became, as Okely has pointed out, a sort of mea culpa for anthropology, despite the fact that many ethnographers found it hard to reconcile Fabian's characterization of the discipline with their own experiences and practices.[8] It was certainly useful ammunition for those doubtful of the intellectual seriousness of ethnographic filmmaking, since "visualism" became an additional stick with which to beat those committed to the enterprise. But, above all, for the observational filmmakers, Fabian's writing—and the alacrity with which it was greeted—cut the ground from under their feet, rendering their position virtually untenable.

The new case for observational cinema hinges on a change in the existing terms of the debate. Hence we propose to put to one side the familiar discussion that has both conflated and reduced the meaning of observation to a narrowly ocular strategy with a tall order of negative features—voyeurism, objectification, surveillance, looking not seeing, assumed transparency, concealed ideology, lack of reflexivity, quasi-scientific objectivity, the ethnographic present, and so on. Our reassessment involves reframing observation as a particular kind of skilled practice, one that has the selective training of the filmmaker's attention at its core.[9] What does it mean to learn to observe as an ethnographic filmmaker? How is one's attention directed to some things (and not others)? What is the epistemological status of observations and how might they constitute anthropological knowledge?

These questions have partly emerged from our own attempts to use observational techniques in a number of fieldwork situations. While personal experiences might appear to give our account a somewhat narrow basis, one of our primary concerns is to ensure that any alternative discourse about observational cinema is anchored in a careful consideration of practice. In shifting to a more subjective stance, we seek to describe in detail what it means as an anthropologist to work in a particular way with a camera. Our apprenticeship in the observational method is intended as a starting point for the development of a broader narrative concerning technique and knowledge in anthropological research.

Learning to Observe

The term "observation" is so commonly used that it is easy to overlook its distinctive meaning and significance across different fields of scholarly practice. Within the natural and social sciences, it is frequently employed to refer to an inquirer who is engaged in activities that are not everyday but are the outcome of specialized training and expertise. But even here, observation is often a taken-for-granted notion that belies its complex and shifting purpose within intellectual inquiry. We noted earlier that recent work in the history of science has brought this question into sharper focus, providing a new set of tools for approaching questions of observation.[10] Such tools are also valuable for anthropologists, since they offer a means for thinking more critically about a notion that is central to the conception of the modern project. Although historians of the discipline have tracked changes in the role of the observer, highlighting its diverse interpretations and rhetorical sway, observation continues to be under-theorized in contemporary discussions about ethnographic practice.[11] For the ethnographic filmmakers, however, it is inescapably at the heart of their enterprise. The use of camera and sound recording technologies forces any practitioner to be acutely aware of countless decisions involved in attending to and documenting social life. The observational filmmakers, however, claimed a heightened commitment to this process, one predicated on the cultivation of a special kind of attention. But what does this mean and how is it acquired? We take up these questions through an examination of the pedagogical practice of Herb Di Gioia. For, following the premature death of his filmmaking partner David Hancock in 1976, Di Gioia directed his energies into teaching, devising an unusual documentary training program that had observational cinema at its core. It shaped a generation of ethnographic filmmakers.[12]

One of Di Gioia's most distinguished former pupils, Molly Dineen, described his approach in the following terms: "Herb taught with passion and conviction. I remember him showing us a film shot of someone inside a car looking out and the next shot showing the car going by. Herb stopped the machine and shouted: 'Can you believe it? Where is the camera supposed to be?' We were confused . . . surely that's how people tell stories? It was just one of the ways he succeeded in breaking down our expectations of how things should be put together. Herb taught us about fluidity, how to choreograph ourselves with the camera, how not to block a doorway or stop a person doing something, how to catch that part of their body or face that expresses mood or reaction. It was all about how you capture reality, not fragmenting it into shots to be cut together in the edit."[13]

Unlike Young, Herb Di Gioia was essentially a practitioner, not a theoretician. If his early collaboration with Hancock had been important in establishing observational cinema as a distinctive genre, his subsequent career as a teacher was crucial in ensuring its continued development through the work of his students. Di Gioia's teaching method was not based upon instruction (least of all technical instruction) in any straightforward sense. It is telling that one of his primary responsibilities, as he saw it, was to undo the damage of professional manuals, technical handbooks, and the customs of the film and television industry. His approach was founded upon a series of exercises that emphasized not only the physical dimensions but also the relational and imaginative dimensions of filmmaking. His teaching was founded in the development by students of *practice,* understood to be—as Dineen pointed out—a complex choreography of consciousness, body, and senses.

Di Gioia's starting point was to remove the nascent filmmakers' reliance on extraneous aspects of filmmaking technology. Without the use of tripod and lights, he encouraged filmmakers to physically embrace the camera and / or microphone and to move in synchrony with their subjects. A second critical element was Di Gioia's insistence that the filmmaker should never speak unless spoken to, challenging the assumption that an inquiry involving people must be speech-driven.[14] The question of human relationships lay at the heart of the filmmaker's emerging practice. In the absence of familiar modes of engagement defined by language, filmmakers had to develop awareness of other kinds of communication between themselves and their subjects, linked to gestures, looks, movement, shape, silence, and so on. To attend to the world observationally meant to shift attention toward one's body and to move with and around one's subjects, allowing one's body in action or repose to become part of filmic space. Through this reorientation of the body came an increased emphasis on the senses of touch, sight, sound, smell as explicit aspects of the filmmaking encounter. Working like this depended on not remaining at a distance from one's subjects but instead moving closer to them. Paradoxical though it at first seemed, proceeding in this way required openness, trust, and intimacy with subjects.[15]

If filmmakers were encouraged by Di Gioia to rely on their embodied knowledge and their senses, then this approach led to a further shift—the abandonment of the shooting script or map. Without it, filmmaking became a process that unfolded over time with no guarantee of what the final piece would look like at the end. Of course, it was never completely open-ended, since the filmmaker's techniques were always shaped by certain questions and concerns. Di Gioia's students, however, learned to pose questions not in the pursuit of definitive answers but as a point of departure in a particular kind of investigation of the world. Crucial was the possibility that practice might reconfigure ideas or serve as the foundation for new theoretical insights.

The reliance on observation required the development of additional skills and discrimination concerning when to start filming and when to cease, how to position oneself, what to point the camera at, when to pan, when to zoom, and when to speak. This depended, in turn, on cultivating sensitivity to social events—a feeling for the ways in which these tend to unfold. Noticing how processes unfold also meant giving time to the film's subjects. It has become commonplace to think of observational cinema as partly defined by long takes, but Di Gioia emphasized not so much the length of the shots as the importance of filming extended sequences. By devoting more time to those being filmed, viewers were also given the means by which to respond actively to situations presented in the film. In order to do this, it was important that the filmmaker remember sequences already recorded. Allowing the material to live in one's imagination was a means of discerning the emerging themes and allowing these to become a catalyst for further decisions. This reflexive strategy followed from the observational filmmaker's relinquishment of a conventional directing role in favor of an approach that took its "mandate" from subjects. In order to be an active observer and yet to hold back from directing, the observational filmmaker had to attend closely to the give and take of the filmmaking encounter in all its different facets, acknowledging its complex choreography, the dynamic of authorship and collaboration, observation, and imagination that constituted the work itself.

Observational footage, with its focus on social processes and its use of extended sequences, required the development of further skills at the editing stage. The emphasis was on discerning resonances in and between different parts of the footage rather than imposing meaning from outside. Di Gioia's approach was again not to instruct student filmmakers but to orient them in a certain way. By asking students to hold image and sound together during their early editing exercises, he drew students' attention to what the footage *already* contained. Editing was about retaining the sense of time devoted to the film subjects, while also providing a rich context for interpretation. The position of each scene was crucial, reflecting the editor's comprehension of the materials. But in shaping materials and interpretation in this way, the task was to resist assertion and the closing down of meaning.

Di Gioia's teaching approach was intended to effect a break in habitual modes of engagement and to foster a new attentiveness to the world. The instruction not to speak and to work only with a handheld camera presented a challenge to the idea that seeing involved only the eyes, since the negotiation of filmic space revealed the degree to which observation occurred with the whole body. Furthermore, moving with and around one's subjects, allowing one's body in action or repose to become part of such space, brought about a strong awareness of one's relationship to those being filmed and of sharing with them the improvisatory character of lived experience. With his exercises, Di Gioia was attempting to cultivate an observational *sensibility* among his students in which the body and senses served as the existential ground of engagement. What this meant was difficult to grasp in abstract terms, since it emerged in and was shaped by specific contexts of practice. By characterizing it as taking up a stance of *respectful witness* risked evoking a filmmaking style of detachment, distance, and passivity. Indeed, early attempts to adhere to Di Gioia's precepts often produced precisely this kind of film. For at the beginning, one could easily make the mistake of interpreting the role of respectful witness to mean hovering on the edge of situations and relationships, filming from the safety of doorways and other marginal spaces for fear of intruding on one's subjects. But gradually one came to recognize that the role Di Gioia envisaged for the observational filmmaker was different. It involved a new set of responsibilities to both the recording process itself and to subjects. Working observationally heightened the sense of the integrity and uniqueness of lived experience, an integrity stolen as it were from the continuous flow of daily events. The challenge was to seek out revelatory moments, those flashes of connection between what would otherwise be lost to flux. The filmmakers had to find ways to clarify situations by holding fast to what unfolded around them, not by generating explanations from an external point. To work in this way was to use a cinematic rather than a textual language, to think with and through visual and aural materials, rather than to use these to give form to an autonomous idea. It was about finding the shape rather than marking the line of a film.

Observing Practice

Given Di Gioia's conception of his task, his resistance to abstract principles in favor of the development of skilled practice, it was not surprising to discover that he made little, if any, distinction between learning how to work observationally and learning how to watch—or more exactly, be receptive to—observational work. For Di Gioia the observational endeavor was not about reifying vision as a separate sense. Instead, the insistence on a close relationship of image and sound was understood as the means by which to stimulate an awareness of sensing bodies—bodies depicted in the film, including the filmmaker's and, as importantly, the bodies of the audience. Hence, the viewer had to learn to be unusually attentive to a look exchanged, a gesture, a pause, a camera movement.

For apprentices of the observational method like ourselves, Di Gioia's own film *Peter Murray* and those of his students, most notably Eva Stefani's *Athene* (1993) and Simon Everson and Marian Stoica's *Room to Live* (1992), became important models, functioning as a valuable reflexive focus for our own evolving practice. It was difficult to say precisely what these films were "about." To do so was to reduce them to something inconsequential or banal (a man making a chair, the housing conditions of a Polish family, a railway station). But, as anthropologists, we found ourselves especially drawn to this work. It offered something subtly different from films more self-consciously fashioned as "ethnographic." The latter strove to be meaningful in substantive anthropological terms—that is, in terms of their content. Their legitimacy depended on being "about" something.

Eva Stefani's *Athene* is set in Athens's main railway station between midnight and the arrival of the first morning train. Edited as if following the events of a single evening, the opening sequences reveal some of the ways in which people inhabit this place. Soldiers, travelers, football fans stand on the platforms or sit in the bar, waiting for the train to come; meanwhile the barmen and station personnel follow their familiar routines; still others drink, socialize, and later settle down to sleep on the station's benches or tiled floors. For the majority, the station is a portal to somewhere else, but for a few it is a makeshift home.

Early on in the film we encounter Florakis, one of the men who sleeps at the station. He talks in enigmatic phrases ("yes, indeed, anyway . . .") as though suspended within his own web of words. Next we follow the movements of a station worker washing down the platform with a hose. "You're from London?" he says to Stefani, his voice inflected with the business-like rhythm of his work. Almost imperceptibly, we register the contrast between these two men. The first hovers over the narrative flow of time with his idiosyncratic interjections, the second is carried by a sense of purpose, finishing his work in steady measure until it is time to go home. The burden on those for whom this place is home is not only the burden of homelessness but of time itself. As people arrive and depart, Florakis and his friends exist in a kind of limbo. For them, the station is a place of waiting.

Locating her documentary firmly within the physical boundaries of the station and its routines, Stefani explores the physical, temporal, and

Still from *Athene* (1993). *Courtesy of Eva Stefani.*

imaginative constraints of life lived in this place at this time. But the film is framed, too, by moments of revelation when those whom she portrays overflow their perceived limits. If *Athene* offers a portrait of a Greek railway station at a moment when nationalisms, poverty, and difference threaten to implode, its power lies in showing how the boundaries between people that arise in such conditions can be temporarily dissolved. This becomes clearer in one of the film's most extended and crucial scenes. Here Stefani documents a series of exchanges that take place between Vangelis, the station's waiter in his starched white jacket, some of his friends, and a long-haired man who wanders into the bar carrying his guitar. Mockingly and with a hint of menace, one of Vangelis's friends asks, "What's your problem?" The musician refuses to rise to the provocation, standing with dignity as he is teased and goaded to prove his talent. Music is an international language, the men say—he must play, since then he will be speaking an international language that all can understand. But the musician is quietly insistent. No, he replies, the point is not about whether music is an international language. What matters is that we all breathe the same air, that we are all human.

The confrontation between the men in the station bar arises spontaneously and unexpectedly. The filmmaker is keenly alert for such moments. Situating herself within this encounter, Stefani holds fast to what is unfolding around her. Neither flinching from it nor over-dramatizing it, she remains inside the scene until it eventually subsides. She is sensitive to the detail of what takes place, to the sounds, inflections, pauses, and silence, to the ebb and flow of language, and to the choreography that unfolds in time and space. Although suffused with tension, the scene nevertheless remains low-key, even un-dramatic. But it encapsulates something of the inner alchemy of the film. For the quality of open attention, what MacDougall calls "open awareness," creates a dilation in the fabric of time—a tiny pause in what otherwise appears to be a continuous series of events—and so Stefani brings us more fully into the presence of her subjects.[16] We can only experience these imaginative moments of overflow because of the relationships the filmmaker herself has created with her subjects and the place in which they dwell. The attitudes and behavior Stefani witnesses—for example, the nationalist sentiments expressed through verbal abuse and sometimes violence—are not subjected to translation or explanation beyond their careful positioning within the film. Again, Stefani is unflinching, showing us things without comment; and yet she is not unmoved.

A second film made in the context of Di Gioia's teaching, *Room to Live,* also allows us to draw attention to some of the distinctive features of an observational sensibility at work. Again, like *Athene,* it appears at first to be deceptively simple—perhaps banal. For what could be interesting about the daily routine of a young Polish couple and their two children who live in Lodz? The opening title of Everson and Stoica's film tells us that Danuta and her husband, Janusz, have been waiting fifteen years for a place in a co-operative housing project. For the last eight years they have rented a one-room flat from their neighbor, Henryk. Janusz works at night as a bus driver, Danuta works during the day dispensing medicines; between them they share the daily tasks of living and raising their children. Their lives are finely balanced, an unfolding series of movements that require precision and skillful calibration. Patiently and scrupulously, Everson and Stoica follow these rhythms, attending to the careful negotiation of time and space that accompanies each moment—sleeping, waking, dressing, cooking, washing, watching TV, and so on. This seamless choreography is broken only momentarily. Their landlord, Henryk, gets drunk on hair lotion. He leaves his kettle boiling, forcing Janusz to break down the door to rescue him.

As its title indicates, *Room to Live* hinges upon a subtle play of meaning—evoking at once the literal and the metaphorical, the material and the existential. Everson and Stoica show us *how* people make their life in its most intimate, everyday detail. There is nothing sentimental, however, in the filmmakers' portrait of Janusz and Danuta, nor is it an expression of social and political indignation. The difficult conditions in post-communist Poland might have seemed an important subject for the filmmakers to address, but to do so didactically would have meant using Danuta and her family to make a point, to illustrate a larger statement about the world in which we live. The beauty of *Room to Live* is that Everson and Stoica resist such a conception of their role, staying close to the ground, so to speak. Instead, through their careful attention to the nuance of daily routine and practice, the filmmakers remind us what constitutes living in its most concrete and yet profound sense.

The distinctive emotional texture of the film emerges from the dense network of relationships between people and place. Far from being intruders, Everson and Stoica learn to inhabit an already confined space, developing relationships of trust and understanding with their subjects that become an integral part of the work itself. Not least, the film renders problematic questions that are often raised in discussion of observational work—namely the supposed detachment and anonymity of the observational filmmaker. In the absence of explicit acknowledgement (verbal exchange) between filmmakers and subjects, it is easy to assume that something is missing, that the work is lacking and unreflexive, indeed voyeuristic. *Room to Live* shows us otherwise. The filmmakers' presence is woven into the fabric of the film and, as such, a richer and more elusive form of inter-subjective relationship emerges than can be articulated through language alone.

Athene and *Room to Live* reveal observational work to be founded upon a particular kind of filmmaking sensibility—one that is fundamentally Bazinian. It is not primarily about the use of certain tools or technologies (a handheld camera, synchronous sound) but it is, instead, a particular way of engaging with the world. As examples, *Athene* and *Room to Live* show us *what* such filmmakers observed and *how* they observed. For instance, we can see that there is a shared interest in the everyday, overlooked spaces of human life approached non-judgmentally, that is, with curiosity and with empathy. Stefani, and Everson and Stoica, seek to render aspects of lived experience, respecting its detail, context, scale, and tempo as meaningful in their own terms rather than understood as a preliminary to more abstract statements about the world. André Bazin once suggested that when we leave the cinema after watching an Italian neorealist film we feel more alive, more humane. It might be said that we experience something similar in the case of *Athene* and *Room to Live,* since we are returned to the world with an expanded sense of what it is to be human. This hinges crucially on the erosion of the boundary between filmmaker, subjects, and audience, such that we glimpse a connection that transcends the limits within which we habitually live. The two films serve to remind us that far from being literal or rendering the world flat, observational work is predicated on an exercise of the imagination. Paradoxically, it is the eschewing of didacticism that makes this possible. For the engaged viewer responds to gaps in filmic discourse by exercising curiosity along similar paths to those followed by the filmmaker. Using observation (seeing, hearing, feeling) and interpretation ("what sense can be made of this?"), the viewer, like the filmmaker, develops a complex relationship with what is being represented. In place of certainty, observational practitioners provoke the intelligence, curiosity, and imagination of their audience, thereby opening up an active space of reflection.

Observational Cinema and Ethnographic Inquiry

Athene and *Room to Live* were both made in the early 1990s. In their modest, low-key manner, these films did not particularly call attention to themselves. The tide had already turned against observational cinema in favor of more explicitly reflexive approaches, and reality television had yet to emerge as a rival form. The significance of this work, however, partly stemmed from the fact that it stood as an alternative to modes of ethnographic filmmaking that at the time were assumed to be more progressive or advanced. Moreover, it was evidence of the continuing saliency of observational work. Far from being examples of a moribund genre, the films of Di Gioia's students were clear statements of a distinctive conception of the documentary project. Not least, they brought into sharp focus limitations in the existing critical discourse on observational cinema.

Although neither *Athene* nor *Room to Live* had been made with disciplinary concerns in mind, they suggested ways of engaging with the world that were recognizably anthropological—raising the possibility that an observational approach might constitute a form of knowing in its own right. Using our own practice, we became interested in clarifying this question—what does observation mean as a particular mode of anthropological inquiry? We embarked on an exploration of this question in a very particular way—namely by interweaving the substance and medium of our research such that the documentation of our subjects' knowledge practices became aligned with our own as anthropologists. In so doing, we were certainly aware of the work produced by earlier anthropological filmmakers identified with the observational moment—for example, John Marshall's *An Argument about a Marriage,* Gary Kildea's *Celso and Cora,* and, of course, David MacDougall's *To Live with Herds.* But, given the prevailing disciplinary paradigms of the 1970s and 1980s, such work was often not recognized for what it was—only for what it was not, as Kildea's exchange with Geertz revealed.[17]

A film by one of us, *The Bracewells* (2000), came out of a broader investigation of vision, landscape, and forms of knowledge. Ravetz was interested in developing a fieldwork project that would allow her to examine claims about the privileged role of vision as a basis for knowledge in Western culture.[18] Taking as her case study the Bracewells, a family who for two generations had rented and worked a 160-acre sheep farm in the Pennine hills that straddle the Lancashire-Yorkshire border, Ravetz used a video camera to explore two sets of questions—the first substantive, the second methodological. How did the Bracewells use vision in their everyday work around the farm? What did they see and what kinds of knowledge did their visual practices confer? Did their "ways of seeing" draw them into the world or constitute an objectification of the world? How might these questions be addressed through an image-based approach? More specifically, how might the use of observational filmmaking techniques serve to align the focus and method of inquiry?

This project was related to Ravetz's earlier work in the context of fine art, where she had been trained to observe and draw "from life," a practice involving the close coordination of hand and eye. For her, drawing observationally was a way of being drawn *into* the world. At the same time, she recognized that within the art world observation was understood as a highly specialized and individualistic practice, connecting artist and viewer not so much to a shared workaday world as to a subjectively experienced transcendent realm. Gravitating toward anthropology, Ravetz continued to be interested in the question of observation, but now posed in a different context. Not only did the camera present ways of extending the social dimensions of her practice, it also suggested the possibility of attending to the observational practices of others.

The Bracewells was made over the course of a year, during which time Ravetz followed the work of the family from winter through to summer. She participated in farming activities, exploring the role of eye, hand, gesture, and voice in tasks such as feeding, mucking out, castration, dehorning, administering medicine, shepherding, dog training, lambing, and dry stone walling. She sought to document the inherent sociality of farmers' labor and the ways observation was used on the farm—not as a specialized *visual* strategy but as a complex of senses, gestures, movement, and language that bound people together in intimate relations with one another, with the animals, and with the land.

Progressively, through filming, the different and conflicting modes of knowledge through which her subjects lived their lives emerged. The Bracewell family was struggling to hold on to what they knew in the face of a crisis in British farming and the resultant political pressure that curbed local practices.[19] Ravetz noticed the incursion of impersonal bureaucratic systems of accounting into a densely woven web of activities based upon contact, relational proximity, and tacit understanding. In particular, abstract categories, lists, numbers, paperwork, rules, and regulations increasingly circumscribed the Bracewells' way of being in the world.

The techniques Ravetz used to make the film were an integral part of her intellectual inquiry. For to work observationally allowed her to take up a situated position alongside different family members, involving herself and the camera in learning to observe and to farm in ways analogous to how the Bracewells learned from each other. The knowledge practices characteristic of farm labor were thus brought into alignment with Ravetz's own anthropological practices so that the farm and the film became intersecting sites. Specifically, Ravetz resisted assuming a role analogous to that of the government's agricultural inspector—someone who asked questions, sought a descriptive overview, summarized ad hoc activity into forms of categorical knowledge. The edited film was intended as a meshing of filming and farming aesthetics—the textures of light and

Still from *The Bracewells* (2000). *Amanda Ravetz.*

dark, of physical and filmic space, and of filming and filmed bodies used as a register of the relationships between vision and knowledge.

It was through observation that Ravetz became part of the Bracewells' social world, since observation was the shared medium of knowledge and communication between them. But the diverse modes of seeing utilized in the film also reflected the tension inherent in observation as an embodied enterprise. Hence, Ravetz's documentation of observation as a social practice went hand in hand with an acknowledgment of the inconstancy of vision, its unreliability. As a filmmaker, she often found herself recording in the dark, in the rain, or with something intruding between herself and the object of her gaze. Increasingly, she recognized that interrupted vision was intimately linked to processes of seeing and knowing on the farm, but equally to acts of translation between the farm and the "wider world." The mechanisms for the translation of the everyday entanglement of bodies and senses into a kind of visualism were seen, for example, in breeding competitions, involving the occlusion of know-how and embodied observation by visual spectacle and ideal. It was precisely through this abstraction, however, that the Bracewells achieved some acknowledgement in the "wider" world. Thus the film's focus on ways of knowing and seeing was pursued under the very conditions in which such practices occur, amounting to a struggle between embodied vision on the one hand and the drive by authorities to control and abstract it on the other. The farm was revealed not as an enclave of one discrete observational mode, but a site where different knowledge modes met—in friction.[20]

Grimshaw's film *Mr. Wade* (2003) was animated by different anthropological questions than the ones that framed *The Bracewells*. But here, too, there was a concern with the senses, knowledge, and forms of skilled practice. In *Mr. Wade,* Grimshaw offered a portrait of a man whose life had been devoted to the breeding and racing of homing pigeons. Her interests as an ethnographic filmmaker were twofold. First of all, she wanted to use the camera to investigate an area of specialized knowledge that was largely embedded in practice. Secondly, she wanted to find a way of approaching the experiential—indeed existential—dimensions of a cultural activity that was highly distinctive and yet largely overlooked.

Mr. Wade was an attempt to explore further a number of questions that had arisen in Grimshaw's earlier research, namely the problem of how to find a medium through which the material, bodily, sensory, and inter-subjective dimensions of fieldwork might be conveyed. How might one render those profoundly non-discursive aspects of ethnographic work that are nevertheless tangible and meaningful? What kind of understanding is generated not from language (talk, interviews, life histories, etc.) but from ongoing shared practice—that is, from the rhythms of living and working, processes of informal learning, attending to gesture, posture, the movement of one's body? Such an inquiry was not about disregarding language but rather about seeking to recontextualize it within a broader communicative landscape. By changing the conventional hierarchy of words and images/sound, one of the intentions behind *Mr. Wade* was the foregrounding of non-discursive practices as constitutive of knowledge; that is, such practices were to be approached not as a step on the way to knowing but as ways of knowing in their own right.

Over the course of more than a year, Grimshaw filmed Wade with his birds. Like Ravetz, she used handheld video technology, making the recording equipment—the camera and microphone—a physical extension of her body. By apprenticing herself to Mr. Wade for an extended period, Grimshaw sought to learn the intricacies of his craft. Her method was not to attempt to acquire skill through instruction but, instead, to try and develop it by means of close observation and imitation—by sensing how to proceed.

In making *Mr. Wade,* Grimshaw came to understand that working observationally was about learning to attend—to her subject and to her own engagement with his world. It began as a process of adjusting her body to the confined space of Wade's loft, following his movements with her own, intuiting where to position herself, when to remain still or be silent, becoming cognizant of the ebb and flow of activity. The camera documented this shaping and honing of attention. The visual and aural material was evidence of a human encounter and of an apprenticeship that involved learning how to look at birds, how to handle them, how to interpret their sounds, how to carry out a sequence of actions, and so on. Through filming, Grimshaw traced the web of tasks that linked Wade to his birds and to a broader community of fellow racers, progressively immersing herself within this sphere of practice. In particular, she revealed that Wade's expertise lay not just in the mastery of tasks that had to be done; it also lay in the sense of *how* things were to be done. Although not initially conceived as such, *Mr. Wade* became a film about devotion— what does it mean to dedicate one's life to keeping birds?

As a reflexive project, the film was built around an investigation of Mr. Wade's practice as a pigeon racer and that of the filmmaker as an ethnographer. The two dimensions of the project were woven together through the observational filmmaking approach itself. It was the means by which Grimshaw tracked the knowledge techniques of Mr. Wade, learning through participatory engagement and self-consciously modeling her actions after her subject's own. The film was an attempt to communicate implicit, non-discursive ways of knowing in their own terms rather than translating them into a different conceptual register. Hence, the final piece *Mr. Wade* did not offer knowledge about, or provide an explanation of, pigeon racing. Instead, Grimshaw sought to draw the viewer into an imaginary encounter where knowledge was not understood to be the outcome of experience but rather was constituted *as* experience. As such, the film rendered it not as sealed and complete but as irreducibly relational and open. In this way, *Mr. Wade* was intended to show that the work of interpretation and analysis in observational cinema is ongoing, generated in the moment of filming and the moment of viewing.

Still from *Mr. Wade* (2003). *Anna Grimshaw.*

Rethinking Observational Cinema

Approaching observational filmmaking as a particular kind of skilled *practice* raises a number of important questions about techniques and forms of knowledge in anthropological inquiry.[21] What areas of human experience might be rendered by means of an observational approach? How might observational work challenge established ways of conceptualizing the anthropological project? In thinking about these questions we have continually come up against the limitations of existing discourses about the genre. Changing the terms of discussion is critical to rethinking observational cinema.

Ever since its appearance, observational cinema has provoked fierce discussion. In nearly every respect it has been deemed inadequate—methodologically, epistemologically, and aesthetically. At best, it has been understood as an early or naïve documentary approach superseded by more advanced techniques (Nichols); at worst, it has been viewed as *the* obstacle to innovation in ethnographic filmmaking (Loizos).[22] Despite these generally negative perceptions, observational cinema has not, in fact, been rendered obsolete by other forms—indeed, quite the opposite. Filmmakers have continued to work observationally—not out of some misguided view of superior truth claims but because to do so offers a particular way of engaging with the world. Moreover, the growing dialogue between artists and anthropologists points to the innovative potential of observational work. But before turning our attention to this matter in the next and final chapter of the book, we want to address the issue that lies at the heart of our engagement with practice—namely, the necessity of finding a language that more effectively describes what we understand the project of observational cinema to be. For if there are some areas of human experience that are better approached by means of observational techniques and if observational practice can serve as the basis for new ideas, how can we begin to talk about these areas and ideas?

Recent changes in anthropology's conceptual paradigms have opened up new perspectives on observational cinema as a distinctive mode of inquiry. Specifically, we refer here to the challenge posed to older analytical frameworks associated with scientific ethnography (data, evidence, truth, objectivity) and semiotics (text, reading, translation) by phenomenologically inflected work and the rise of what has come to be known, following Stoller, as "sensuous scholarship."[23] For over the last decade, there has been a renewed concern with questions of the body, the senses, experience and emotion, skilled practice, and forms of knowledge. Changes in the discipline's theoretical orientation linked to these questions have, in turn, stimulated debate about the techniques and forms by which anthropological work has traditionally been conducted. Visual anthropology— and ethnographic filmmaking in particular—has increasingly come to the fore in discussions of this kind. Once acknowledged to be more than merely an illustrative or pictorial endeavor, the field has been understood as a potential site in which alternative modes of anthropology might be pursued. As David MacDougall has put it, "instead of simply adding to anthropology's fields of study [visual anthropology] poses fundamental challenges to anthropological ways of 'speaking' and knowing."[24] We have come to understand observational cinema as an important example of this shift.

Critical to rethinking observational cinema is the body of anthropological work that has called for a fundamental reorientation of disciplinary thought. Over the last decade or so, writers such as Ingold, Stoller, Taussig, and MacDougall have, in different ways, sought to challenge many of the assumptions at the core of the modern project—the "matter of a fact," dualities of biology and culture, body and mind, individual and society, practice and theory. Jackson, for example, has argued for a phenomeno-logical anthropology that is focused above all on the "lifeworld"—the everyday sphere of sociality, practical activity, and consciousness that encompasses conceptual understanding but is not primarily driven by it. Such a project does not approach experience as raw material that can be mined for some underlying truth or reality. Rather it moves the focus to the existential and practical uses of meaning and belief, asking "what is the knowledge with which people live?"[25]

This move away from categorical conceptions of the world to the practicalities of what it is to know finds particular expression in Ingold's notion of a "sentient ecology."[26] This new mode of anthropology takes as its starting point "a conception of the human being not as a compos-ite entity made up of separable but complementary parts, such as body, mind and culture, but rather as a singular locus of creative growth within a continually unfolding field of relationships."[27] Drawing on notions of skill, embodied practice, and tacit knowledge, Ingold's approach brings into focus questions of perception and "know-how" or ways of being and knowing the world that emerge from practical activity rather than from formal instruction or the adherence to abstract rules. Ingold characterizes the processual nature of learning as *enskillment,* a sort of apprenticeship involving the active and ongoing participation by the developing subject-as-organism in the world. This hinges upon what Ingold calls, borrowing from James Gibson, "the education of attention." By this he refers to the subtle adjustments and realignment of the sensing subject that follow from observation and imitation of skilled practitioners. It involves learn-ing to attend to the complex sensory experience of gestures, looks, colors, and textures as much as to propositional forms of language. For Ingold, the skilled practitioner acts in the world as a way of knowing it.[28]

Ingold's commitment to enskillment is linked in turn to a *relational* perspective, one that conceives of the human subject as a complex organ-ism enmeshed in a dense web of relationships that includes other sen-tient beings, non-human animals, and the material environment itself. Through this relational approach, development and change are under-stood as ongoing, reciprocal processes in which the human subject-as-organism both shapes, and is shaped by, its exploratory engagement with the lifeworld.

The emphasis on experience—on the consciousness of being fully engaged in activity—can appear to exclude other forms of cultural knowledge, rational intellectual reflection, or explanation. Indeed, one of the criticisms leveled at Ingold's work and at phenomenological anthropology in general is that by becoming immersed in processes and relationships, the anthropologist is cut off from the conceptual, the non-local, and the imaginative dimensions of life. To accept this is to misunderstand phenomenology that does not exclude the conceptual and the pre-given but rather seeks to view these *as* experience. As Jackson has argued, rather than being treated as static forms of knowledge that occlude or over-determine practical domains of experience, existing cultural knowledge, virtual worlds, and imaginaries are all weighted in terms of how they are perceived and used. Understanding how apparently established knowledge and forms are *experienced* requires a sensitivity to the strategic, contingent relational ways in which what is given is addressed via processes of knowledge-in-the-making. This requires attending to the flux of experience, allowing it to show itself.[29]

The writing of Jackson and Ingold has been important in establishing the intellectual ground for our reevaluation of observational cinema. By identifying the fundamentally phenomenological scope of the enterprise, it becomes possible to more effectively grasp what observational cinema *is* as a mode of anthropology. Hitherto observational filmmakers have struggled to persuade critics to engage with their work on its own terms instead of subjecting it to judgments according to different (textually oriented) criteria. The phenomenological turn in anthropology offers a new language through which the genre might be critically approached.[30]

But what does the development of an anthropological perspective grounded in theoretical approaches to knowledge and skill mean for established patterns of working and for the communication of anthropological knowledge? If the transformation in theoretical perspective is, as Ingold insists, fundamental, then surely anthropologists must go about pursuing their practice in entirely new ways? These questions have been taken up by those covering similar intellectual terrain to Ingold's—such as Stoller (sensuous scholarship), Jackson (radical empiricism), MacDougall (the corporeal image), and Taussig (mimesis).[31] Such writers, in seeking to move anthropological attention away from the conventional objects of social scientific inquiry—structures, systems, text, theory—in favor of a renewed engagement with lived experience, have acknowledged the challenge posed to the familiar conventions of scholarly practice. For them the commitment to a certain philosophical perspective on human activity in the world can only profoundly influence and shape the techniques and representational forms by which inquiry is pursued.

One effect of the phenomenological turn and consequent interrogation of anthropological method and form has been a renewed engagement on the part of some anthropologists with questions of mimesis and the mimetic faculty. Drawing on the work of Walter Benjamin and the Frankfurt School, a number of attempts have been made to investigate and to recuperate mimesis as a particular way of knowing, perceived to have been displaced historically by the rise of more "advanced" theories, most notably by codified, symbolic systems of knowledge. Proposing that mimesis be understood as a mode of sensuous knowledge, Taussig has argued passionately against the prevailing prejudices associated with imitation or copying. "Today it is common to lambast mimesis as a naïve form or symptom of Realism," he has declared. Taussig continued: "mimesis has become that dreaded, absurd or merely tiresome Other, that necessary straw-man against whose feeble pretensions poststructuralists prance and strut."[32]

For Taussig, Benjamin's essays provided the foundation for an investigation into the distinctive nature of mimesis as a contemporary mode of knowledge, what he refers to as the capacity to Other or to take hold of something by means of its likeness. His conception of the operation of mimesis involves two key elements—*copy* and *contact,* understood as a sensuous or visceral connection between perceiver and perceived, subject and object.[33] Taussig makes the tactility of vision critical to his conception of the mimetic. For, in place of the Enlightenment model of vision predicated on detachment, distance, and mastery, he posits a form of knowledge yielded through proximity such that "the concept of *knowing* something becomes displaced by a *relating to.*"[34] By this he refers to a process of "active yielding."[35] But, as Taussig points out, Benjamin's notion of the mimetic was inseparable from its antithesis, alterity, the dialectical movement, or push and pull, between merging and separation, sameness and difference, self and other. The slippages between these polarities were, however, filled with transformative possibilities.[36]

The work of Taussig enables us to recognize the challenge observational cinema presents to established methods and forms of communication in anthropology. The emphasis by observational filmmakers on techniques such as the long take, deep-focus photography, and extended sequences can be seen as embedded within what, following Ingold, we can call a relational perspective—that is, a way of bringing into focus the relational and experience-rich character of a lifeworld. Understood in these terms, observational filmmaking begins to appear as a potential model of the kind of anthropology that Ingold, Jackson, and others are advocating. It is a way of exploring human relations in the world from the perspective of skilled practice and a way of conceiving of anthropology itself as a form of skilled practice.

Observational cinema has been accused of feigning transparency and the adoption of a detached stance. Certainly it is the case that observational filmmaking is about following, indeed respecting, the unfolding of the real. This is reflected partly in the way such works are filmed and edited. But rather than defining it in stylistic terms, we have suggested it is the particular interweaving of epistemology and ethics that distinguishes the approach. We refer here to the commitment by the observational filmmaker to the opening up of a distinctive kind of inter-subjective space in which new anthropological understandings might emerge. Hence practice is neither about the pragmatic placement of the camera nor the execution of highly controlled maneuvers in pursuit of a complete film. The placement of the camera is determined by skill, judgment, and a sensibility that is shaped both by "prior" knowledge and by the spontaneous response to what is unfolding moment by moment. The co-presence of filmmaker and subjects, the creation of shared time and space between them (co-evalness), serves as the basis for creating a world for the viewer that has its own spatial and temporal coherence. The observational filmmaker models this world through an active process of engagement. Events, relationships, spaces press against him or her, shaping the contours of the work and affecting the viewer's capacity to imagine or to be lifted beyond the limits of his or her own experience.[37]

Taussig has talked of mimesis as a sensuous movement of thought. In *Athene* this literally involves the filmmaker being moved in a way that challenges the separation of self and other or of what Taussig calls alterity. The filmmaker's sensuous intelligence results in raw and yet delicate face-to-face encounters. The camera moves like a human face and indeed is an extension of Stefani's face. This is about the interpenetration of subjectivities but in a way that does not excise moments of difficulty or resistances to engagement. In such encounters by experiencing what it feels like to look and by feeling the look of another upon us, we experience our own intentions, that is, our *ethics;* and through sense apprehension or aesthesis, we encounter and infer the intentions of others.[38]

By privileging the sensory, the observational filmmaker refuses to abstract from the particular. In each of the examples we have discussed, there is a visceral presence that speaks of the materiality of the world. Observational cinema foregrounds the power of sensuous detail, its ability to enter the viewer's consciousness and stay there—as Buck-Morss says, mimesis is memorable.[39] For Taussig the two-layered nature of mimesis—the entwining of contact and copy, the viscerality of perception with the aloofness of the copy—is the means by which the object of perception and the body of the perceiver merge, allowing reality to be slowed down: "We see and comprehend hidden details of familiar objects . . . ," and thus, "we become aware of patterns and necessities that have hitherto invisibly ruled out lives."[40]

Observational cinema, contrary to much critical opinion, is not then about creating an accurate transcription of the world. Instead it hinges upon connection, expressed in an almost intangible, empathic moment. How to render this moment concrete is the problem that confronts the observational filmmaker. Taussig reminds us that mimesis is never a straightforward process of mirroring. It has a marked visionary—indeed, magical—aspect (Benjamin's "flash of recognition"—transformation wrought in an instant of contact). Hence, once we take seriously the possibility of knowledge through contact, we are able to recognize the imperative of an imaginative leap at the heart of observational cinema. In proposing that observational cinema be considered as an example of a phenomenological anthropology, we do not, of course, suggest that it is the only or definitive model of such an endeavor. Our interest is in how it contributes to the developing debate about what is involved, concretely, in the reorientation of anthropological work. Interpreted as such, the distinctive techniques and aesthetic of observational filmmaking no longer appear as evidence of a simple-minded scientism or old-fashioned ethnographic realism. Instead they can be appraised as constitutive of a reflexive praxis, a way of *doing* anthropology that has the potential to creatively fuse the object and medium of inquiry.

CHAPTER 6

Toward an Experimental Anthropology

Debates about observational cinema continue to reverberate through the fields of anthropology and film studies, despite the passage of time and the emergence of new, hybrid forms. For some commentators, observational techniques remain valuable as "tools" in the training of novice filmmakers—considered a first step on the way to the development of a more mature or self-conscious practice. For those more critical of the enterprise, such techniques are regarded as nothing more than an expression of conceptual and methodological simple-mindedness. But, as we have already noted, notwithstanding all the claims and counter-claims, observational work has neither disappeared nor has it been replaced by more "advanced" forms. Indeed it continues to develop and expand. In this final chapter of the book, we seek to chart some of the new directions in which observational work is moving.[1] Building on the case articulated in the previous chapter, we argue for the creative potential of the observational strain in ethnographic research and we evaluate its role in an emerging non-textual or experimental anthropology.[2] Using selected examples, we will suggest that contrary to popular perception, the continuing commitment to observational work should not be considered as evidence of theoretical naïveté. It is central to an innovative project that challenges conventional disciplinary assumptions, opening up "other ways of speaking and knowing."[3]

In the first part of the chapter, we take up a number of issues raised at the beginning of the book about the observational turn in ethnographic filmmaking. We return to the question of its Bazinian roots as an essential initial step in understanding the aesthetic character of contemporary observational work. Although we have consistently highlighted its distinctiveness, we are anxious not to be perceived as advocating a tight, prescriptive framework by which different approaches might be judged legitimately "observational" or not. There is something of a paradox here. For if indeed the observational enterprise in its current phase is marked by fluidity and innovative diversity, why continue to hold on to the idea that there is something unique about it? Linked to this question is the shift in terminology employed in our discussion. Hence, in talking less about a genre called "observational cinema" and more about an "observational sensibility," we indicate an impulse or orientation toward the world that runs through certain bodies of work. By making this change, we intend to convey the openness and expansiveness of the project, and to underline the fact that its representational form is not conceived in advance but generated by the process of making and viewing. Understood in this way, observational work appears not so much as a point of arrival but one of departure in anthropological inquiry.

Drawing on a series of case studies, the second part of the chapter deals with recent innovations that are identifiably "observational," while at the same time posing a significant challenge to expectations hitherto associated with the genre. Filmmaking remains an important thread in our narrative, but we are especially interested in the ways that contemporary practitioners, notably Eva Stefani, David MacDougall, and Ilisa Barbash and Lucien Castaing-Taylor have attempted to move beyond the production of a particular kind of ethnographic representation—for instance, by relocating their work from the context of the cinema into the site of the gallery, by foregrounding the aesthetic possibilities of the medium, by self-consciously using observational techniques to open up a space between art and anthropology. Not least the pronounced aesthetic self-consciousness of the work is suggestive of a new interest in, and engagement with, certain kinds of contemporary art.[4]

The final part of the chapter considers observational cinema as a mode of experimental anthropology. This may seem something of a bold claim, given the prevailing stereotypes of the genre. A decade ago, one commentator complained that the "predictability," "the flat-footed truth claims," "the automatic adherence to the austerities of naturalistic, observational 'plain style'" had seriously inhibited innovation in the field of ethnographic filmmaking.[5] Critics have long linked observational approaches to the literal rather than to the imaginative, to the conservative rather than to the avant-garde, to (bad) science rather than to art. However, in articulating a case for the significance of the observational impulse in contemporary ethnographic work, our concern is to precisely claim it for art—or, at the very least, raise the possibility of a convergence between new observational work and certain kinds of artistic endeavor. In so doing, we are not advocating an appropriation of art or the making of anthropology that "looks like art." Instead how might an observational sensibility serve as a catalyst in a new configuration of art and anthropology—one that might lead to the radical reconceptualization of anthropology itself?

The previous chapter proposed a rethinking of observational cinema. Our case was built around observational filmmaking as a form of skilled practice linked to a phenomenological anthropology. We suggested it be considered as a way of being, moving, and relating that hinged upon a particular training or education of attention. Crucial to our case was a shift in interpretive paradigms—one that in turn raised questions about the kind of knowledge yielded by working in this way. Taussig's recuperation of the mimetic (following Benjamin) becomes valuable in understanding the unusual dynamic at the heart of observational work.[6] It enables a characterization of observational knowing not as involving a *translation* of the other but as, instead, a sensuous movement of thought—an unplanned-for overflowing of categories, flashes of recognition yielded by the slowing down of perception effected by slippages of contact and copy.

Given the distinctive nature of this inquiry, one of the critical questions facing the observational filmmaker is how to persuade viewers to engage with the work on its own terms. This has often been problematic. Anthropological audiences have tended to resist—or at least be impatient with—the openness and density of observational work, interpreting such qualities as evidence of the inadequacy of the film medium to convey ideas or articulate abstract concepts. These qualities are, however, what the observational filmmaker attempts to render, viewing them not as a preliminary to anthropology "proper" but as constitutive of a different sort of knowledge practice. However, the dislodging of certain expectations about what comprises legitimate disciplinary knowledge in favor of the acceptance of interpretive possibilities framed by means of an observational aesthetic has been surprisingly difficult to achieve. It invites misunderstanding and cultural projections of many kinds. But, as we will see in the cases discussed below, it is precisely here that the challenge and creative potential of observational work lies.

Changing the anthropological ground on which observational film-making has traditionally stood brings into renewed focus its Bazinian foundations. This is central to the task here. For, although the importance of Bazin's ideas was highlighted in an earlier section of this book, his influence on developments in ethnographic cinema has yet to be fully explored or articulated. His conception of a cinema of reality and its *profoundly aesthetic character* are, however, at the heart of any evaluation of contemporary observational practice.

The essays of Bazin, long considered unfashionable and unjustly neglected, are now undergoing a renaissance as the dominance of semiotic and psychoanalytical frameworks slowly wanes within the field of film studies.[7] As a number of recent writers have noted, critics traditionally made heavy rhetorical use of Bazin in their repudiation of cinematic realism. Inevitably, this involved the caricaturing of much more subtle and interesting ideas about the evolution of cinematic language. Crucial to the new case for Bazin has been an acknowledgment of his "modernism." Such a notion, flying in the face of older interpretations, has hinged upon drawing a distinction between an "old" or archaic and a "new" realism.[8]

Taking as their starting point Bazin's examination of the work of Rossellini and his contemporaries as an aesthetic event (rather than a moment defined by subject matter), commentators have pointed to his concern with the radically different spatio-temporal organization of Italian neorealist cinema. Despite his deep commitment to a cinema of reality, what made Bazin's approach also "modernist" was his acknowledgement of the fundamental instability and ambiguous quality of the real. It eluded apprehension by means of representational or perspectival conventions—or, as Deleuze explained it, "the real was no longer represented or reproduced but 'aimed at.' Instead of representing an already deciphered real, neorealism aimed at an always ambiguous, to be deciphered real."[9] Understood in these terms, Bazin's writings on the structure of the image, the development of sound, the distinctive configurations of time, space, and narrative construction, the nature of viewer engagement—and his notion of an a posteriori rather than an a priori cinema ("the sense that the film is being made as you watch it, that film is a process in which it seeks its own shape as it forms itself rather than imposing a shape beforehand")[10]—have taken on a fresh significance in recent attempts to grapple more seriously with cinematic realism.

The renewal of observational cinema's Bazinian foundations brings back into focus the crucial question of realism—and the aesthetics of realism. For, from the outset, Bazin's conception of a new cinema of reality turned on the use of specific techniques. It was not, he emphasized, simply "found" but actively fashioned. "Realism in art can only be achieved in one way—through artifice," he once declared.[11] Bazin understood the kind of artifice with which filmmakers worked to be an expression of their particular philosophical stance toward the world. As we have already seen, he discussed this question in terms of a general contrast he drew between those filmmakers who, as he put it, placed their faith in the image and those who placed their faith in reality. For Bazin, the classic cinematic technique associated with the former was montage. By contrast, those filmmakers who rejected what Bazin called "photographic expressionism and the tricks of montage" worked with a set of different techniques. Central were extended shots and deep-focus photography.[12]

Although the observational turn in ethnographic filmmaking has often been linked to changes in recording technology, we have been concerned with the fundamental epistemological shift that it represented. The new approach developed by David and Judith MacDougall, David Hancock and Herb Di Gioia, and others drew extensively on the range of techniques discussed by Bazin in his writings on cinematic realism.[13] However, in breaking with previous forms of ethnographic filmmaking that involved the fragmentation of reality as an initial stage in its reconstitution as "knowledge" (whether organized according to a framework of science, salvage anthropology, or universal humanism), the observational filmmakers were neither epistemologically nor methodologically naïve. Quite the reverse. From the outset, they were struggling with the aesthetic challenge of how to render the real in ways that were not reductive or static but instead opened up exploratory possibilities.

Three Case Studies

The debate about Bazinian modernism that we have briefly highlighted here offers an important framework for approaching the observational sensibility in recent work. Not least, it helps move the discussion beyond an older discourse that has tended to simplify—often for rhetorical reasons—questions about realism and about the aesthetics of realism.

In the previous chapter, we outlined a number of critical positions articulated with respect to observational cinema—each one (MacDougall's by his own admission) perhaps also tending toward the reductive.

By overlooking the central place accorded to the ambiguity of the real in observational cinema, it has been easy enough to dismiss the approach as a form of "old" realism. A closer look at particular examples of recent work, however, immediately serves to challenge such a perception. For, understood as experiments in a phenomenological anthropology, they propose new ways of presenting human experience. The radical nature of the challenge follows from pushing further into the real—not seeking to more effectively represent it. It has also meant a willingness to work more radically with the "open" nature of the inquiry—that is, not seeking to overcome perceived weaknesses by adding, for example, interview, supplementary text, and so on.[14] This is a somewhat daring move, since it runs contrary to the impulse of conventional intellectual inquiry. Hence, rather than attempting to explain the real or subordinate it to established discursive frameworks, contemporary observational practitioners have sought to render, ever more fully, its ambiguous, mobile nature. In so doing, their work raises interesting issues about the aesthetics of realism and the project of an experimental anthropology. Specifically, it calls into question any simple opposition between realism and modernism, between what is generally considered to be a "conservative" aesthetic and what is considered a "progressive" one.

Our discussion is built around three case studies—Eva Stefani's *The Box* (2004), David MacDougall's *SchoolScapes* (2007), and *Sheep Rushes* (2007) by Ilisa Barbash and Lucien Castaing-Taylor. Each of the examples is marked by the process of "undoing" that has marked earlier work in the tradition of realist cinema—namely, the relinquishing of theatrical or expository conventions such as conflict-based drama, characters, the foregrounding of action or event, linear narrative, interviews, and voice-over narration. It should be emphasized at this point, though, that Stefani, MacDougall, and Barbash and Castaing-Taylor (like their forerunners in Bazinian cinema), in seeking to "undo" established conventions, are not laboring under any illusion of transparency. Instead, they are fully cognizant of the *aesthetic* nature of their task. But if, on the one hand, they are skeptical of anthropological and filmic conventions, they are, on the other hand, equally skeptical of formal innovation pursued for its own sake. Hence it is important to understand the experimental quality of projects selected for discussion not as abstractly conceived but driven by particular human encounters located in specific time and space.

THE BOX

An elderly woman lies with her head propped on cushions, looking up at the ceiling. In the background, we hear the sound of rain and the faint echo of voices from elsewhere in the building. With each shot, Stefani draws us into the world of her subject, patiently accumulating small and seemingly insignificant gestures—how the subject's hands move slowly and arthritically across the cloth as she ties back the curtains, the careful deliberation with which she smoothes the covers of a neatly made bed, the arrangement of her modest possessions—a chair, a small table, a television set, a washbasin and mirror. She struggles to read an old French grammar book, regretful of how she has let the language go and lamenting the fact that she no longer reads.

Stefani's subject, unnamed in the film, lives and waits and passes time. But, as the filmmaker suggests, Marika's life is not meaningful only in reference to the past. Stefani shows her, a slight stooping figure, standing before the mirror as she delicately brushes her face and combs her fine hair into place. There is a coy, momentary flicker of pleasure in her expression before the scene cuts to the luminous blue screen of the television with the sound turned down. Quiz presenters jostle with advertisements, images of Turkish women are replaced by images of a political demonstration in Latvia, heavily made-up women peer out of the screen, men in formal suits energetically gesticulate to unknown audiences.

Commenting on everything that passes before her, Marika hovers by the television set, expectant. A male newscaster reads through the day's headlines. She seems transfixed, moving closer, caressing the screen as though she were touching the man's cheek. When the newsreader's face disappears for a moment she waits impatiently for him to return, whispering, conspiratorially, "We've got friends, Niko, visitors" (the filmmaker and viewers). Later, she asks: "Niko, will you go dancing, Niko dear?" once more placing her hand lovingly against the image of the newsreader's face and touching her heart. But television moves inexorably on. One image follows another in rapid succession, the newsreader is replaced by other faces, empty faces that flash across the screen smiling at everybody and nobody.

Eva Stefani's eleven-minute video, *The Box* (2004), was completed

Still from *The Box* (2004). *Courtesy of Eva Stefani.*

some ten years after *Athene*.[15] It was originally part of a longer documentary made in 1998 for Greek television about people living in institutional accommodations. Stefani found herself especially drawn to Marika and to the challenge of how, as a filmmaker, she might evoke something of her subject's existence without overly dramatizing or sentimentalizing it. She was dissatisfied with her earlier film and decided to rework the material into a new piece.[16] It involved a gradual stripping away of extraneous matter—subjects, situations, interactions, events, even emotion—until all that remained was an elderly woman alone in one room with a television set.

  The Box presents a historical subject located in time and place. At the same time, however, Stefani invokes the complex intersections of her subject's small-scale world and the larger forces of global communications by exploring the fragmented densities and textures of experience. From the outset, we are made aware of how the room is cut off, separated from the institutional sounds of feet and voices in the corridor. Contrasted with these anonymous workaday noises we hear the woman's rasping breath, her whispering of the word *belle* as she tries to remember her beloved French. She recalls how once she was able to keep up with her understanding and reading of another language; she invokes the falsity of time in her talk of life passing; she enters the imaginative world of the television, talking to the newsreader as if he were her real rather than virtual companion. This collision of times and places is mirrored in the phenomenon of television broadcasting itself, which, with its incessant juxtaposing of myriad kinds of difference, appears to reduce it to equivalent units—whether entertainment, information, or politics.

The attention to scale, detail and texture distinguishing Stefani's film is evidence of her continuing commitment to an observational approach. So, too, her subject matter—slight and seemingly insignificant, that we might impatiently shrug our shoulders and say, "So what?" The scale of *The Box*, carefully judged and finely calibrated, reflects that of its subject, the intimate sensibility created from camera movements that are delicate, responsive, and fluid. The use of extended shots invites the viewer to look into the image and to explore the existential space that opens up around Stefani's subject. Here, details such as the woman's arthritic hands, the battered book of French, the moving mouth of the newsreader and the gummy sounds of the woman's mouth as she mimics him, unsettle with their fractured vividness.

Stefani's techniques in *The Box* are closely linked to those used in her earlier film *Athene,* but a number of new features distinguish her more recent observational work. The first relates to the scale of the piece. Questions of scale have always been central to experiments in cinematic realism (serving as an important counter-weight to cinema's tendency toward the grandiose). With *The Box*, Stefani signals her interest in experimenting with this notion. Running at eleven minutes, Stefani's film—like its subject—might seem to be something negligible, easily overlooked, or quickly discarded. Secondly—and related to the question of scale—is the way that Stefani now seeks to engage her audience. For the deliberation with which she resists extension, explanation and elaborate contextualization create an unusual tension within the work, intensifying and foregrounding the problem of meaning.

From the beginning, one of the challenges presented by the observational approach in ethnographic filmmaking has been the openness of the final representation. Stefani takes this one step further. Stripped down in every way, the beguiling quality of *The Box* lies precisely in its brevity, in its simplicity. The viewer is forced back onto himself or herself—

encountering *The Box* not as an introduction to something else (a longer film, an explanation, an intervention) but as complete in and of itself. Stefani's intention is not to "capture" her subject but instead raise questions about the feelings we attach to experience *before* the point at which we invest it with meaning. What do I need this to mean? What am I projecting onto Stefani's subject? Is my relationship with Marika a mirror of her relationship with the newscaster?

The gauging of experience prior to categorical meaning poses a particular challenge to documentary filmmaking in its conventional form, dependent as it is on linear sequential narrative and a respect for cause and effect as a way of showing how a situation changes over time. *The Box* undermines the idea that narrative must lead from one place to another. Stefani's focus on the unfinished aspects of experience allows her to build a narrative and sensory filmic space in which gaps, inconsistencies, and disorientations come, paradoxically, to the fore. It is Stefani's ability to approach experiential time as something fractured, bland, and affecting that suggests an expansion of the observational cinematic approach. The logic of action and reaction, cause and effect is displaced; instead there is a sense of something bubbling up—as if reality were like small pockets of air that burst when they reach the surface.

Stefani's short work has been screened at a number of documentary film festivals. Significantly, it has also been exhibited within an art gallery context. Although Stefani herself has expressed some reservations about the latter site, it is perhaps within the space of the gallery that *The Box* is most fully realized. Here, whether in a small darkened space or displayed in a bright gallery on a television screen, viewers make choices about how to engage with work that differs from that of the cinema. Not least, it allows the viewer to move toward and around the image—indeed to touch the screen. For to "know" this piece is to resist translating its "meaning" and to be receptive to a mimetic connection with the sensuous knowledge it may yield.

On the one hand, the shift into a gallery space makes possible different experiences, ones that are usually filtered out or subsumed into abstract categories by anthropology on the grounds of being literal, unruly, unsorted, under-theorized. But, on the other hand, as Stefani recognizes, by moving work into the gallery there is a danger of aestheticizing one's subjects, or using subjects in the service of an artistic vision. These are issues that reverberate through the other examples of contemporary observational work that we wish to consider here. They cannot be easily resolved but they are usually to be found at the heart of exchanges between artists and anthropologists.

SCHOOLSCAPES

David MacDougall's *SchoolScapes* (2007) is one of several pieces made as part of what he calls "An Observation Project" pursued at the Rishi Valley School in South India. It represents an interesting new phase in MacDougall's long-standing engagement with the question of observation understood to be a particular way of investigating the world as an anthropological filmmaker. With the Rishi Valley films, MacDougall makes observation itself the focus of his investigation. He sets out to explore how pupils at a school established by the twentieth-century Indian philosopher Krishnamurti perceive the world around them. Specifically, he seeks to discover how the camera might both facilitate and document this process. Taking Krishnamurti's writing as a point of departure, MacDougall asks students to find out, through filming, how they might learn to see familiar things in novel ways.[17]

SchoolScapes, MacDougall's own film, comprises forty single shots or scenes, assembled into a piece with a running time of seventy-seven minutes. It was shot in high-definition video and, because of the detail rendered through this technology, the film was intended to be viewed as a projected work rather than one screened on a television monitor. By looking closely at the opening scenes of *SchoolScapes,* it is possible to identify some of the distinctive features that characterize MacDougall's new project. We examine how MacDougall works with observation both as the object and medium of his inquiry, one that challenges the existing forms of anthropological representation. The innovative quality of the piece, like Stefani's, followed from and was an expression of the filmmaker's particular engagement with the real. Moreover, the techniques of cinematic realism, far from circumscribing his project, facilitated his break with linearity and with the familiar spatial and temporal conventions of anthropological inquiry.

The first scene of *SchoolScapes* comprises a single, wide shot of a rocky hillside. The gray sky is squeezed into upper part of the frame, while the landscape itself fills the remainder of the frame. We see large rocks clustered at the top of a gently sloping edge that runs left to right. Smaller rocks are more loosely scattered at the lower levels of the hillside.

Folds and lines mark the texture of the terrain; a dark track into the hillside is just about discernible. The reddish hue amid the grays, greens, and browns of the landscape suggests that the scene was filmed at dawn. The shot lasts a minute, during which time the camera is completely motionless. Throughout, however, the image is animated by the sounds of natural life—the harsh squawking of crows mixed in with the higher and sweeter tones of small birds.

MacDougall positions his camera at a distance from the scene. It is still and steady. The shot has no obvious beginning or end. Through precise framing, the camera demarcates a particular space—but it is one that is neither static nor unchanging, since it unfolds in real time. Moreover, although the camera remains stationary, the scene is extraordinarily alive. Not least, the viewer becomes aware of his or her own perceptual activity—the processes of looking and listening, of scanning, exploring, focusing, pausing, moving in and out of the picture, traversing its surface, and so on.

The duration of the film's second scene is also one minute. The camera is again motionless. However, the content and composition of the shot stand in marked contrast to the preceding one. No longer looking onto a landscape from a distance, the camera is now in the midst of trees. We do not see ground or sky. A complicated tangle of branches and leaves fills the frame. Again we experience the stillness of the camera and the movement around it—the breeze that animates the vegetation, the soft shimmering sound of the leaves, the delicate changing light, and the ripples of movement through the trees. MacDougall isolates a small, everyday moment and asks us to attend to it—fully and openly.

The third scene of *SchoolScapes* lasts almost five minutes. Mac-Dougall's camera is located in a school dormitory. There are five beds, four unmade and a fifth still occupied. There is the sound of a noisy fan, a door opening and closing, the voice of a man sent to rouse a sleeping boy. A curtain flutters on the edge of the frame. Patiently and without moving, MacDougall's camera observes the boy as he slowly unzips his sleeping bag. Unhurried, he yawns and stretches, and eventually moves to sit on the edge of his bed. He leaves the frame of the camera. We glimpse him in the wall mirror, returning with his shoes and socks. Slowly the boy puts on his socks, pausing frequently. He ties his laces, rests, scratches his face—and then lies down on his bed once more. Again MacDougall asks us to observe a process we might conventionally regard as unremarkable—

and yet the detail and intensity of the filmmaker's engagement with the scene transforms it into something remarkable—compelling, even—in its complexity.

The film is comprised of single scenes. Each scene is a long, unbroken shot. Discrete narratives unfold within individual scenes; there is movement within the shot, between foreground and background, rather than between shots. The viewer is positioned in front of the scene and is asked to engage directly with what the camera frames and presents. Through this kind of cinematic aesthetic, MacDougall sets out to explore a notion of observation or awareness that underpins the Rishi Valley School. Founded by the twentieth-century Indian philosopher Krishnamurti, the school seeks to foster a skepticism among its pupils of what might be called established "ways of seeing"—that is, ideologies, systems, religions, faiths. In keeping with Krishnamurti's teachings, pupils are encouraged to discover the world for themselves, to see it with their own eyes. This hinges upon the development of a particular kind of looking or observation that Krishnamurti called "awareness."

According to Krishnamurti, awareness is about learning "to observe what is actually taking place in our daily life, inwardly and outwardly."[18] Crucial to this is the ability of being open to the world, seeing it with new eyes, observing it as if for the first time. Each of the scenes in MacDougall's *SchoolScapes* may be considered an experiment in observation understood in Krishnamurtian terms—that is, the individual shot, the extended unbroken take, comprises a self-consciously defined moment of attention. MacDougall seems to be asking something like the following: What happens if we stop and attend carefully to the things that surround us, to everyday, overlooked moments? What happens if we really try to engage with them fully and openly in a Krishnamurtian sense—that is, not by concentrating on them but by observing them? How might a film render this engagement such that the viewer becomes an observer in the Krishnamurtian sense of the word?

MacDougall draws upon a cinematic aesthetic derived from the early Lumière films as the medium through which to pursue his research. Here, in the deliberate placing of the camera and the use of the long, unbroken shot as a complete film in and of itself, *SchoolScapes* seeks to recapture something of the cinematograph's original promise to reveal the world anew. The camera is active and exploratory—not through its movement but through an attentive engagement with the world we might describe

Still from *SchoolScapes* (2007). *Courtesy of David MacDougall.*

as characterized by "awareness." Crucial to *SchoolScapes* is MacDougall's attempt to align the audience's eye with his own eye as an anthropological filmmaker, since we can only properly engage with his project if we bring the kind of awareness to bear on our viewing that he has brought in making the film. With each scene, MacDougall challenges us to look—what do we look at and how do we look? By presenting the viewer with an artifact of his own process of looking, he seeks to persuade us that filming/looking is not a preliminary to editing/knowing but constitutes its own mode of investigation. Moreover, running parallel to it but separate from it are forms of understanding that emerge from juxtapositions of moments of attention or individual scenes. The connections are not causal, predicated on linear forms of argument and exposition. They are intended to be resonant or suggestive, serving as points of departure for further questioning and discovery.

With *SchoolScapes,* MacDougall questions the conventional hierarchy of shooting and editing where the former is equated to open exploration, the latter to finished analysis. This has, of course, been implicit in all of his earlier work. Now he brings it fully into focus. Shooting and editing are revealed to be different forms of interpretive work—and both stand in contrast to that underlying text-based inquiry. Approached in this way,

SchoolScapes might best be understood as a matrix—an anthropological web that emerges from and coalesces around experiential or affective ways of knowing. In employing the notion of "ways of knowing," we underline the *relational* quality of what MacDougall engages as an anthropological filmmaker. For *SchoolScapes* represents an attempt to create an artifact that is continuous with, rather than a translation of, observation or looking. Here knowledge is expressed not as an object, an outcome of reflection on experience, but instead as a *process* in which experience is inseparable from knowing.

SHEEP RUSHES

Ilisa Barbash and Lucien Castaing-Taylor's video installation *Sheep Rushes* (2007) is part of a larger film project that documents the lives of the last remaining sheep herders in America who practice transhumance on a significant scale. Located in the vast, inhospitable terrain of Montana, Barbash and Castaing-Taylor found themselves drawn to an observational approach as a way of communicating the distinctive texture of their subjects' experience.[19] In their attempt to evoke something of the *affective* and *elemental* dimensions of a human existence forged in the struggle with animality and an unforgiving mountain landscape, they began exploring the techniques and aesthetic possibilities of cinematic realism.

Sheep Rushes comprises three extended film sequences: *Hell Roaring Creek* (nineteen minutes), *The High Trail* (five minutes), and *Fine and Coarse* (nine minutes). The installation was included as part of the exhibition Equal, That Is, to the Real Itself, held at the Marian Goodman Gallery in New York. The idea of presenting work within a gallery space had not been part of Barbash and Castaing-Taylor's original conception of their project. However, in viewing and assembling their film material, they had become dissatisfied with a number of decisions they were making as editors of a more conventional linear piece (*Sweetgrass*). In particular, they became interested in finding ways to foreground the spatial and temporal qualities of the extended sequences and long unbroken takes that made up a good deal of their footage. The invitation to participate in the Goodman show stimulated Barbash and Castaing-Taylor to think again about the formal possibilities of an observational approach. For, as they discovered, using observational techniques did not necessarily lead to a single outcome—the production of a certain kind of ethnographic film. Indeed, as they sought to move beyond the initial aesthetic scope of their research, they embarked on an exploration of new representational forms and exhibition sites from those usually associated with the presentation of anthropological work.

At the Goodman Gallery, Barbash and Castaing-Taylor's *Sheep Rushes* was projected onto large-size floor-to-ceiling screens in a darkened room. The three segments of the installation ran consecutively on a continuous loop, but the viewer was free to enter or leave the space at any time during the screening. Hence the work had no definitive beginning or end, and the parts could be seen as a linear sequence or as small, isolated segments. The different pieces that made up the installation were all marked by a developed observational sensibility, but each was distinctive in the manner of its expression.

Hell Roaring Creek, the longest part of the installation, is made up of just three extended takes. It begins with the sound of water flowing under a black screen. The carefully composed first image is a static wide shot from a tripod-mounted camera placed in the midst of a fast-flowing stream. In the hazy dawn light, it is possible to make out the shadowy outlines of herders on horseback and sheep—hundreds of sheep huddled together on the bank to the right. A dog growls, there are muffled shouts, but it is the bleating of the sheep that is insistent, urgent even. Anticipation grows. Sheep move cautiously toward the edge of the bank, bunched together, bleating incessantly, goaded by the growls of dogs and shouts of men. Eventually, before daylight begins to break, they start to cross—hesitantly, one by one, some scrambling, others walking or jumping. And they keep crossing, a seemingly endless flow of animals. The effect is hypnotic, mesmerizing. A fade to black between the first seven-minute and the second eight-minute shot, the shift in camera position, and the gradual seeping of daylight into the image indicates the passage of time. And still the sheep keep on crossing. With the final unbroken shot, the herders and their dogs follow the last remaining animals as they splash through the water to the other side. The river continues to flow, its sound reverberating long past the final frame.

The High Trail, the shortest of the installation segments, also opens with a static wide shot—this time we see a rocky mountain ridge framed against a brilliant blue sky. Again we hear the rich and familiar sound of sheep bleating, now mixed with the rasping, gravelly voice of a herder praising his dog. In the far distance, we begin to see a line of animals snaking down the steep mountainside. A wild mountain goat watches from a high ledge as the sheep reach lower pasture. The camera zoom draws attention to scale and distance, the early panoramic shots standing in stark contrast to later, tightly focused shorter ones of sheeps' hooves passing over the dry, dusty ground.

The third segment of *Sheep Rushes* stands close to the things it depicts. In *Fine and Coarse,* the camera is encompassed by the scene rather than standing back to frame it. Sheep mill around two large sheds in the early morning light. A sharp cut to a handheld camera abruptly moves us into the middle of the action. Inside the shed a man is grabbing hold of one of the sheep waiting in the run above the shearing corridor. The shed is a mass of throbbing sounds—the electric shears, music—and movements as animals are skillfully flipped and turned and fleeced. The camera pans up and down the men, carefully mirroring their skillful choreography. The wool peels off like butter, leaving rippled shorn skin. Toward the end of the shot, a deep-focus lens offers a view of a long portion of the shed with several men moving at once. One of the men stops to change the blade and oil the electric shears. The metal-encased jointed arms containing electric wires swing high above the men, bent to their task. It is dark in the shed, lending a carnal, erotic density to the entire sequence. Another shot takes us back outside to a carefully framed landscape. Here a hundred or so sheep, newly shorn, stand hunched in falling snow.

As an example of the contemporary observational sensibility in anthropological work, *Sheep Rushes* contains a number of interesting features. Especially notable is Barbash and Castaing-Taylor's extensive use of a tripod that enables them to generate carefully composed static wide shots that serve to draw the viewer's attention to the self-conscious framing and to the movement unfolding within the frame itself. There are also individual, extended sequences that serve to spatialize time—that is, the viewer's exploration of space becomes also an experience of time. In breaking with the conventions of linear narrative in which temporality is generated through a succession of shots, *Sheep Rushes* represents a further extension of the innovation pursued by MacDougall in his *SchoolScapes.* The visual aesthetic of *Sheep Rushes* is highly developed and meticulously crafted; so too the work's soundscape. In particular, Barbash and Castaing-Taylor set up a suggestive contrast between the distance and formality of the tripod-mounted camera and the intimate guttural quality of the audio track.

The overall shape of the piece, *Sheep Rushes* as a video *installation,* and the nature of its location (an art gallery) represents, of course, a

Still from *The High Trail* (2007). *Courtesy of Ilisa Barbash and Lucien Castaing-Taylor.*

significant departure from existing observational forms. *Sheep Rushes* invites the viewer to explore the material through active bodily engagement, moving in and around the film space itself. Moreover, there is no fixed order to the three sections of the piece. Hence it might be viewed in whole or in part and in any sequence of parts. One of the hallmarks of observational work—its open, unfinished texture—is here given new emphasis. For *Sheep Rushes* exists only for the duration of its installation. It is reconfigured as a different work with each subsequent exhibition, made and remade according to the particular constraints and possibilities inherent in any given site.

Like Stefani and MacDougall, Barbash and Castaing-Taylor share a profound commitment to the real and to the problem of how, aesthetically, to render the real. Their video installation is not an inquiry into the subject of sheep farming. Instead, the filmmakers seem to be asking, "What flows and circuits of experience occur around sheep farming? What are the feelings that attach to these experiences? How can their medium be used to create an equivalent for these?"

Art, Anthropology, and the Observational Sensibility

Looked at as films "about" something, the work of Stefani, MacDougall, and Barbash and Castaing-Taylor immediately presents a challenge—namely, why should we feel that there is something worth attending to here? The examples discussed above cannot be adequately encompassed by an account of their content—an old lady in a small room with a television set, everyday scenes from an Indian school, the herding of sheep across a mountainous terrain. In each case, the filmmaker is concerned with what might be considered unremarkable, the neglected, the everyday, rendering it not as an object of scrutiny but as a space to be opened up between seer and seen. Moreover, by attempting to forge a correspondence between their own observational sensibilities and the mobile character of such a reality, the filmmaker becomes ever more invested in preserving the openness and ambiguity of the image, since this is a way of evoking reality's relational character—its unfinished, shifting form.

The commitment by Stefani, MacDougall, and Barbash and Castaing-Taylor to engaging the real in an open and exploratory manner represents an important extension of the Bazinian project—that is, the creation of a cinema that is not reductive but expansive or "modernist" in its approach to the real. Indeed, *The Box, SchoolScapes,* and *Sheep Rushes* may be seen as evidence of what Jayamanne, in her discussion of Bazin, has termed "new" realism.[20] Interpreted in these terms, its distinguishing features are again not primarily its content or subject matter but its aesthetic—and what makes the aesthetic of the new cinematic realism distinctive is its unusual spatial and temporal qualities. Specifically, there is a break with the conventions associated with "old' or "traditional" realism—most notably, linear narrative, character, action, and reaction identified by Deleuze as characteristic of "sensory-motor" cinema. Instead, a new kind of ethnographic cinema has begun to form around "purely optical and sound situations" in which "motor helplessness" gives way to an intense sensory awareness, dissolving structures of causality in favor of indeterminacy and the imaginary. It is, Deleuze declares, "a cinema of the seer and not of the agent."[21]

The filmmaking projects pursued by Stefani, MacDougall, and Barbash and Castaing-Taylor are characterized by very different inflections and concerns, expressing highly distinctive interpretations of the observational task. Not least, these differences challenge the view that observational filmmaking approaches are predicated on the disavowal of the aesthetic or the perpetuation of the illusion of a style-less style that effaces individual authorship. *The Box, SchoolScapes,* and *Sheep Rushes* serve as a reminder of the centrality of authorship to the observational project, extending in significant ways Bazin's radical conception of the filmmaker as "filter" (rather than director) in the new cinema of reality.

At the same time the recent work by Stefani, MacDougall, and Barbash and Castaing-Taylor shares a pronounced formal inventiveness in anthropological terms. Does this signal an abandonment of anthropology in favor of the making of "art"? Certainly their work runs counter to existing conventions of ethnographic representation and its developed aesthetic self-consciousness risks seeming "arty," an indulgence in formalism for its own sake. Exhibiting such work in a gallery or museum context raises difficult questions for anthropologists. It evokes aspects of an uncomfortable history in which human subjects are put on show or turned into objects of aesthetic scrutiny. But the question of what this means in terms of contemporary anthropology is made more complicated by virtue of the fact that the filmmakers themselves are interested, to a greater or lesser degree, in exploring convergences with art practice. These convergences include a shared concern with "the real," an attention to and mining of the everyday, an interest in the transformative possibilities of the mundane, the careful siting of work and considered engagement with the viewer, and a commitment to interrogating the formal possibilities of the medium—as seen in the deliberate play with the look, the framing, the sound, and the tempo of the work.

Filmmaker and photographer Sharon Lockhart is one of the contemporary artists most often cited by anthropologists interested in the creative possibilities that might follow from a convergence of different fields of practice. For example, in a recent essay, Schneider argued for the importance of Lockhart in the development of a new dialogue between art and anthropology.[22] Certainly it is not hard to identify characteristics that might be considered expressive of an anthropological sensibility in works such as Lockhart's *Teatro Amazonas* or *Goshogaoka,* including a commitment to cultural performance, to the use of ethnographic methods, and to the forging of collaborative relationships with anthropologists in the field. But, as Schneider points out, Lockhart is not alone in making art that in some important sense resembles anthropology. He also names Juan Downey and Michael Oppitz. Of course, the potential list is much longer. One might also add Antony Gormley, Susan Hiller, Rosalind Nashashibi, Sonia Boyce, Erika Tan, Daniel Peltz, Mohini Chandra, Jeremy Deller, Steve McQueen, Roy Villevoye, and Fiona Tan, to name but a few.

Calls for greater dialogue between art and anthropology are nothing new, having stretched back over a century to the early phases of the modern discipline.[23] If there was always a good deal of exchange between these two fields of practice in twentieth-century French anthropology, the Anglo-American school was marked by greater circumspection, traditionally aligning itself with science (as indicative of a collective disciplined inquiry) rather than with art (understood to be about the individual imagination or creativity). Although for many anthropologists today the notion of science is deeply problematic, disciplinary anxieties about art have remained largely unchanged.[24] The publication of Hal Foster's essay, "The Artist as Ethnographer," however, reignited the debate about art and anthropology, at the same time as it served to push it in new directions.[25] Hitherto anthropology had offered the "primitive" as an object of Western artistic appropriation, while art itself (initially as non-Western or tribal art) had been constituted as an object for anthropological appropriation (as the anthropology of art). Following Foster's intervention, discussion shifted, becoming increasingly focused around what has been termed the "ethnographic turn" in contemporary art.[26] One of the critical issues to emerge concerned the status of ethnography. Was it a specialized set of disciplinary techniques, something "belonging" primarily to anthropology, or was it a more general epistemological orientation guiding work that might be pursued according to very different parameters?

Anthropologists have explored relationships between art and anthropology in a number of different ways. For example, Schneider and Wright, while acknowledging the institutional and historical differences between the two fields, have pointed out that disparities between examples of practice were often more a reflection of differences between sites of display rather than ones of intention or technique.[27] Approached as self-evident or stable categories, art and anthropology have acted as a foil for one another in past exchanges. But, as Schneider and Wright have argued, to hold to such a position means to overlook their fundamental instability as categories and the possibility of creative borrowings or appropriation.

Another position may be found in the work of Ingold and others.[28] It, too, hinges upon according a central place to art practice over discourse or rhetoric. Ingold has proposed "exploratory knowledge practices" as a framework for approaching art and anthropology as deeply social endeavors—ones, moreover, that are not inherently different from one another but comprise analogous modes of investigating the world. In particular, he highlights the open-ended character of art and anthropology *as practices in the world,* seeking thereby to distinguish them from art objects or ethnographic texts that involve a distancing from the world and a finishing off of experience. For Ingold, the skill of artists or anthropologists is anchored in how they come to know "a site"; that is, in the ways that they move through and actively engage an environment, and in how effectively they are able to channel the attention of the audience in accordance with their own knowledgeable practice.

There is a problem, however, with each of these positions. On the one hand, the danger of appropriation, crucial to Schneider and Wright's case, is that it foregrounds the striving after aesthetic effect or what is sometimes called the making of anthropology that "looks like art."[29] This position involves the privileging of the aesthetic over the social, form over content. It implies that what is required is the borrowing of artistic techniques rather than the development of new techniques and representational forms in response to specific obstacles encountered within the anthropological process—and considered to be an integral part of the anthropology itself. It has strong echoes of the "envy" that Foster identified in his writing about art and anthropology. In Foster's case, it was the artist who envied the anthropologist. Here the situation is reversed. Now it is the anthropologist who, trapped within a position of disciplinary confinement and accountability, looks longingly at the perceived freedom and creativity of the artist.

On the other hand, the stance taken by Ingold is predicated on the denial or downplaying of the aesthetic. Far from proposing appropriation or borrowings, both art and anthropology are understood to be fundamentally analogous ways of engaging with an environment. However, this kind of approach cannot account for particular historical and cultural traditions that emerge from the privileging of certain sensibilities, techniques, forms, and affects over others. Nor, in its exclusive focus on skill and process, can it encompass questions relating to the nature of the representational object itself (as art or anthropology).

The importance of contemporary observational work is that it offers an example of how anthropologists might begin to develop a different sort of dialogue with artists. This would involve neither an appropriation of aesthetic effects nor a repudiation of them. It coalesces around an impulse in both fields toward what Jackson has called the "existential imperative"—that is, the creative transformation of what seems given.[30]

Epilogue: Observational Cinema and Experimental Anthropology

Over the last twenty years or so, notions such as "experimental anthropology" or "experimental ethnography" have increasingly emerged within disciplinary discourse. Although hotly disputed—and in many cases summarily rejected—these terms have proved useful in describing efforts to move beyond the established conventions of anthropological representation—specifically, the production of a certain kind of academic text or monograph. The publication of *Writing Culture* in the mid-1980s is most often cited as the key moment in the development of anthropology's aesthetic self-consciousness.[31] As an expression of the profound dissatisfaction with the literary devices of scientific ethnography, Clifford and Marcus's edited volume stimulated a new interest in the techniques of writing and in forms of textual construction. For those working in the field of visual anthropology, there was a certain irritation that innovations pursued in non-textual media were not acknowledged as an integral part of this experimental moment. Indeed, commentators like Ginsburg were quick to point out that work by Jean Rouch, Robert Gardner, and David MacDougall had much earlier addressed the very same questions that had come to animate the debates associated with *Writing Culture.*[32]

Given the entrenched positions of the so-called textual and visual anthropologies, it was not perhaps surprising that questions about ethnographic representation were pursued largely within the existing disciplinary parameters. What both constituencies shared, however, was a profound skepticism toward forms of anthropological realism. Hence to claim that the observational sensibility may serve as the foundation of an experimental anthropology may seem far-fetched. But this is precisely the case we have attempted to outline here.

At best, observational approaches in ethnographic cinema have been seen as a necessary stage on the way to more "advanced" filmmaking. At worst, they have been seen as an obstacle in the way of more innovative practice. The commitment to the real, and to the aesthetic possibilities of a new ethnographic cinema founded in the real, have long been assumed to be at odds with discourses of anthropological experimentation. The latter have focused, almost exclusively, on the techniques of montage understood to exemplify a modernist (and by implication, radical, dialogic) sensibility.[33] But there is, in fact, nothing inherently progressive or reactionary about either realism or modernism and, as the recent commentary on Bazin has revealed, the categories are themselves unstable and porous. Each of the examples discussed above poses a challenge to the normal conventions of ethnographic representation—both textual and visual. Crucially, this challenge emanates from a position of realism and, as such, it calls into question assumptions that a montage-based aesthetic is synonymous with progressive inquiry, while an extended sequence–shot aesthetic is necessarily harnessed to a conservative one.

Our case for considering Stefani, MacDougall, and Barbash and Castaing-Taylor as key figures in an experimental anthropology is not made on the grounds that their work resembles art or that it is formally innovative in its aesthetic character. It stems from the fact that it is representative of an inquiry in which epistemology, ethics, and aesthetics are mutually constituted. Important to any understanding of the innovative quality of the examples presented above is the question of its motivation. The experiments we have highlighted with medium, narrative, site, scale, duration, linearity, framing, and so on all followed from particular problems encountered by the filmmakers in the course of their observational practice. They were not abstractly conceived, pursued for their own sake, or developed as a means of personal expression. Evolving in the space *between* makers and sites, they opened up the possibility that *other* viewpoints might emerge as an integral part of the anthropological endeavor—the works' formal qualities developing in conjunction with, and expressive of, the shaping of knowledge itself.

At the beginning of this chapter we suggested that observation, understood as a mode of skilled practice, might serve as a basis for a new engagement between artists and anthropologists. For the latter, this means the pursuit of an anthropology that is not undertaken from a place of theory but from the perspective of everyday life and, as such, it comprises an ongoing practice (moving, relating, being) forged through collaborative exchange with particular human subjects. Crucial, as we have seen in the examples of Stefani, MacDougall, and Barbash and Castaing-Taylor, is the problem of how to approach and render other experiences of the world. Specifically, what kind of perceptual readjustment is necessary in order to bring different subjective perspectives into alignment or proximity? This active, continuous process is what we call "observation." In referring to it as a *skilled practice,* we seek to draw attention to the fact that the perceptual process is not separated out from its "final" anthropological form—that is, the perceptions of others and the anthropologist's ways of attending to them are inseparable elements of the inquiry.

What kind of dialogue with the visual arts might an anthropology of this sort make possible? Of all human endeavors, art is pre-eminently about perception and the education of perception.[34] Even during its most "conceptual" phases, artists have attended carefully to how an audience might engage with their work. The forging of a closer relationship with art practice enables anthropologists to think more expansively about questions of perception. For those working observationally, such questions are already at the forefront of their approach. They serve to facilitate a change in the terms of exchange—away from mere instrumentality (appropriation) and from the conflation of art and anthropology as generalized human perception. The observational strain in contemporary inquiry opens up a new dialogue about how two grounded perceptual practices, art and anthropology, might be calibrated in innovative ways.

Although aesthetics—by which we mean attention to the formal qualities of work—are important here, it would be a mistake to assume that this is indeed the ground on which artists and anthropologists meet. The cultivation of an observational sensibility brings the anthropologist closer to certain kinds of contemporary artist by virtue of a shared interest in the being of others in the world—encompassing experiences that run counter to accepted models of perception, questioning where the world ends and the imagination begins—and the aesthetic challenge thereby raised.

The radical nature of the observational project for anthropology lies in the questions it poses to existing disciplinary forms of speaking and knowing. Founded in a new relationship between those with whom anthropologists work and learn, it has at its center a resistance to the categorization or commodification of knowledge. *The Box, SchoolScapes,* and *Sheep Rushes* offer a glimpse of what might be involved in pursuing an anthropology of this kind. For, as "image-and-sequence" rather than a "word-and-sentence" modes of inquiry,[35] these examples reveal that the shift from the latter to the former is not just about a change of medium. It involves a profound epistemological and aesthetic move. By attending to the real and to the aesthetics of the real, observational practitioners have from the beginning signaled their commitment to an anthropology tuned to what MacDougall has termed "being."[36] By this he refers to an expansive humanist project founded upon the complexity and irreducibility of subjects in the world. In place of the impulse to translate, there is instead a yielding to phenomena, or what Jackson calls an attention to the small gestures that human beings make "toward opening up a space in which to live."[37] It does not follow from this, however, that the problem of meaning is ignored. For being stands in a position of continual tension with representational conventions and interpretative frameworks ("meaning"). The work of Stefani, MacDougall, and Barbash and Castaing-Taylor (and that of their predecessors in the observational tradition) manifests an active resistance to the neat folding of experience into theory, or the simple equation between perception and cognition. An anthropology constituted in this way has the potential to puncture our assumptions and to undermine habitual action, catalyzing thereby a reconfigured relationship with the material world.

NOTES

PREFACE

1. Of course, Jean Rouch was an early pioneer, developing an innovative anthropological cinema that challenged many of the assumptions of both the discipline of anthropology and the practices of documentary filmmaking. His films of the late 1950s and early 1960s (*Les Maîtres Fous, Jaguar, Moi, Un Noir,* and *Chronique d'un été*) built around his notions of the *ciné-transe* and ethno-fiction offer important evidence of the radical nature of his project. See, for example, Feld 2003, Grimshaw 2001, and Stoller 1992.

2. See Grimshaw 2001.

3. See Grimshaw and Ravetz 2005. See also www.miriad.mmu.ac.uk/caa (Connecting Art and Anthropology Workshop website, accessed December 1, 2008).

4. We draw here on a framework articulated by the the History of Scientific Observation Project directed by Lorraine Daston and Fernando Vidal at the Max Planck Institute for the History of Science in Berlin, www.mpiwg-berlin.mpg.de.

5. The terms "observation" and "observational" were often invoked by documentary filmmakers and commentators during the 1960s. It was only later, from the mid-1970s onward, that "observational cinema" was coined to designate a distinctive *genre* of anthropological work.

6. In taking a handful of filmmakers associated with the UCLA program as our examples, we are not suggesting that observational cinema was invented by a coterie of people around Young. The observational movement was always a broad and eclectic project, one that quickly developed in different parts of the world with distinctive local interpretations and emphases.

The rationale for the particular focus of this book is two-fold. Firstly, it reflects our desire to examine instances of filmmaking practice in detail, something that would be impossible if we were to broaden the scope of our discussion. Secondly, there is a distinctive anthropological lineage associated with Colin Young—one in which we are ourselves located. Although this might appear to disqualify our account or make it seem overly self-interested (or worse, self-congratulatory), we have treated it as an unusual fieldwork opportunity. By placing Young and the filmmakers associated with him at the center of our study, we have looked at observational cinema as a particular site of practice. The book may thus be taken as a case study. Its anthropological inflection is to be found as much in its methodological approach as its substantive concerns.

By choosing to highlight this lineage, however, we are acutely aware of neglecting many other examples of observational practice—past and present. This could include, for example, the early work of Lumière, Flaherty, Wright, Rouquier, and Renoir; the innovations of John Marshall during the 1950s and 1960s; and, of course, the contributions of contemporary filmmakers—Eliane de Latour (France), Johan van der Keuken (Netherlands), Kim Longinotto (UK), Dumitru Budrala (Romania), and Kersti Uibo (Estonia), to name but a few.

1. WHAT IS OBSERVATIONAL CINEMA?

1. Sandall 1972, Young 1995 (originally written in 1975).

2. Its importance and significance as an enduring point of reference derives partly from Young's central position in the observational movement but also from the inclusion of his essay in Paul Hockings's edited volume, *Principles of Visual Anthropology*. This collection was crucial in gaining legitimacy for visual anthropology. Reprinted in 1995, it remains a widely used book.

3. Sandall 1972, p. 194.

4. Ibid., p. 196.

5. Young 1995, pp. 100–102.

6. Ibid., p. 102.

7. Ibid., p. 105.

8. Mamber 1974, for example.

9. Young 1995, p. 107.

10. Young was not as bold as Sandall, who suggested Orson Welles's masterpiece *Citizen Kane* as an important model in the development of a new filmmaking approach built around observation. Sandall wrote: "The concern with seeing rather than assertion did not derive from documentary: it came with the exploration of deep focus photography found in *Citizen Kane*. This was a reaction against the photography of the day in which focus was more often soft than deep. Scene complexity or richness, anything which approached the richness of reality itself, this only hampered the telling of the tale" (1972, p. 194). Bazin also discussed Welles's importance to the development of a cinematic aesthetic not driven by montage (1967 and Bazin and Truffaut 1992).

11. Observation is often understood as *only* about "seeing." Sandall's and Young's conception was not reductive in this way.

12. Original emphasis, Crary 1990, pp. 5–6.

13. This not to suggest, of course, that the filmmakers at UCLA were unaware of Bazin and the cinema of Italian neorealism. In his memoir, MacDougall recalls reading Hugh Gray's translations of *What Is Cinema?* in proof form. He also notes that Rossellini was teaching in the United States during this time (MacDougall 2001). But the influence of Bazin's work on changes in anthropological filmmaking has not before been explicitly acknowledged.

14. For scholarly work on Bazin, see Andrew 1990, Deleuze 1989, Forgacs et al. 2000, Jayamanne 2001, Margulies 2003.

15. There were of course important exceptions—for example, Béla Balázs and André Breton.

16. Andrew 1990, pp. 190–191.

17. These two essays are included in Bazin 1967.

18. This essay is included in Bazin 1972.

19. Bazin's letter in included in Bazin 1972.

20. As Millicent Marcus observes, neorealism began as a term designating a literary movement (1986, p. 18). From the outset, there has been intense debate among filmmakers and critics alike as to the defining features of neorealist cinema. Features most often cited have included location shooting, the use of non-professional actors, handheld cam-

era work, low production values, and an interest in a particular kind of subject matter (working or poor people). Today, however, there is a growing recognition that many of these features were an important part of fascist cinema too (Ben Ghiat 2000; Bondanella 1990). To what extent, critics now ask, did postwar Italian cinema represent a radical break with existing conventions? Rossellini's own career as a filmmaker began under Mussolini's regime. It developed, rather than abruptly changed direction, as war, occupation, and liberation followed in fascism's wake. The continuities in Rossellini's work lead Ben Ghiat to characterize *Rome, Open City* a "transition film": "one that builds on the aesthetics and themes of Rossellini's previous movies and works out his relationship to past ideologies and identities" (2000, p. 30).

21. Bazin 1972, pp. 19–20. Many contemporary critics have followed Bazin's lead here. Attention has shifted away from a concern with identifying a unified set of aesthetic features. Instead writers have begun to explore the nature of the moral or political stance that linked different figures in Italian neorealist cinema; see, for example, Marcus 1986, Nowell-Smith 2000.

22. However, as more contemporary commentators have pointed out, despite the attempt to bring coherence to the film's elements through the imposition of a conventional storyline, the oppositions upon which *Rome, Open City* is built (those of class, gender, morality, as well as fiction/documentary, melodrama/ethnographic detail, and studio and "real" locations) are intact at its end. Indeed, as Forgacs emphasizes these dualities are inherent to the filmmaker's conception of the city itself (2008, pp. 38–39). For Rome exists as both a centralized and decentralized space, a site of surveillance and one of resistance in which the vertical and horizontal planes of action remain unresolved. See also Wagstaff 2000.

23. Bazin 1972, p. 27. Other commentators have followed Bazin's lead in considering *Paisà* to be Rossellini's most innovative work. The film's documentary qualities, evoked through the deployment of maps and newsreel-like footage, its fluid camera work, and its open-ended, ambiguous nature, have been widely celebrated. It is understood to have extended in significant ways the cinematic innovations begun by Rossellini in *Rome, Open City*. For example, the landscape—conceived not as a backdrop to experience and action but as integral to them—plays a fuller and more elaborated role in *Paisà*. In the first of Rossellini's war trilogy films, the bomb-scarred city is inseparable from the narrative that unfolds around Manfredi, Pina, and Don Pietro. Rome is the site of specific historical events, but it is also a locus of universal human values. In *Paisà*, too, Rossellini uses the landscape to tell the different stories that comprise the film—most strikingly, as just noted, in its final part. The terrain is now greater and more diverse, its communicative function more nuanced and elusive than that of *Rome, Open City*. See Forgacs et al. 2000.

24. Bazin 1972, p. 20.

25. Ibid., pp. 34–38. Bazin explained this in the following terms:

> The unit of cinematic narrative in *Paisà* is not the "shot," an abstract view of a reality which is being analyzed, but the "fact." A fragment of concrete reality in itself multiple and full of ambiguity, whose meaning emerges only after the fact, thanks to other imposed facts between which the mind establishes certain relationships . . . Man himself is just one fact among others, to whom no pride of place should be given a priori. (pp. 37–38)

26. Ibid., p. 33.

27. Ibid., p. 26.

28. Although Bazin's attention subsequently shifted to De Sica as an exemplar of a more developed or later neorealism, he never lost his admiration for Rossellini as a filmmaker—defending his later work (e.g., *Voyage to Italy*) in the face of much critical hostility. He recognized Rossellini's unusual ability to evoke intangible and yet compelling aspects of subjectivity—perhaps more fully developed and elaborated in the later cinema of Antonioni. See "In Defense of Rossellini," Bazin 1972.

29. Ibid., pp. 47–49.

30. Ibid., pp. 67 and 76.

31. Many of these ideas were articulated by De Sica's collaborator, Cesare Zavattini, in his important manifesto of neorealist cinema, "Some Ideas on the Cinema."

32. Although Bazin does not include the question of language in his list of neorealist characteristics, it is an important aspect of the new Italian cinema. For example, in his discussion of Visconti's portayal of Sicilian fishermen, *La Terra Trema,* he noted the use of the local dialect. As more recent critics have noted, language is central to Rossellini's war trilogy. The way that Rossellini addressed this issue in the second film of the trilogy both built upon and extended the treatment of language in its first part. In her discussion of *Rome, Open City,* Millicent Marcus highlights the film's "anti-rhetorical stance" (1986, p. 34). The matching of words and deeds in the case of partisan hero Manfredi, she suggests, is crucial to any interpretation of the film's meaning. For it is the expression of Rossellini's own refusal as a filmmaker to engage in hyperbole, his repudiation of the bombast and grandiosity that marked an earlier cinema. Rossellini took this further in *Paisà.* The question of language, indeed communication itself, lay at the heart of the film. Increasingly, Rossellini explored moments of insight in which human connection is made across boundaries of language and culture; see, for example, Nowell-Smith 2000, p. 11.

33. Bazin 1972, pp. 52–53.

34. Ibid., p. 60.

35. Ibid., p. 81.

36. Ibid., p. 76.

37. Ibid., pp. 80–81.

38. Ibid., p. 24. This distinction cut across the conventional categories of fiction and documentary, enabling Bazin to bring together Robert Flaherty, Jean Renoir, and Orson Welles as important examples of directors of the latter category. In the former category, he included the Russian documentarist Dziga Vertov alongside Sergei Eisenstein.

39. Bazin 1967, p. 25.

40. Ibid., pp. 26–27.

41. Aitken 2001, p. 184, and Bazin 1967, p. 27.

42. The term "objective" or "objectivity" is often used to describe this stance. It refers to the attempt to allow things to exist for their own sake rather than suffuse them with the subjectivity of the observer or appropriate them to rhetoric and argument.

43. His biographer, Dudley Andrew, describes Bazin's new conception of the film director in the following terms: "Of neither Flaherty nor Renoir can we say that the filmmaker has erased his own vision. He has instead erased his direction of the action while retaining his style of vision as witness to that action. The audience may then watch an actual event and a considered perspective oriented toward that event. . . . His [Renoir's] style is part of an instinct that first chooses what to watch and then knows how to watch it—more precisely how to coexist with it. Under the subtle pressure of

this approach, relationships within reality become visible, bursting into the consciousness of the spectator as a revelation of a truth discovered" (1990, p. 109). He goes on to describe this kind of cinema as one of "disclosures," in contrast, we might say, to a cinema of assertion (p. 117).

44. Forgacs 2008, p. 24.

45. Andrew 1990, p. 114.

46. Bazin 1972, p. 48.

2. SOCIAL OBSERVERS

1. See interviews with many of the leading figures, Levin 1971. Also O'Connell 1992 and Saunders 2007.

2. For a more detailed discussion of these debates, see Winston 1995, Nichols 1981, Bruzzi 2000, and Hall 1991. See also the early study by Mamber 1974.

3. In the discussion that follows, we use the term *cinéma vérité* to describe developments in American documentary during the 1960s. This may seem unusual given that the term "direct cinema" is often used to distinguish North American documentary from the work of French filmmakers like Jean Rouch. In the interests of general consistency we have decided to employ the terminology that is used by the major writers we work with in this book. Colin Young and others describe the work of Drew, Leacock, and so on as *cinéma vérité*.

4. See, in particular, Hall 1991, p. 27, and Bruzzi 2000.

5. Constraints of space lead us to select only a handful of films from a rich array of possibilities. The three films we have chosen are emblematic of where the project began in 1960 and where it reached almost decade later. Moreover, our choice reflects work of some of the key players in the *cinéma vérité* movement, allowing us to highlight different interpretations, sites, and sensibilities.

6. In this we have drawn on the work of the History of Observation Project run by Lorraine Daston and Fernando Vidal at the Max Planck Institute for the History of Science, Berlin.

7. Original emphasis, 1992, p. 1.

8. Young 1995.

9. Quoted in Hall 1991, p. 29.

10. If O'Connell 1992 has remained an enthusiast, Nichols 1988, Waugh 1985, and Winston 1995 and 2000 are more skeptical.

11. O'Connell 1992, p. 32.

12. This is a recurrent theme in many of the films made by Drew and his associates; for example, *Crisis, Happy Mother's Day, Don't Look Back*. The mediated nature of American experience is one of the central issues being explored in the *cinéma vérité* work. See Rothman's discussion of this question 1996.

13. O'Connell 1992, p. 71.

14. This is a point also discussed by Hall 1991, p. 41.

15. Quoted in O'Connell 1992, p. 126.

16. See the Maysles' interviews in Levin 1971, Rosenthal 1971, and Dixon 2003. In the commentary added to the DVD version of *Salesman*, Al Maysles explains that growing up as a Jewish boy in the Boston suburbs brought him into endless conflict with Irish boys. This often involved fighting—establishing an unusual physical connection that serves as a basis for approaching the lives of Brennan and his fellow salesmen. Rouch

was interested, too, in the disjuncture between the jobs that people do in the world and other dimensions of their subjectivity. He posed this question most dramatically in *Les Maîtres Fous*, but it is to be found in other films such as *Jaguar; Moi, Un Noir;* and *Chronique d'un été*.

17. DVD commentary. Also, Maysles explains that he came to understand the centrality of relationships with subjects partly as a result of making a film about Truman Capote as Capote was completing *In Cold Blood*. Capote's relationships with key characters were the foundation for writing what he called a "non-fiction novel."

18. The Maysles ask us to follow them in not looking on judgmentally but with empathy. This aspect of the film is strongly reminiscent of De Sica's attitude in *Bicycle Thief*. The connection between the films is also underlined in the distinctive scale of drama (it is never inflated but intensifies along with a growing sense of anxiety for the key protagonists—and it is from their desperation that unethical actions follow).

19. Many of the leading *cinéma vérité* filmmakers made these kind of ad hoc adaptations—Rouch, Pennebaker, Leacock, Marshall—and so, too, MacDougall.

20. Rosenthal 1971, p. 82.

21. See Rothman on the centrality of speaking to *cinéma vérité* 1996, p. 110.

22. Their later film *Grey Gardens* is an important example of this distinctive approach toward subjects.

23. It could be argued, and it was certainly Zwerin's belief, that the use of dramaturgical devices of this kind were necessary in helping the film reach a broader audience than might normally be available for observational documentary.

24. Bazin 1967, p. 25. See also our discussion in chapter 1.

25. The term "privileged" is MacDougall's 1998. We discuss it further in chapter 4.

26. See Anderson and Benson 1991, Grant 1992, Lucia 1994.

27. *Titicut Follies* is perhaps one of most controversial and extensively debated documentary films. Despite his high prolific output, the critical literature on Wiseman is surprisingly thin. Important studies of his cinema include Anderson and Benson 1991, Atkins 1976, Grant 1992, 1998, and Mamber 1974.

28. Rosenthal 1971, p. 67.

29. John Marshall was a distinguished filmmaker in his own right and a figure of particular significance in the tradition of ethnographic cinema. During the 1950s he began his work with the Ju/'hoasi people (also known as !Kung San) that continued until his death in 1995. But he was also an important pioneer of *vérité* filmmaking in America. In addition to collaborating with Wiseman on *Titicut Follies* (he was originally credited as co-director as well as cameraman), he worked with Richard Leacock and D. A. Pennebaker. During the late 1960s, he made the acclaimed Pittsburgh Police series that is widely recognized to have laid the ground for later *vérité*-style television cop shows. Unfortunately, given the focus of this book, it is not possible here to examine Marshall's work in any detail. See Ruby 1993.

30. This is, of course, where he is able to assert his directorial authority. Wiseman in Rosenthal 1971, p. 72. See also Grant 1998.

31. Nichols 1978, p. 18.

32. Ibid., p. 18.

33. Again, this is reflected in Wiseman's own position—he records sound and edits but he does not engage his subjects directly through the camera.

34. Wiseman in Rosenthal 1971, p. 320. For more details on his working methods, see interviews with Wiseman—in particular Levin 1971, Rosenthal 1971, and Lucia 1994.

35. MacDougall 1998.

36. Quoted in Grant 1998, p. 239.

3. OBSERVATIONAL CINEMA IN THE MAKING

1. *Dogme* was the movement launched in 1995 by the Swedish filmmakers Lars Von Trier and Thomas Vinterberg. In its rejection of high-budget, high-tech, spectacular filmmaking, it shared many of the same features as the earlier *vérité* and observational movements. However, unlike their precursors, the founders of *Dogme* issued a written manifesto or what they called "A Vow of Chastity." It established a set of rules that were intended to circumscribe filmmaking practice—including handheld equipment, synchronous sound, and other techniques common to earlier forms of cinematic realism.

2. MacDougall 2001, pp. 81–82.

3. For further details, see Henley's interview with Young in Henley 2007, MacDougall 2001, and Grimshaw and Papastergiadis 1995.

4. See Di Gioia's conversation with Grimshaw 2006b.

5. The wife of Welsh-born Hancock was from Stowe, Vermont. This helped cement an interest in pursuing film work in this particular locality.

6. Other projects included, most notably of course, David and Judith MacDougall's work with the Jie in Uganda. While in East Africa, they also collaborated with Suzette Heald and Richard Hawkins in the making of a film on Bagisu initiation (*Imbalu*). In addition, Richard Hawkins made a film in Chile, *La Tirana*, and filmmaker Mark McCarty and anthropologist Paul Hockings produced *The Village*, a film based in Ireland.

7. A fifth film in the Vermont People series had been shot (a portrait of a stained glass window maker), but it has never been edited.

8. In this, we might say his approach paralleled that of Bazin as a film critic. We take up the question of Di Gioia's pedagogy more fully in chapter 5.

9. The use of subjects' own reflections on their lives, in their own voice and in their own terms, can be found in a number of other films made around this time—for example, Tanya Ballantyne's *The Things I Cannot Change* (1966) and Shirley Clarke's *Portrait of Jason* (1967).

10. Colin Young later expressed this problem in the following way: "There is a grandeur to the images that Flaherty produced of everyday life, from *Nanook* on. There's a grandeur about the images that Balikci produced of the Netsilik . . . It's difficult to replicate this in the context of urban society but it's still there. You can only appreciate this grandeur by being witness to it. And properly employed, film can make that possible. I don't mean by making another life exotic, but by knowing how to be close to what is actually happening in that other person's life," Young in Henley 2007, p. 150. But, as Ballantyne discovered in making *The Things I Cannot Change,* this was a risky business. For what she intended to be a sympathetic portrait of her main subject was interpreted very differently by the audiences of the film.

11. See Di Gioia's conversation with Grimshaw, 2006b, p. 49.

12. Ibid., p. 50.

13. There are only two pieces of voice-over in the final film.

14. For details of the series—its aims and objectives, geographical and cultural scope, methods and particular conception of the camera within this inquiry—see Miller's *Faces of Change* study guide. His description is couched in the language of science—evidence, data, testing, observation, replication, scientific method, and so on.

15. Hancock cited in Young 1995, p. 101.

16. Ibid., pp. 108–109.

17. See Grimshaw 2006b, p. 55.

18. Hancock quoted in Young 1995, p. 109.

19. Grimshaw 2006b, pp. 53–54.

20. This emerges in an unusual way, through the changing positions the filmmakers take up with respect to their subject. At times they film him through the frame of the chair, at other times moving alongside him. The process of making a chair and making a film mirror one another.

21. For the film theorist Siegfried Kracauer, the potential of film lay in its ability to make visible aspects of the material world otherwise overlooked, redeeming the world "from its dormant state, its state of virtual nonexistence, by endeavoring to experience it through the camera" (1960, p. 300). See also Aitken 2001.

22. See Hancock 1975 and Young 1995.

23. Hancock 1975, p. 107.

24. Bazin 1972, p. 38.

25. Originally published in *Sight and Sound*, October 1953, pp. 64–69. Reprinted in 1966.

26. Zavattini 1966, p. 225.

27. Here, too, we can locate serious differences between a cinematic project of this kind and the one pursued in the documentaries of Leacock, Drew, and Wiseman.

28. In calling such moments "spectacular" as Zavattini does in his discussion of the film of a woman buying a pair of shoes, he uses the term deliberately to signify a specific quality to be found in the new work. He explains it thus: "Upon this elementary situation [shoe buying] it is possible to build a film. All we have to do is discover and then show all the elements that go to create this adventure, in all their banal "dailiness" and it will become worthy of attention, it will even become spectacular not through its exceptional, but through its *normal* qualities; it will astonish us by showing so many things that happen every day under our eyes, things we have never noticed before." Original emphasis, Zavattini 1966, p. 221.

29. See Grimshaw 2006b, p. 52.

30. Zavattini 1966, p. 220. It is interesting that this term was taken up much later by anthropologists—most notably by Abu-Lughod 1991, p. 157.

31. See MacDougall 2001 and Henley 2007.

32. Grimshaw 2006b.

4. OBSERVATIONAL CINEMA ON THE MOVE

1. See Taylor 1998.

2. Inseparable from MacDougall's practice, and running parallel to it, is a body of writing through which he has explored broader questions concerning film, anthropology, and non-textual forms of inquiry. His collected essays, *Transcultural Cinema* (1998) and *The Corporeal Image* (2006), are an integral part of any evaluation of MacDougall's place within the observational tradition.

3. Originally published in Hockings 1975, it was reprinted with an epilogue in MacDougall 1998.

4. Other projects by David MacDougall have involved the completion of a *set* of films. The individual films exist as stand-alone pieces but they also are related in

important ways with others in the set. As the Turkana trilogy shows (*Lorang's Way, A Wife among Wives, Wedding Camels*), the connections between the different parts are not straightforward or progressive but more diffuse and open-ended. Hence, although this aspect of the Doon School project is not new, it is important not to overlook its significance.

In this chapter we use the term "film" in reference to the Doon School Project, at the same time as we are cognizant of MacDougall's recent shift from celluloid to digital video. Despite important differences between these media, "film" and "filmmaker" continue to be used by MacDougall in describing his own practice. These terms are also used by many others to encompass work made by means of the moving image, whether celluloid or video. In the remainder of the book we also follow this convention.

5. This aspect of observational work may be taken as an exemplification of the distinction between what MacDougall has called "external" and "deep" reflexivity (1998 pp. 89–91).

6. MacDougall 2001, p. 82.

7. Ibid., p. 87.

8. Ibid., p. 87.

9. Although made in collaboration with Judith MacDougall, David MacDougall is credited as the film's director.

10. The shift in our language here reflects David MacDougall's role as the director of *To Live with Herds.*

11. Although the MacDougalls were not the first to use subtitles, the key role played by subtitling in *To Live with Herds* stands as an important reminder of the centrality of sound and speech to observational filmmaking.

12. MacDougall 1998.

13. It involved, MacDougall explained, "bearing witness to the 'event' of the film and making strengths of what most films are at pains to conceal" (1998, p. 134). He continued: "Here the filmmaker acknowledges his or her entry upon the world of the subjects and yet asks them to imprint directly upon the film aspects of their own culture. This should not imply a relaxation of purposefulness, nor should it cause filmmakers to abandon the perspective that an outsider can bring to another culture. But by revealing their role, filmmakers enhance the value of the material as evidence. By entering actively into the world of their subjects, they can provoke a greater flow of information about them. By giving them access to the film, they make possible the corrections, additions, and illuminations that only the subjects' response to the material can elicit. Through such an exchange a film can begin to reflect he ways in which its subjects perceive the world."

14. For Young's co-founder of the Ethnographic Film Program, Walter Goldschmidt (and Mead), the potential of observational cinema lay in its augmentation of scientific data. See Henley 2007.

15. Ibid.

16. MacDougall 1998, pp. 136–138.

17. MacDougall 2006, p. 120.

18. Ibid., pp. 68–69.

19. Ibid.

20. Ibid., p. 125.

21. Ibid.

22. Vaughan 2005, p. 458.

23. Echoing, of course, such classic films as Tony Richardson's *The Loneliness of the Long Distance Runner* and François Truffaut's *The 400 Blows,* Vaughan 2005, p. 460.

24. Nichols 1991, p. 40.

25. In working in this way, MacDougall also reminds us of language and conversation as a social practice. He takes seriously his subjects as intellectuals who work out ideas through dialogue and verbal exchange. This is evident in his first film, *To Live with Herds.* In the Doon School series he shows us that children are not just engaged in *doing* but also in thinking. See also MacDougall 2006, p. 142.

26. Extended scenes are often assumed to be synonymous with long takes. But they are, in fact, distinctive elements within an observational aesthetic and used for different reasons, with different consequences.

27. MacDougall 2006, pp. 133–40.

28. Vaughan 2005, p. 463.

29. Bazin quoted by Sandall 1972, p. 196.

30. MacDougall 2006, pp. 121–122.

31. This work seems, above all, to be in dialogue with MacDougall's essay "The Fate of the Cinematic Subject," in MacDougall 1998. Here MacDougall notes that films are often thought to be "concrete work rather than complex cross-points of thoughts and feelings." He explores the complex and ever-shifting ground between filmmaker, subject, and film—of extension and retraction, the imaginary and the concrete, contact and loss, present / future and past, confinement and escape. Although written before MacDougall made *The Age of Reason,* the essay speaks very directly to it.

32. It is interesting and instructive to consider MacDougall's Doon School Project alongside Wiseman's *High School.* As observational films, they reflect starkly different interpretations of the task.

33. MacDougall in conversation with Ravetz, July 2007.

34. MacDougall 2006, p. 4.

35. MacDougall 1998, p. 65.

5. RETHINKING OBSERVATIONAL CINEMA

1. Grant 1992, pp. 1–2.

2. The literature on observational cinema is extensive. Given our interest in refocusing attention on practice rather than discourse, we have framed our discussion with reference to key critical positions as represented by MacDougall 1998, Nichols 1991, and Fabian 1983.

3. MacDougall 1998; see also a discussion of MacDougall's position in chapter 4.

4. Nichols 1991, pp. 40–41.

5. Nichols 1991, p. 93.

6. The presentation of documentary cinema's history in the form of a "family tree," that is, an evolutionary or progressive narrative often linked to changes in recording technology, has been importantly contested by writers such as Bruzzi 2000.

7. Fabian 1983, p. 106.

8. Okely 2001.

9. Again we draw here on work in the history of science, particularly the approach pursued in the History of Observation Project directed by Lorraine Daston and Fernando Vidal at the Max Planck Institute, Berlin. We also acknowledge, too, the growing interest among anthropologists in questions of situated learning and apprenticeship, particularly Lave and Wenger 1991, Grasseni 2007, and Herzfeld 2004.

10. See preface.

11. Stocking 1983 is an important exception. Also Schaffer 1993.

12. The anthropologists who studied with Di Gioia at the National Film and Television School during the late 1980s and early 1990s—John Baily, Marcus Banks, Anna Grimshaw, Paul Henley, and Felicia Hughes-Freeland—became involved in different ways with the establishment of visual anthropology as a distinctive field of study within Britain, even if their initial focus around ethnographic filmmaking was gradually displaced by a more diverse range of interests and practices (see Banks and Morphy 1997). Henley and Grimshaw were part of the Granada Centre for Visual Anthropology at the University of Manchester that became an important focus for observational work.

13. Dineen 2003, p. 22. After graduating from the National Film and Television School, Dineen quickly established herself as one of Britain's most gifted observational filmmakers. Working largely in television, her films are unique in offering an ethnography of contemporary society. Perhaps most notable is *The Ark,* her five-part series on London Zoo. Committed to the development of long-term projects founded in ethical practice, Dineen has found it increasingly difficult to hold her ground in the face of cheap reality programming that has both appropriated and compromised the techniques of observational filmmaking.

14. This is often misunderstood. Di Gioia's techniques were not about the privileging of image over sound—or reifying the non-verbal. They were an attempt to redress the conventional hierarchy of image and sound in documentary. As we have seen in earlier parts of this book, the observational approach involved a break with the conventions of the word-driven film. This meant, in turn, *not* the marginalization of language but crucially its reinsertion into cultural practice such that it was more comprehensively contextualized. Hence contrary to popular belief, a new importance was given to language—necessitating the filmmaker to attend closely not just to what people said but also to how they said it. Nevertheless this prescription has always presented difficulties for the filmmaker, since it runs counter to the norms and expectations of social exchange.

15. Again this question has long been misunderstood. What is the nature of the interaction between filmmaker and subjects in this kind of work? Di Gioia's techniques fostered an enhanced understanding of inter-subjective communication—one that crucially includes the verbal but at the same time is not exclusively defined by it.

16. MacDougall 2006, p. 7.

17. Kildea quoted in MacDougall 1998, p. 78.

18. Fabian 1983, Cosgrove 1984.

19. In 1996, the British government announced links between BSE (bovine spongiform encephalopathy) and vCJD (variant Creutzfeldt-Jakob disease). Farmers faced new levels of government intervention aimed, for example, at tracing cattle from birth to slaughter.

20. Ravetz's doctoral research into the role of the senses in daily practice connects, in significant ways, with Cristina Grasseni's study of dairy farmers in northern Italy. The latter project was also pursued at the University of Manchester. See Grasseni 2004 and 2007.

21. See also Lave and Wenger 1991, Herzfeld 2004, and Grasseni 2007.

22. Nichols 1991, Loizos 1997.

23. Stoller 1997, also exemplified by the work of Jackson 1996, Ingold 2000, Csordas 1994.

24. MacDougall 1998, p. 63.

25. Jackson 1996, p. 12.

26. Ingold 2000, p. 25. It is somewhat ironic that Ingold articulated his new agenda for anthropology while based at the University of Manchester, since the Granada Centre for Visual Anthropology, one of the key sites for observational filmmaking, was located there too. It is an unfortunate reflection of the deep, and ultimately spurious, divide between "textual" and "visual" anthropologies that the shared creative possibilities raised by this conjunction of interests were not fully grasped at the time. There were some exceptions—Ravetz's work, for example—but on the whole the two projects were pursued independently.

27. Ingold 2000, pp. 4–5.

28. Ingold 2000, pp. 36–37.

29. Jackson 1996.

30. Although our focus here is anthropology, we have already noted that film studies has also seen a resurgence of phenomenologically oriented work—for example, Sobchack 1992 and Marks 2000 and 2002.

31. Stoller 1997 and MacDougall 1998 and 2006 have been especially prominent in the call for new anthropological techniques and forms.

32. Taussig 1993, p. 44.

33. Taussig 1993, p. 21.

34. Taussig 1993, p. 26, original emphasis.

35. Taussig 1993, pp. 45–47.

36. Benjamin's writing on the resurgence of the mimetic faculty within modernity now also forms an important part of the discourse of contemporary film studies. Not surprisingly, his interest in the potential of mimetic technologies to reawaken a sensuous connection between self and the world has been taken up by certain scholars as a counterweight to the semiotic and psychoanalytical frameworks that have long dominated the field. Benjamin's influence has been especially manifest in the work of Marks 2000, who has drawn significantly on his notion of the mimetic in her investigation of the distinctive qualities of intercultural cinema. In particular, it has offered her a way of thinking about what she has called "haptic" or tactile epistemologies; that is, ways of knowing located in the body and senses that have been lost within conventional hierarchies of knowledge and theories of representation. Careful to avoid both mysticism and primitivism, Marks argues that at the heart of cinematic engagement lies mimesis, activating a complex tactile encounter that unfolds through the process of film viewing.

37. Taussig 1993, p. 8. There are important overlaps here with the cinematic project pursued by Jean Rouch; see Stoller 1992. Of course, the question of power remains central to an anthropology pursued in this way. Herzfeld's discussions of power, hierarchy, and knowledge in the context of apprenticeship models of social learning are important here; see Herzfeld 2004 and 2007.

38. "Our meetings with artworks are embedded in the meanings and conventions we bring to encounters with other persons, and all non-monumental art is a means of figuration in this sense. Yet, specifically, this meeting with an artwork that is in itself and for itself is analogous to that free ethical stance in which persons are encountered in themselves and for themselves—without prior determination of outcome or goal." Stewart 2005, p. 18.

39. Cited in Taussig 1993, p. 2.

40. Taussig 1993, p. 25.

6. TOWARD AN EXPERIMENTAL ANTHROPOLOGY

1. In this chapter we continue to focus on the observational sensibility as expressed and developed through film. Of course this medium is not the only one through which this particular kind of phenomenological anthropology might be pursued, and the examples chosen represent only a tiny sample of a much broader range of experimental work that is pertinent to anthropology. Many of the questions we have raised here might also be explored through the work of other contemporary filmmakers such as Leonard Retel Helmrich, Jana Ševčíková, and Sergei Dvortsevoy. Moreover, they have served to stimulate analogous forms of experimentation and innovation in textual anthropology, creating new hybrid forms that include poetry, the photo-text, and so on. Notable examples include: Michael Jackson's *Rainshadow* (1988) and *Dead Reckoning* (2006); Michael Taussig's *My Cocaine Museum* (2004); Kirin Naryan's *My Family and Other Saints* (2007); Paul Stoller's *Gallery Bundu* (2005) and *Stranger in the Village of the Sick* (2004); and Ruth Behar's *An Island Called Home* (2007).

2. For a different discussion of the experimental impulse in ethnographic work, see Russell 1999.

3. MacDougall 1998, p. 63.

4. Our interest in possible convergences between art and anthropology is part of a broader move among practitioners in both of these fields to establish terms for a new dialogue—as evidenced, for example, in the high-profile public events held at Tate Modern in London (Fieldworks, 2003) and the Carpenter Center at Harvard University (Setting Up the Document, 2004). See also Schneider and Wright 2006 and Schneider 2008.

5. Loizos 1997, pp. 83–84

6. Taussig 1993; see our fuller discussion in chapter 5.

7. We have noted elsewhere that this conceptual turn mirrors the one found in the discipline of anthropology—namely, there has been a shift away from an exclusive reliance on discursive or textual frames of reference and an interest in exploring other perspectives that might more effectively encompass affect, embodied experience, and sensory knowledge; see Sobchack 1992, Marks 2000 and 2002.

8. In particular, see Deleuze 1989, Jayamanne 2001, Rohdie 1995.

9. Deleuze 1989, p. 1. See also Rohdie 1995, p. 84, and Jayamanne 2001, pp. 135–137.

10. Rohdie 1995, p. 84.

11. Bazin 1972, p. 26.

12. Bazin 1967, pp. 25–27.

13. In their commitment to a Bazinian cinema, the observational filmmakers approached the act of filming as analytical work in its own right—and not merely a preliminary to editing. Hence, as our examples have revealed, it does not involve a working through of materials or "data" previously obtained. It is comprised of countless decisions made in the moment of filming itself. The finished film becomes an artifact of this unfolding process.

14. For example, Henley 2004.

15. For a discussion of *Athene*, see chapter 5.

16. After six years when watching again the documentary I had made on the old people's home I was very annoyed by how I had incorporated various characters and so many things in it to communicate the sense of loneliness in the institution. Marika, just by herself, expressed this feeling

with nothing more but her presence in her little room. So I just sat in the cutting room for a week and cut out everybody else. I didn't care how long the film would be as long as it had a clear form. While I was editing it I kept thinking of it as a monologue in a modern play, treating it more as fiction than documentary. I cut out any information related to Marika's personal history—it wasn't a rational decision—but it seemed the right thing to do. I believe that this lack of facts and this anonymity gave Marika more strength as a character. (Stefani, personal communication)

17. From these experiments, a number of small films were shot and edited by students at the Rishi Valley School. They may be considered as companion pieces to MacDougall's own film, *SchoolScapes*.

18. Krishnamurti 1969, p. 16.

19. *Sheep Rushes* represents an interesting break with earlier work by Barbash and Castaing-Taylor, especially their film *In and Out of Africa*, that depended heavily on interview and montage editing. In his review of *In and Out of Africa*, Nichols particularly highlighted the filmmakers' use of "collage-like juxtapositions." Understanding it as appropriate to their particular research interests (the traffic in African art), he also takes it as evidence of an important break with forms of ethnographic realism. It is, he suggests following Marcus, an expression of a "modernist sensibility." Nichols 1997, p. 819.

20. Jayamanne 2001, pp. 136–137.

21. Deleuze 1989, pp. 2–7. Of course, there are interesting echoes here of Rouch's project.

22. Schneider 2008.

23. See, for example, Marcus and Myers 1995, Morphy and Perkins 2006, Schneider and Wright 2006.

24. Margaret Mead's famous outburst during her debate with Gregory Bateson exemplifies this position (Bateson and Mead 1977). The strength of feeling provoked by Robert Gardner is also evidence of the uneasiness that surrounds art and anthropology. His film *Forest of Bliss* is perhaps one of the most intensely debated works, sharply dividing its anthropological commentators. For different responses to the film, see Chopra 1989, Moore 1988, Östör 1989, Parry 1988, and Ruby 2000. A different perspective is offered by Clifford in his exploration of art and anthropology in interwar Paris, 1988. Gell's book *Art and Agency* is also much cited in discussions of these kinds. In recognizing the strength of feeling provoked by "art," Gell called for anthropologists to develop what he called "methodological philistinism." See Gell 1992, p. 42, and 1998.

25. Foster 1995. Originally published as a short essay in Marcus and Myers 1995, it was subsequently expanded and included in Foster 1996.

26. The so-called "ethnographic turn" was a small part of broader changes in contemporary art. Most notably, it was the movement from "studio to situation" that significantly changed the relationship between anthropology and art. From the creation of collaborative artworks involving members of the public to the appropriation of areas once considered the domain of other professions (e.g., science, health, urban planning), contemporary artists, like anthropologists, began to take social situations as their subjects. As a consequence, artists increasingly developed techniques that resembled those used by the anthropologist. They often embarked on fieldwork; they self-consciously used "documentary" approaches in video and sound recording; they practiced participant-observation. This area of contemporary art involved a reorientation on the part of the artist, creating the conditions in which vernacular or lay understandings could give

way to something less familiar, more surprising. The growing interest in social worlds—indeed, in ethnographic subjects—meant that artists found themselves sharing many of the same concerns as their anthropological counterparts.

27. Schneider and Wright 2006, also Schneider 2008.

28. See Ingold 2008, Gunn forthcoming.

29. Making work that "looks like art" is a criticism sometimes leveled by artists and art tutors at those who do not possess what is considered a coherent art practice. According to this view, an artist is expected to develop a distinctive approach toward perception, conception, technique, and subject matter. To be judged a competent artist depends not only on the production of work but also on the recognition of a coherent practice. See Ravetz 2007.

30. "In the interstices of everyday life, whenever we realize our practical and imaginative capacity to transform the events that befall us into scenarios of our own choosing." Jackson 2005, p. xxii.

31. Clifford and Marcus 1986.

32. See Ginsburg 1998 and Wright 1998.

33. Marcus 1990, Loizos 1997.

34. The term "art" is, of course, problematic given its historical and cultural connotations. In employing it here, we do not wish to suggest a universal concept. We use it to identify questions of perception and the particular shaping of perception that is often known as "art" but has much broader cross-cultural resonance. For example, Morphy's discussion of Aboriginal painting has a particular perceptual experience at its center, even though it is conceptualized in different cultural terms (Morphy 1989).

35. MacDougall 1998, p. 63.

36. MacDougall 2006, p. 6.

37. "My interest [here] is in the ways people effectively redistribute being within the most intimate spaces of their lives, and imaginatively, practically, and socially negotiate new relationships between external constraints and inner potentialities . . . Though revolutions may not be born of such small gestures toward opening up a space in which to live, life consists of them. This is why anthropology that simply describes categorical modes of being—male/female, elder/younger, oppressor/oppressed—fails to do justice to those miniscule details of everyday life that determine how a person's lot is actually lived." Jackson 2005, pp. 188–189.

FILMOGRAPHY

The Age of Reason. 2004. David MacDougall. Centre for Cross-Cultural Research. Australian National University. Australia. 87 mins.

An Argument about a Marriage. 1969. John Marshall. Film Study Center. Harvard University. USA 18 mins.

The Ark. 1993. Molly Dineen. BBC Television. Great Britain. 239 mins.

Athene. 1993. Eva Stefani. National Film and Television School. Great Britain. 40 mins.

Bicycle Thief (Ladri di Biciclette). 1948. Vittorio de Sica. PDS/ENIC. Italy. 90 mins.

Bitter Melons. 1971. John Marshall. Film Study Center, Harvard University. USA. 30 mins.

The Box. 2004. Eva Stefani, Greece, 11 mins.

The Bracewells. 2000. Amanda Ravetz. The Granada Centre for Visual Anthropology, University of Manchester. Great Britain. 49 mins.

Bread Day. 1998. Sergei Dvortsevoy. Russia. 55 mins.

Celso and Cora: A Manila Story. 1983. Gary Kildea. Australia. 109 mins.

Character Formation in Different Cultures Series (*Childhood Rivalry in Bali and New Guinea,* 17 mins.; *First Days in the Life of a New Guinea Baby,* 15 mins.; *A Balinese Family,* 20 mins.; *Karba's First Years,* 20 mins.; *Bathing Babies in Three Cultures,* 13 mins.). 1952. Gregory Bateson and Margaret Mead. Institute for Intercultural Studies. USA.

Chester Grimes. 1972. Herbert Di Gioia and David Hancock. The Vermont Center for Cultural Studies Inc. USA. 50 mins.

Chronique d'un été (Chronicle of a Summer). 1960. Jean Rouch and Edgar Morin. Argos Films. France. 90 mins.

Citizen Kane. 1941. Orson Welles. RKO Radio Pictures. USA. 119 mins.

Crisis: Behind a Presidential Commitment. 1962. Drew Associates. ABC News. USA. 53 mins.

Dead Birds. 1963. Robert Gardner. Film Study Center, Harvard University. USA. 84 mins.

Don't Look Back. 1967. D. A. Pennebaker. Docurama. USA. 96 mins.

Doon School Chronicles. 2000. David MacDougall. Centre for Cross-Cultural Research. Australian National University. Australia. 140 mins.

Duwayne Masure, 1971. Herb Di Gioia and David Hancock. University of California at Los Angeles Motion Pictures Division, MFA Thesis Film. USA. 40 mins.

The Eye of the Day. 2001. Leonard Retel Helmrich. The Netherlands. 94 mins.

Familiar Places. 1980. David MacDougall. Australian Institute of Aboriginal Studies. Australia. 53 mins.

Forest of Bliss. 1985. Robert Gardner. Film Study Center, Harvard University. USA. 91 mins.

The 400 Blows (Les quatre cents coup). 1959. François Truffaut. Films du Carrosse/ SEDIF. France. 94 mins.

Germany Year Zero (Germania, anno zero). 1947. Roberto Rossellini. Tevere/Sadfilm. Italy. 78 mins.

Goshogaoka. 1997. Sharon Lockhart. USA. 63 mins.

Grey Gardens. 1976. Albert and David Maysles. Portrait Films. USA. 95 mins.

Happy Mother's Day. 1963. Leacock-Pennebaker Inc. USA. 26 mins.

High School. 1968. Frederick Wiseman. Osti Films. USA. 75 mins.

The Hunters. 1958. John Marshall. Film Study Center, Harvard University. USA. 72 mins.

Imbalu: Ritual of Manhood of the Gisu of Uganda. 1988. Richard Hawkins. University of California at Los Angeles. USA. 70 mins.

In and Out of Africa. 1992. Ilisa Barbash and Lucien Taylor. University of California, Extension Center for Media and Independent Learning. USA. 59 mins.

Jaguar. 1954/1966. Jean Rouch. Les Films de la Pléiades. France. 93 mins.

Jakub. 1992. Jana Ševčíková. Czech Republic. 46 mins.

Karam in Jaipur. 2001. David MacDougall. Centre for Cross-Cultural Research. Australian National University. Australia. 54 mins.

Kenya Boran. 1974. James Blue and David MacDougall. American Universities Field Staff. USA. 66 mins.

The Loneliness of the Long Distance Runner. 1962. Tony Richardson. Woodfall Films. Great Britain. 103 mins.

Lorang's Way. 1979. David MacDougall and Judith MacDougall. Fieldwork Films. Australia. 70 mins.

Les Maîtres Fous. 1954. Jean Rouch. Les Films de la Pléiades. France. 29 mins.

Moi, Un Noir. 1957. Jean Rouch. Les Films de la Pléiades. France. 70 mins.

Mr. Wade. 2003. Anna Grimshaw. The Granada Centre for Visual Anthropology, University of Manchester. Great Britain. 63 mins.

Naim and Jabar. 1974. David Hancock and Herb Di Gioia. American Universities Field Staff. USA. 50 mins.

The New Boys. 2003. David MacDougall. Centre for Cross-Cultural Research. Australian National University. Australia. 100 mins.

The Nuer. 1971. Robert Gardner, Hilary Harris, and George Breidenbach. Film Study Center, Harvard University. USA. 73 mins.

Old Believers. 2001. Jana Ševčíková. Czech Republic. 46 mins.

Paisà. 1946. Roberto Rossellini. OFI. Italy. 115 mins.

Peter Murray. 1975. David Hancock and Herb Di Gioia. The Vermont Center for Cultural Studies Inc. USA. 50 mins.

Peter and Jane Flint. 1975. David Hancock and Herh Di Gioia. The Vermont Center for Cultural Studies Inc. USA. 120 mins.

Photo Wallahs. 1991. David MacDougall and Judith MacDougall. Fieldwork Films. Australia. 59 mins.

Piemule. 1984. Jana Ševčíková. Czech Republic. 46 mins.

Portrait of Jason. 1967. Shirley Clarke. Filmmakers Co-Operative. USA. 105 mins.

Primary. 1960. Drew Associates. Time-Life Broadcast. USA. 50 mins.

Rivers of Sand. 1975. Robert Gardner (with George Breidenbach and Hilary Harris). Film Study Center, Harvard University. USA. 84 mins.

Rome, Open City (Roma, città aperta). 1945. Roberto Rossellini. Excelsa. Italy. 105 mins.

Room to Live. 1992. Simon Everson and Marian Stoica. National Film and Television School. Great Britain. 50 mins.

Salesman. 1968. Albert and David Maysles. Maysles Films Inc. USA. 91 mins.

SchoolScapes. 2007. David MacDougall. CCR Media Works/Fieldwork Films. Australia. 77 mins.

Sheep Rushes (*Hell Roaring Creek*, 19 mins.; *The High Trail*, 5 mins.; *Fine and Coarse*, 9 mins.). 2007. Ilisa Barbash and Lucien Castaing-Taylor. USA.

Song of Ceylon. 1934. Basil Wright. Ceylon Tea Propaganda Board/GPO Film Unit. Great Britain. 40 mins.

Sweetgrass. 2008. Ilisa Barbash and Lucien Castaing-Taylor. Film Study Center, Harvard University. USA. 115 mins.

Teatro Amazonas. 1999. Sharon Lockhart. USA. 38 mins.

Tempus de Baristas. 1993. David MacDougall. Instituto Superiore Regionale Etnografico/Fieldwork Films/BBC Television. Italy, Australia, Great Britain. 100 mins.

La terra trema: episodio del mare. 1948. Luciano Visconti. Universalia. Italy. 160 mins.

The Things I Cannot Change. 1966. Tanya Ballantyne. National Film Board of Canada. Canada. 58 mins.

Titicut Follies. 1967. Frederick Wiseman. Bridgewater Film Co. Inc. USA. 89 mins.

To Live with Herds. 1972. David MacDougall. University of California at Los Angeles. USA. 70 mins.

Umberto D. 1952. Vittorio de Sica. Dear Films. Italy. 89 mins.

The Village. Mark McCarty. 1969. Ethnographic Film Program, University of California. USA. 70 mins.

Voyage to Italy (Viaggio in Italia). 1953. Roberto Rossellini. Sveva Films. Italy. 80 mins.

The Wedding Camels. 1977. David MacDougall and Judith MacDougall. Rice University Media Center/Fieldwork Films. USA/Australia. 108 mins.

A Wife among Wives. 1981. David MacDougall and Judith MacDougall. Rice University Media Center/Fieldwork Films. USA/Australia. 75 mins.

With Morning Hearts. 2001. David MacDougall. Centre for Cross-Cultural Research. Australian National University. Australia. 110 mins.

FILM DISTRIBUTION

The distribution details of the films that we discuss at length in this book are as follows: *Athene* and *Room to Live* are available from the National Film and Television School (www.nftsfilm-tv.ac.uk). *The Box* is distributed by the filmmaker, Eva Stefani (evastefani @gmail.com). David MacDougall's Doon School series is available from Berkeley Media (www.berkeleymedia.com); so, too, are the later Rishi Valley films including *SchoolScapes*. *Primary* (Drew Associates, drewassociates.net) and *Salesman* (Albert and David Maysles, www.mayslesfilms.com) have been issued on DVD by New Video Group and Criterion, respectively. *Titicut Follies* may be purchased from Zipporah Films (www .zipporah.com). *Naim and Jabar* (Di Gioia and Hancock) is distributed by Documentary Educational Resources (www.der.org). Copies of the Vermont films by Di Gioia and Hancock are not currently available for distribution. For availability of *Sheep Rushes,* contact Lucien Castaing-Taylor (lucien_castaing-taylor@harvard.edu).

BIBLIOGRAPHY

Abu-Lughod, Lila. 1991. "Writing Against Culture." In Richard G. Fox, ed., *Recapturing Anthropology: Working in the Present*. Santa Fe, N.M.: School of American Research, 137–162.

Aitken, Ian. 2001 *European Film Theory and Cinema: A Critical Introduction*. Edinburgh: Edinburgh University Press.

Anderson, Carolyn, and Thomas W. Benson. 1991. *Documentary Dilemmas: Frederick Wiseman's Titicut Follies*. Carbondale: Southern Illinois University Press.

Andrew, Dudley. 1990. *André Bazin*. New York: Columbia University Press.

Atkins, Thomas R. 1976. *Frederick Wiseman*. New York: Monarch Press.

Banks, Marcus. 2001. *Visual Methods in Social Research*. London: Sage.

Banks, Marcus, and Howard Morphy, eds. 1997. *Rethinking Visual Anthropology*. New Haven, Conn.: Yale University Press.

Bateson, Gregory, and Margaret Mead. 1977. "Margaret Mead and Gregory Bateson on the Use of the Camera in Anthropology." *Studies in the Anthropology of Visual Communication* 4(2): 78–80.

Bazin, André. 1967. *What Is Cinema?* Vol. 1, edited by Hugh Gray. Berkeley: University of California Press.

———. 1972. *What Is Cinema?* Vol. 2, edited by Hugh Gray. Berkeley: University of California Press.

Bazin, André, and Francois Truffaut. 1992. *Orson Welles: A Critical View*. Rev. ed. London: Acrobat Books.

Behar, Ruth. 2007. *An Island Called Home*. New Brunswick, N.J.: Rutgers University Press.

Ben Ghiat, Ruth. 2000. "The Fascist War Trilogy." In David Forgacs, Sarah Lutton, and Geoffrey Nowell-Smith, eds., *Roberto Rossellini: Magician of the Real*. London: British Film Institute, 20–35.

Bondanella, Peter. 1990. *Italian Cinema: From Neo-realism to the Present*. New York: Continuum.

Bruzzi, Stella. 2000. *New Documentary: A Critical Introduction*. London and New York: Routledge.

Chopra, Radikha. 1989. "Robert Gardner's *Forest of Bliss*: A review." *Society for Visual Anthropology Newsletter* 5(1) (Spring): 2–3.

Clifford, James. 1988. *The Predicament of Culture*. Cambridge, Mass.: Harvard University Press.

Clifford, James, and George Marcus, eds. 1986. *Writing Culture: The Poetics and Politics of Ethnography*. Berkeley: University of California Press.

Cosgrove, Denis E. 1984. *Social Formation and Symbolic Landscape*. London: Croom Helm.

Crary, Jonathan. 1990. *Techniques of the Observer: On Vision and Modernity in the Nineteenth Century*. Cambridge, Mass.: MIT Press.

Csordas, Thomas, ed. 1994. *Embodiment and Experience: The Existential Ground of Culture and Self*. Cambridge: Cambridge University Press.

Deleuze, Gilles. 1986. *Cinema 1: The Movement-Image*. Translated by Hugh Tomlinson and Barbara Habberjam. Minneapolis: University of Minnesota Press.

———. 1989. *Cinema 2: The Time-Image*. Translated by Hugh Tomlinson and Robert Galeta. Minneapolis: University of Minnesota Press.

Dineen, Molly. 2003. Interview. In David A. Goldsmith, ed., *The Documentary Makers: Interviews with 15 of the Best in the Business*. Crans-Près-Céligny, Switzerland: RotoVision, 22–31.

Dixon, Wheeler Winston. 2003. "An Interview with Albert Maysles." *Quarterly Review of Film and Video* 20: 177–192.

Fabian, Johannes. 1983. *Time and the Other: How Anthropology Makes Its Other*. New York: Columbia University Press.

Feld, Steven, ed. 2003. *Ciné-ethnography: Jean Rouch*. Minneapolis: University of Minnesota Press.

Forgacs, David. 2008. *Rome, Open City (Roma, città aperta)*. London: BFI Film Classics.

Forgacs, David, Sarah Lutton, and Geoffrey Nowell-Smith, eds. 2000. *Roberto Rossellini: Magician of the Real*. London: British Film Institute.

Foster, Hal. 1995. "The Artist as Ethnographer." In George Marcus and Fred Myers, eds., *The Traffic in Culture: Refiguring Art and Anthropology*. Berkeley: University of California Press, 302–309.

———. 1996. *The Return of the Real: The Avant-Garde at the End of the Century*. Cambridge, Mass.: MIT Press.

Gell, Alfred. 1992. "The Technology of Enchantment and the Enchantment of Technology." In Jeremy Coote and Anthony Shelton, eds., *Anthropology, Art and Aesthetics*. Oxford: Oxford University Press, 40–66.

———. 1998. *Art and Agency: An Anthropological Theory*. Oxford: Oxford University Press.

Ginsburg, Faye. 1998. "Institutionalizing the Unruly: Charting a Future for Visual Anthropology." *Ethnos* 63(2): 173–196.

Grant, Barry Keith. 1992. *Voyages of Discovery: The Cinema of Frederick Wiseman*. Urbana: University of Illinois Press.

———. 1998. "Ethnography in the First Person: Frederick Wiseman's *Titicut Follies*." In Barry Keith Grant and Jeanette Sloniowski, eds., *Documenting the Documentary: Close Readings of Documentary Film and Video*. Detroit, Mich.: Wayne State University Press, 238–253.

Grasseni, Cristina. 2004. "Video and Ethnographic Knowledge: Skilled Vision in the Practice of Breeding." In Ana Isabel Alfonso, László Kürti, and Sarah Pink, eds.,

Working Images: Methods and Media in Ethnographic Research. London: Routledge, 15–30.

———, ed. 2007. *Skilled Visions: Between Apprenticeship and Standards*. New York: Berghahn Books.

Grimshaw, Anna. 1992. *Servants of the Buddha: Winter in a Himalayan Convent*. London: Open Letters Press.

———. 2001. *The Ethnographer's Eye: Ways of Seeing in Modern Anthropology*. Cambridge: Cambridge University Press.

———. 2006a. "A Case Study in Early Observational Cinema: The Work of Herb Di Gioia and David Hancock." *Visual Anthropology Review* 22(1): 34–45.

———. 2006b. "Conversations with Anthropological Filmmakers: Herb Di Gioia." *Visual Anthropology Review* 22(1): 45–59.

Grimshaw, Anna, and Nikos Papastergiadis, eds. 1995. *Conversations with Anthropological Filmmakers: David MacDougall*. Cambridge: Prickly Pear Pamphlets.

Grimshaw, Anna, and Amanda Ravetz. 2005. *Visualising Anthropology: Experiments in Image-Based Practice*. Bristol: Intellect Books.

———. Forthcoming. "Rethinking Observational Cinema." *Journal of the Royal Anthropological Institute*, n.s.

Gunn, Wendy, ed. Forthcoming. *Fieldnotes and Sketchbooks: Challenging the Boundaries between Descriptions and Processes of Describing*. Frankfurt: Peter Lang.

Hall, Jeanne. 1991. "Realism as a Style in Cinéma Vérité: A Critical Analysis of *Primary*." *Cinema Journal* 30(4): 24–50.

Hancock, David. 1975. "Disappearing World: Anthropology on Television." *Sight and Sound* 44(1–4): 103–107.

Henley, Paul. 2004. "Putting Film to Work: Observational Cinema as Practical Ethnography." In Ana Isabel Alfonso, László Kürti, and Sarah Pink, eds., *Working Images: Methods and Media in Ethnographic Research*. London: Routledge, 109–130.

———. 2007. "The Origins of Observational Cinema: Conversations with Colin Young." In Beate Engelbrecht, ed., *Memories of the Origins of Visual Anthropology*. Frankfurt: Peter Lang, 139–161.

Herzfeld, Michael. 2004. *The Body Impolitic: Artisans and Artifice in the Global Hierarchy of Value*. Chicago: University of Chicago Press.

———. 2007. "Deskilling, Dumbing Down and the Auditing of Knowledge in the Practical Mastery of Artisans and Academics: An Ethnographer's Response to a Global Problem." In Mark Harris, ed., *Ways of Knowing: New Approaches in the Anthropology of Knowledge and Learning*. Oxford: Berghahn, 91–112.

Hockings, Paul, ed. 1975. *Principles of Visual Anthropology*. Berlin: Mouton de Gruyter.

———, ed. 1995. *Principles of Visual Anthropology*. 2nd ed. Berlin: Mouton de Gruyter.

Ingold, Tim. 2000. *The Perception of the Environment: Essays on Livelihood, Dwelling and Skill*. London: Routledge.

———. 2008. "Anthropology Is Not Ethnography." *Proceedings of the British Academy* 154: 69–92.

Ingold, Tim, with Ray Lucas. 2007. "The 4 A's (Anthropology, Archaeology, Art and

Architecture): Reflections on a Teaching and Learning Experience." In Mark Harris, ed., *Ways of Knowing: New Approaches in the Anthropology of Experience and Learning*. Oxford: Berghahn, 287–305.

Jackson, Michael. 1988. *Rainshadow*. Dunedin: McIndoe.

———. 1994. *Pieces of Music*. Auckland: Random House.

———. 1996. *Things As They Are: New Directions in Phenomenological Anthropology*. Bloomington: Indiana University Press.

———. 2005. *Existential Anthropology: Events, Exigencies and Effects*. New York: Berghahn.

———. 2006. *Dead Reckoning*. Auckland: Auckland University Press.

Jayamanne, Laleen. 2001. *Toward Cinema and Its Double: Cross Cultural Mimesis*. Bloomington: Indiana University Press.

Kracauer, Siegfried. 1960. *Theory of Film: The Redemption of Physical Reality*. London: Oxford University Press.

Krishnamurti, J. 1969. *Freedom from the Known*. Edited by Mary Lutyens. London: Gollancz.

Lave, Jean, and Etienne Wenger. 1991. *Situated Learning: Legitimate Peripheral Participation*. Cambridge: Cambridge University Press.

Levin, G. Roy. 1971. *Documentary Explorations: 15 Interviews with Film Makers*. New York: Doubleday.

Loizos, Peter. 1997. "First Exits from Observational Realism: Narrative Experiments in Recent Ethnographic Film." In Marcus Banks and Howard Morphy, eds., *Rethinking Visual Anthropology*. New Haven, Conn.: Yale University Press, 81–104.

Lucia, Cynthia. 1994. "Revisiting High School: An Interview with Frederick Wiseman." *Cineaste* 20(4): 5–11.

MacDougall, David. 1997. "The Visual in Anthropology." In Marcus Banks and Howard Morphy, eds., *Rethinking Visual Anthropology*. New Haven, Conn.: Yale University Press, 276–295.

———. 1998. *Transcultural Cinema*. Princeton, N.J.: Princeton University Press.

———. 2001. "Colin Young, Ethnographic Film and the Film Culture of the 1960s." *Visual Anthropology Review* 17(2): 81–88.

———. 2006. *The Corporeal Image: Film, Ethnography and the Senses*. Princeton, N.J.: Princeton University Press.

Mamber, Stephen. 1974. *Cinema Verite in America: Studies in Uncontrolled Documentary*. Cambridge, Mass.: MIT Press.

Marcus, George. 1990. "The Modernist Sensibility in Recent Ethnographic Writing and the Cinematic Metaphor of Montage." *Visual Anthropology Review* 6(1): 2–12.

Marcus, George, and Fred Myers, eds. 1995. *The Traffic in Culture: Refiguring Art and Anthropology*. Berkeley: University of California Press.

Marcus, Millicent. 1986. *Italian Film in the Light of Neorealism*. Princeton, N.J.: Princeton University Press.

Margulies, Ivone, ed. 2003. *Rites of Realism: Essays on Corporeal Cinema*. Durham, N.C.: Duke University Press.

Marks, Laura. 2000. *The Skin of the Film: Intercultural Cinema, Embodiment and the Senses.* Durham, N.C.: Duke University Press.

———. 2002. *Touch: A Sensuous Theory and Multisensory Media.* Minneapolis: University of Minnesota Press.

Miller, Norman N. n.d. *Faces of Change Series: A Study Guide.* American Universities Field Staff/Cambridge, Mass.: Documentary Educational Resources.

Moore, Alexander. 1988. "The Limits of Imagist Documentary: A Review of Robert Gardner's *Forest of Bliss.*" *Society for Visual Anthropology Newsletter* 4(2): 1–3.

Morphy, Howard. 1989. "From Dull to Brilliant: The Aesthetics of Spiritual Power among the Yolngu." *Man,* n.s., 24(1): 21–40.

Morphy, Howard, and Morgan Perkins, eds. 2006. *The Anthropology of Art: A Reader.* Oxford: Blackwell.

Narayan, Kirin. 2007. *My Family and Other Saints.* Chicago: University of Chicago Press.

Nichols, Bill. 1978. "Fred Wiseman's Documentaries: Theory and Structure." *Film Quarterly* 31(3) (Spring): 15–28.

———. 1981. *Ideology and Image.* Bloomington: Indiana University Press.

———. 1988. "The Voice of Documentary." In Alan Rosenthal, ed., *New Challenges for Documentary.* Berkeley: University of California Press, 48–63.

———. 1991. *Representing Reality: Issues and Concepts in Documentary.* Bloomington: Indiana University Press.

———. 1997. "Dislocating Ethnographic Film: In and Out of Africa and Issues of Cultural Representation." *American Anthropologist* 99(4) (December): 810–824.

Nowell-Smith, Geoffrey. 2000. "North and South, East and West: Rossellini and Politics." In David Forgacs, Sarah Lutton, and Geoffrey Nowell-Smith, eds., *Roberto Rossellini: Magician of the Real.* London: British Film Institute, 7–19.

O'Connell, P. J. 1992. *Robert Drew and the Development of Cinema Verite in America.* Carbondale: Southern Illinois University Press.

Okely, Judith 2001. "Visualism and Landscape: Looking and Seeing in Normandy." *Ethnos* 66(1): 99–120.

Östör, Ákos. 1989. "Is That What *Forest of Bliss* Is All About? A Response." *Society for Visual Anthropology Newsletter* 5(1) (Spring): 4–8.

Parry, Jonathan. 1988. "A Comment on Robert Gardner's *Forest of Bliss.*" *Society for Visual Anthropology Newsletter* 4(2) (Fall): 4–7.

Ravetz, Amanda. 2001. "Vision, Knowledge and the Invention of Place in an English Town." Unpublished Ph.D. thesis, University of Manchester.

———. 2007. "A Weight of Meaninglessness about Which There Is Nothing Insignificant: Abjection and Knowing in an Art School and on a Housing Estate." In Mark Harris, ed., *Ways of Knowing? New Anthropological Approaches to Method, Learning and Knowledge.* Oxford: Berghahn, 266–286.

Rohdie, Sam. 1995. *The Passion of Pier Paolo Pasolini.* London: British Film Institute; Bloomington: Indiana University Press.

Rosenthal, Alan, ed. 1971. "*Salesman:* Albert Maysles." In Alan Rosenthal, ed., *The New*

Documentary in Action: A Casebook in Film Making. Berkeley: University of California Press, 76–91.

Rothman, William. 1996. *Documentary Film Classics.* Cambridge: Cambridge University Press.

Ruby, Jay. 1993. *The Cinema of John Marshall.* London: Routledge.

———. 2000. *Picturing Culture: Explorations of Film and Anthropology.* Chicago: Chicago University Press.

Russell, Catherine. 1999. *Experimental Ethnography: The Work of Film in the Age of Video.* Durham, N.C.: Duke University Press.

Sandall, Roger. 1972. "Observation and Identity." *Sight and Sound* 41(4): 192–196.

Saunders, Dave. 2007. *Direct Cinema: Observational Documentary and the Politics of the Sixties.* London: Wallflower Press.

Schaffer, Simon. 1993. *From Physics to Anthropology—and Back Again.* Cambridge: Prickly Pear Pamphlets.

Schneider, Arnd. 2008. "Three Modes of Experimentation with Art and Anthropology." *Journal of the Royal Anthropological Institute,* n.s., 14: 171–194.

Schneider, Arnd, and Chris Wright, eds. 2006. *Contemporary Art and Anthropology.* Oxford: Berg.

Sobchack, Vivian. 1992. *The Address of the Eye: A Phenomenology of Film Experience.* Princeton, N.J.: Princeton University Press.

Stewart, Susan. 2005. *The Open Studio: Essays on Art and Aesthetics.* Chicago: University of Chicago Press.

Stocking, George. 1983. *Observers Observed: Essays on Ethnographic Fieldwork.* Madison: University of Wisconsin Press.

Stoller, Paul. 1992. *The Cinematic Griot: The Ethnography of Jean Rouch.* Chicago: University of Chicago Press.

———. 1997. *Sensuous Scholarship.* Philadelphia: University of Pennsylvania Press.

———. 2004. *Stranger in the Village of the Sick: A Memoir of Cancer, Sorcery and Healing.* Boston: Beacon Press.

———. 2005. *Gallery Bundu: A Story about an African Past.* Chicago: University of Chicago Press.

———. 2008. *The Power of the Between: An Anthropological Odyssey.* Chicago: University of Chicago Press.

Taussig, Michael. 1993. *Mimesis and Alterity: A Particular History of the Senses.* New York: Routledge.

———. 2004. *My Cocaine Museum.* Chicago: University of Chicago Press.

Taylor, Lucien. 1998. Introduction. In David MacDougall, *Transcultural Cinema.* Princeton, N.J.: Princeton University Press, 3–21.

Vaughan, Dai. 2005. "The Doon School Project." *Visual Anthropology* 18: 457–464.

Wagstaff, Christopher. 2000. "Rossellini and Neo-realism." In David Forgacs, Sarah Lutton, and Geoffrey Nowell-Smith, eds., *Roberto Rossellini: Magician of the Real.* London: British Film Institute, 36–49.

Waugh, Thomas. 1985. "Beyond *Vérité:* Emile de Antonio and the New Documentary of the Seventies." In Bill Nichols, ed., *Movies and Methods,* vol. 2. Berkeley: University of California Press, 233–257.

Winston, Brian. 1995. *Claiming the Real: The Griersonian Documentary and Its Legitimations.* London: British Film Institute.

———. 2000. *Lies, Damn Lies and Documentary.* London: British Film Institute.

Wright, Chris. 1998. "The Third Subject: Perspectives on Visual Anthropology." *Anthropology Today* 14(4): 16–22.

Young, Colin. 1995. "Observational Cinema." In Paul Hockings, ed., *Principles of Visual Anthropology,* 2nd ed. Berlin: Mouton de Gruyter, 99–113.

Zavattini, Cesare. 1966. "Some Ideas on the Cinema." In Richard Dyer MacCann, ed., *Film: A Montage of Theories.* New York: E. P. Dutton, 216–228.

INDEX

ANNA GRIMSHAW trained as an anthropologist and filmmaker. She is Associate Professor in the Graduate Institute of the Liberal Arts, Emory University. She is author of *Servants of the Buddha* and *The Ethnographer's Eye: Ways of Seeing in Modern Anthropology*. With Amanda Ravetz, she co-edited *Visualizing Anthropology: Experiments in Image-Based Practice*.

AMANDA RAVETZ trained as a painter at the Central School of Art and Design and later completed a doctorate in Social Anthropology with Visual Media at the University of Manchester. She is Research Fellow at MIRIAD (Manchester Institute for Research and Innovation in Art and Design), Manchester Metropolitan University.

Printed and bound by CPI Group (UK) Ltd, Croydon, CR0 4YY

25/03/2025

14647343-0003